16th International PEAT Congress (IPC 2021)

Poster Presentations

Tallinn, Estonia
3-6 May 2021

ISBN: 978-1-7138-3867-8

Printed from e-media with permission by:

Curran Associates, Inc.
57 Morehouse Lane
Red Hook, NY 12571

Some format issues inherent in the e-media version may also appear in this print version.

Printed by Curran Associates, Inc. (2021)

For permission requests, please contact International Peatland Society (IPS) at the address below.

International Peatland Society (IPS)
Vapaudenkatu 12
40100 Jyvaskyla Finland

Phone: 358 14 3385 440
Fax: 358 14 3385 410

ips@peatlands.org

Additional copies of this publication are available from:

Curran Associates, Inc.
57 Morehouse Lane
Red Hook, NY 12571 USA
Phone: 845-758-0400
Fax: 845-758-2633
Email: curran@proceedings.com
Web: www.proceedings.com

International Peatland Society

IPC 2021

16th INTERNATIONAL PEATLAND CONGRESS

3-6 May 2021 • Tallinn, Estonia

Poster presentations

Argo Argel • Suru bog, Estonia

THANK YOU TO ALL SPONSORS AND EXHIBITORS

Gold sponsor

Silver Sponsor

Bronze sponsor

PEAT Talks Sponsor

Exhibitors

Proceedings of the 16th International Peatland Congress

Publisher: Publicon PCO, Kastani 42, Tartu, Estonia
Published: June 2021

FOREWORD

When in April 2019 we invited the international peatlands community to join the next big event - the 16th IPS International Peatland Congress (IPC2020) in Tallinn, Estonia - we had no idea about the global challenges ahead. Due to the COVID-19 pandemic, various international events, including the IPC2020, had to change their traditional ways of planning and management completely.

As a result, the first fully virtual IPC in history - the 16th IPC2021 - was launched in Tallinn in May 2021.

The main theme of the Congress, PEATLANDS AND PEAT - SOURCE OF ECOSYSTEM SERVICES, proposed by the Organising Committee of the Congress already in 2012, remained the same. In collaboration with executive Board of the IPS the Programme was structured into 27 sub-topics of seven key topics.

Initially, 429 abstracts were accepted by the Scientific Committee of the Congress, out of which 220 presentations (including 58 poster presentations) were made in the virtual environment. During the four Congress working days, it was possible to enjoy excellent presentations by eight international keynote speakers, six Peat Talks, 12 intriguing talks from the Industry Summit programme and six from the Peatwise Session. In total, the 16th IPC2021 had presentations from 31 countries and participants from 34 countries.

The Congress left a clear impression that there is a consensus among wide range of stakeholders about the uniqueness of peatland ecosystems and their services.

The *Carbon sequestration and climate regulation* sessions attracted the largest number of presentations, clearly influenced by the global carbon neutrality policy. Significant changes in land-use in tropical peatlands have led scientists and stakeholders to adopting innovative techniques and research methods to raise awareness about these unique ecosystems in the world.

Several presentations emphasised that the use of peat as an energy source is rapidly declining. At the same time, the demand for peat-based growing media and the high value of peat-based products is increasing. In addition, the COVID-19 crisis has shown that the importance of locally produced food cannot be underestimated. Therefore, we are still in a situation where the challenges in developing high-quality and cost-effective growing substrates have remained, while companies are actively turning their attention to the climate policy and society needs.

In recent decades, great developments have taken place in the collection of experiences and scientific know-how in the field of restoration and reclamation of peatland ecosystems. In Europe, such activities have been financially supported by continuous contributions from different base and applied science funds. However, there are still several tasks which need to be tackled in relation to changes in climate, freshwater resources, GHG emissions, aquatic and terrestrial biodiversity, and anthropogenic pressure. Furthermore, it seems that it is time look toward such integrated research areas such as socio-ecology or socio-hydrology, aiming to involve social scientists more deeply into the research and management policy of ecosystem services of peatlands or peat, for example.

With this publication, we aim to maintain the ideas and experiences shared in the 16th IPC2021 for future use and to contribute closer communication development between scientists, peat industry professionals, conservationists, officials and other stakeholders of peatlands and peat.

We thank all participants of the Congress and the Secretariat for realising our ideas in a 100% online environment.

May 15, 2021

Elve Lode
Chair of the Scientific Committee

Martin Küttim
Deputy Chair of the Scientific Committee

Erki Niitlaan Chairman

Jaanus Paal Congress General

ORGANISING COMMITTEE

Erki Niitlaan Chair of the Congress, Estonian Peat Association
Jaanus Paal Scientific Congress General, University of Tartu
Elve Lode Chair of the Scientific Committee, Tallinn University
Martin Küttim Vice-Chair of the Scientific Committee, Tallinn University
Edgar Karofeld University of Tartu
Marko Kohv Estonian Wetlands Society
Gilbert Ludwig International Peatland Society
Susann Warnecke International Peatland Society

SCIENTIFIC COMMITTEE

Rachel Carmenta University of Cambridge, England
Gerald Jurasinski The University of Rostock, Germany
Marko Kohv University of Tartu, Estonian Fund for Nature, Estonia
Randall Kolka USDA Forest Service Northern Research Station, USA
Aino Korrensalo University of Eastern Finland, Finland
Marika Kose Estonian University of Life Sciences, Estonia
Ingrida Krigere Latvian Peat Association, Latvia
Ain Kull University of Tartu, Estonia
Liisa Küttim Tallinn University, Estonia
Martin Küttim Tallinn University, Estonia
Anna Laine University of Eastern Finland, Finland
Elve Lode Tallinn University, Estonia
Aleksei Lotman Estonian Fund for Nature, Estonia
Lars Lundin Swedish University of Agricultural Sciences, Sweden
Shailendra Mishra Asian School of the Environment, Singapore
Katri Ots Estonian University of Life Sciences, Estonia
Jaanus Paal University of Tartu, Estonia
Jan Peters Michael Succow Foundation, Germany
Piret Pungas-Kohv University of Tartu, Estonian Fund for Nature, Estonia
Mart Reimann Tallinn University, Estonia
Jack Rieley The University of Nottingham and UK Peatland Society, United Kingdom
Line Rochefort Laval University, Canada
Jüri-Ott Salm Estonian Fund for Nature, Estonia
Hannu Salo Bioenergia ry, Finland
Budi Indra Setiawan Bogor Agricultural University, Indonesia
Dace Silina Latvia University of Life Sciences and Technologies, Latvia
Pete Whittington Brandon University, Canada
Meng Xianmin Northeast Normal University, China Humic Acid Industry Association, China

ID 62309

EVALUATION OF PHYSICAL AND CHEMICAL PROPERTIES OF PROCESSED SPHAGNUM PALUSTRE BIOMASS AS A POSSIBLE ADDITIVE IN HORTICULTURAL SUBSTRATES

*Raphael Müller[1] & Stephan Glatzel[1]

[1]Faculty of Earth Sciences, Geography and Astronomy, Department of Geography and Regional Research, Geoecology, University of Vienna, Vienna, Austria

raphael.mueller@univie.ac.at

SUMMARY

Provisioning of raw material is an important ecosystem service provided by restored and rewetted peatlands. Using materials produced on re-established peatland sites can help to increase the interest of stakeholders to expedite further restoration measurements. Therefore, the cultivation and extraction of peat moss, the so-called Sphagnum farming, offers a promising way of paludiculture. In this study physicochemical properties of harvested and processed Sphagnum palustre were evaluated to identify possible uses in horticultural substrates. Effects of processing steps on the maximum water holding capacity (MWC) of Sphagnum palustre were evaluated, followed by a comparison of specific mixtures including peat and coir in different volumetric ratios. The wettability of the materials was analysed using standardised hydration experiments. Mixtures were fertilised and incubated for four weeks. Measurements using bomb calorimetry, thermogravimetry and elemental analysis of H, C, N, S and O were carried out for treated and untreated substrates. Results show that different processing steps reduce the MWC of processed Sphagnum biomass significantly compared to fresh moss, except for one treatment. All mixtures that include processed Sphagnum biomass have higher MWC than mixtures without it and rewetting of mixtures including Sphagnum is faster and more efficient. Fertilisation of processed Sphagnum decreased the stability of organic matter leading to a loss of total carbon, a shift of thermogravimetric peaks towards lower temperatures and a reduction of gross heat values. Processed Sphagnum biomass shows advantageous physical properties that enhance water holding and rewetting characteristics of mixtures while the stability of Sphagnum palustre decreases rapidly after fertilisation.

Keywords: *Sphagnum palustre, peat, wettability, substrate, provisioning service, horticulture*

INTRODUCTION

The concept of ecosystem services aims to link biological and physical properties of ecosystems to human well-being. Therefore, functions offered by ecosystems are transformed into measurable economic values resulting in a classification containing three main categories which are provisioning, regulating and cultural services (Boerema et al., 2017). Intact peatlands offer a great variety of ecosystem services and especially its regulating services (e.g. regulation of climate on different scales, carbon storage, water quality regulation) are well known. Next to intact peatlands also formerly degraded, restored and rewetted peatlands (e.g. former peat cutting sites) offer valuable provisioning services. Paludiculture on rewetted peatlands and especially Sphagnum farming combines regulating and provisioning services as it permits the production of an agricultural product (i.e. Sphagnum biomass) under sustainable conditions (Gaudig et al., 2014). Increasing the interest in Sphagnum farming by finding more possible fields of applications may help to rise attention amongst decision-maker to push forward further restoration measurements. Therefore, the use of harvested Sphagnum biomass as a renewable material used in horticultural substrates and growing media might be a promising alternative to non-renewable peat-based substrates, but research results especially on physical and chemical properties of pre-processed Sphagnum biomass are very limited (Kämäräinen at al., 2018). For this reason, the aim of our study is the evaluation of harvested and pre-processed Sphagnum palustre biomass as an additive material for substrates used in horticulture, namely peat and coir, focusing on hydrophysical properties such as MWC and wettability as well as on thermochemical features.

MATERIALS AND METHODS

Fresh Sphagnum biomass was harvested and purchased from a local reed farmer in the Netherlands (8377 HD Kalenberg) in 25 L bags. After transportation in a cooled flower transporter mosses were air-dried indoor on a metal grid placed on euro-palettes for 6 weeks. To guarantee aeration the material was turned twice a week. Peat (Latvian bog-peat, weak to medium decomposition (H3-H4), pH 3-4, 250 L) and coir (washed and pressed bales, fibre lengths: 3-30 mm) were bought from "Franz Kranzinger GmbH" (5204 Straßwalchen, Austria). All three materials were oven-dried at 40 °C for 2 weeks (except for Sphagnum biomass dried at 60 °C used for pre-processing comparisons), cut using a scissor and rubbed through a 2 mm sieve to remove unwanted material and impurities (e.g. reeds, leaves, remains of coconut shell). Sphagnum biomass was exposed to microwave radiation (450 W, 4:30 minutes) to decrease moulding during wetting experiments (except for Sphagnum used in pre-processing comparisons). Prepared mixtures were formulated based on a percentage volume (vol.-%) using two materials for each mixture (i.e. 50/50 vol.-%) resulting in mixtures containing coir/peat, Sphagnum/peat and Sphagnum/coir. MWC was detected using standardised metal cylinders (0.1 × 10^-3 m3) which were filled with mixtures and soaked with deionised water for 3 days. After drainage for 10 minutes on a sand bath cylinders were oven-dried at 105 °C until constant weight. The gravimetric water content was calculated according to Marshall et al. (1996). Wettability of substrates was determined according to an adapted version of Fonteno et al. (2013) and Fields et al. (2014) using 4 × 10^-3 m3 substrate hydrated 10 times using 4 kg deionised water. Differences of stability between materials were evaluated using elemental analysis (H, C, N, S and O), bomb calorimetry and thermogravimetry following Worrall et al., (2017) and Worrall et al., (2018). Therefore, all mixtures were fertilised weekly and incubated at 40 °C for 4 weeks. After drying all samples at 60 °C until dry, the materials were milled using a mixer mill. Powdered material for elemental analysis was dried at 105 °C for 24 hours. Statistical analysis was performed with RStudio (1.2.5019). For the detection of significant differences between materials a non-parametric Man-Whitney test for unpaired data was used.

RESULTS

MWC results of different pre-processing steps for Sphagnum show that specific steps (i.e. drying, sieving, microwave radiation) of Sphagnum biomass reduces the MWC significantly compared to fresh, unprocessed biomass, except for one procedure (i.e. drying at 40 °C, sieving < 2 mm, exposure to microwave radiation (450 W, 4:30 minutes)) which was therefore chosen as the standard treatment. MWCs for different mixtures (see Figure 1.) show that coir stores significant lower amounts of water (mean ± SD, 3.3 ± 1.3 kg/kg dry weight) compared with peat alone (6.4 ± 0.3 kg/kg dry weight), while coir/peat shows no significant differences (6.3 ± 1.1 kg/kg dry weight). All mixtures which contain processed Sphagnum biomass store significant higher amounts of water then peat alone, while especially pure Sphagnum (28.4 ± 2.2 kg/kg dry weight) holds nearly 5 times more water then peat.

The addition of Sphagnum to peat increases the amount of water to a mean of 15.1 ± 0.8 kg/kg dry weight while an addition of Sphagnum to coir increases the mean MWC to 9.9 ± 0.3 kg/kg dry weight.

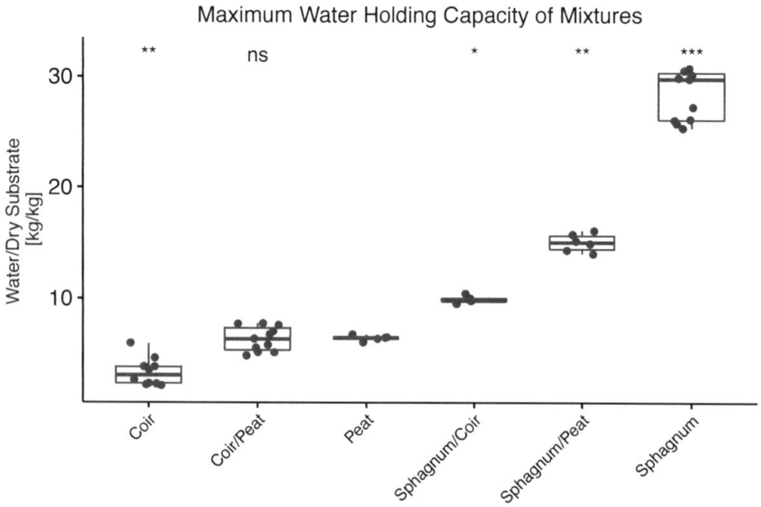

Figure 1. Boxplots of maximum water holding capacities (MWC) for different mixtures presenting amounts of water in kg per kg dry substrate. Results for each group are pairwise compared with peat to detect significant differences (Man-Whitney test, p-values < 0.05 indicated as *, p < 0.01 as **, p < 0.001 as ***)

Results for wettability measurements of all mixtures are reported in Figure 2. Sphagnum and Sphagnum/peat mixtures show the highest increases after each hydration event, while coir, peat and coir/peat show a general increase at lower levels. Mean amounts of water held by the substrate after the last hydration event are highest for Sphagnum (1.47 ± 0.09 kg) followed by Sphagnum/peat (1.37 ± 0.35 kg) and Sphagnum/coir (1.01 ± 0.26 kg), while amounts are lower for mixtures without Sphagnum. Results for coir/peat amount up to 0.88 ± 0.29 kg, for peat alone 0.82 ± 0.19 kg and for coir 0.62 ± 0.21 kg

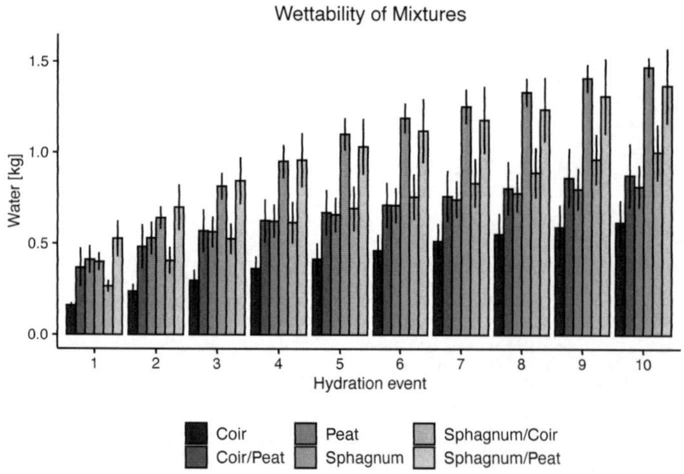

Figure 2. Wettability of mixtures for each hydration event (1-10). Amounts of water within hydration column stated in kg water. Error bars indicate standard error of the mean, n=3

Normalized mean results of thermogravimetric analysis (TGA) are presents in Figure 3 for fertilised and unfertilised substrates. TGA for Sphagnum shows a peak of mass loss at 140 °C, a second at 300

°C and a third at 340 °C. After fertilising Sphagnum, there is a shift of the third peak towards 300 °C. Unfertilised peat has similar peaks at 145 °C, 300 °C and 320 °C while peaks of fertilised peat appear at 154 °C and 304 °C. For coir peaks occur at 140 °C, 306 °C and 373 °C and for fertilised coir peaks at 140 °C, 312 °C and 372 °C were detected.

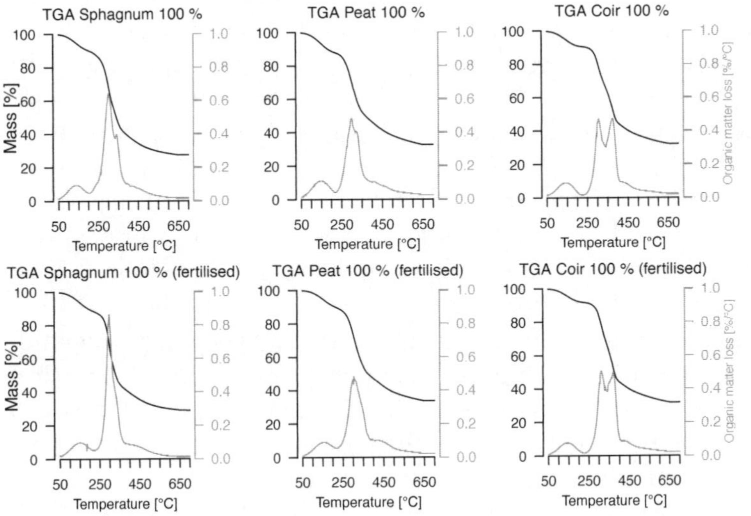

Figure 3. Results of thermogravimetric analysis. Black line indicates the relative mass loss while grey line represents derivative thermogravimetry (DTG). Results indicate means of triple measurements normalized to a temperature range between 50-700 °C

Results for elemental analysis and bomb calorimetry are shown in Table 1. Fertilisation increased total amounts of N for all 3 materials while total C decreased for Sphagnum and peat and increased for coir. S contents decreased slightly for Sphagnum and increased for coir after fertilisation. Amounts for H contents decreased for Sphagnum and coir after incubation and O contents for Sphagnum decreased while values for other materials stay stable. Gross heat values increased for all materials after fertilisation treatment except for Sphagnum where a reduction is detectable.

Table 1. Summary of elemental analysis and bomb calorimetric values for unfertilised and fertilised mixtures

Mixture	**C**	**N**	**S**	**H**	**O**	**Gross heat value**
	%	%	%	%	%	MJ/kg ± SD
Sphagnum	44.3	1.0	0.6	6.2	46.0	17.09 ± 0.01
Sphagnum fertilised	42.6	1.4	0.4	5.7	45.8	16.44 ± 0.09
Peat	46.4	0.8	0.2	4.9	42.9	16,77 ± 0.33
Peat fertilised	46.2	1.2	0.2	4.9	42.6	17.29 ± 0.05
Coir	45.3	0.4	0.2	4.1	42.1	16.87 ± 0.22
Coir fertilised	46.9	0.6	0.5	3.8	42.1	17.63 ± 0.19

DISCUSSION

MWCs presented in Figure 1 demonstrates the high amount of water held by pre-processed Sphagnum compared to other materials. The morphology of Sphagnum species facilitates these high amounts of water held by the biomass as big parts of leaves consist of dead, large hyaline cells, while minor parts consist of smaller chlorophyllose cells (Thompson and Waddington, 2008). Therefore, peat moss can store 20-30 times of its own dry weight of water (Yoshikawa et al., 2004). As our results show similar ranges for peat moss, we argue that our pre-processing steps of Sphagnum biomass (i.e. drying and sieving) had no significant effect on hydrophysical properties. Pure Sphagnum and all mixtures containing 50 vol.-% moss increased the MWC significantly compared with peat alone while mixtures without Sphagnum biomass show no significant differences or even lower MWC levels. Similar effects were discussed by Jobin et al. (2014) who showed that the addition of Sphagnum fibres to different peat-based substrates increased the amount of easily available water and improved the overall quality of brown peat. Wettability (see Figure 2) indicates that pre-processed Sphagnum biomass has the ability to rehydrate quickly and can hold high amounts of water by hydration alone (i.e. no soaking over longer periods). For pure peat and coir, the opposite is the case as for both materials only slow mass increases after each hydration were detected. Effects of hydrophobicity due to drying may lead to a decrease water infiltration and are well known for organic materials including peat and findings of Michel et al. (2017), who used a comparable wettability approach, showed similar wettability patterns for peat with initial moisture contents of 25% and 50%. Mixtures including Sphagnum increased wettability of peat and coir and are therefore enhancing the mixtures rehydration capacity. All DTG-curves show a distinct peak between 100-150 °C, a typical phenomenon which can be related to a loss of hygroscopic moisture (Méndez et al., 2011). After the incubation of Sphagnum biomass and peat, higher rates of mass loss at lower temperatures (at 300 °C) were detected and Rovira et al. (2008) related these patterns to a typical process of decomposition of organic matter. Mendez et al. (2011) relates mass losses between 200-375 °C to losses of less condensed, labile carbon compounds (i.e. cellulose, lignocellulose and carbohydrates) while mass losses at higher temperatures (400-600 °C) account for more condensed organic substances. DTG-curves for coir indicate that the material is less susceptible to decomposition after incubation while peat and especially Sphagnum biomass are less robust possibly due to the lack of lignin-containing vascular tissue (Maksimova et al., 2013; Taskila et al., 2016). Measured gross heat values are in accordance with results from literature where averages of 16.7 MJ/kg dry biomass are reported (Paine, 1971). Incubation of substrates increased gross heat values except for Sphagnum where a reduction was detected which was also the case for total carbon contents. Due to fertilisation N contents after incubation increased in all substrates.

CONCLUSION

Summarised, our results showed that the use of pre-processed Sphagnum palustre biomass as an additive or substitute material for coir and peat shows advantages, especially when comparing hydrophysical properties, namely MWC and wettability, as it increased the amounts of water held by a mixture and its rehydration capacity. On the other hand, a fertilisation followed by a 4-week incubation of Sphagnum palustre pointed out disadvantages of the material as the stability of carbon compounds were lower and the susceptibility to decomposition were higher compared with coir and peat.

ACKNOWLEDGEMENTS

Special thanks to Fred Worrall for giving the possibility of using the laboratory at Durham University, Department of Earth Sciences and “bellaflora Gartencenter GmbH” (Austria) for financial support.

REFERENCES

1. Boerema A., Rebelo A.J., Bodi M.B., Esler K.J., Meire P. (2017) Are ecosystem services adequately quantified?. *Journal of Applied Ecology*, 54: 358–370.
2. Fields J.S., Fonteno W.C., Jackson B.E. (2014) Hydration Efficiency of Traditional and Alternative Greenhouse Substrate Components. *HortScience*, 49, 336–342.
3. Fonteno W.C., Fields J.S., Jackson B.E. (2013) A Pragmatic Approach to Wettability and Hydration of Horticultural Substrates. *Acta Horticulturae*, 1013: 139–146.
4. Gaudig G., Fengler F., Krebs M., Prager A., Schulz J., Wichmann S., Joosten H. (2014) Sphagnum farming in Germany – a review of progress. *Mires and Peat*, 13: 1–11.
5. Jobin P., Caron J., Rochefort L. (2014) Developing new potting mixes with Sphagnum fibers. *Canadian Journal of Soil Science,* 94: 585–593.
6. Kämäräinen A., Simojoki A., Lindén L., Jokinen K., Silvan N. (2018) Physical growing media characteristics of Sphagnum biomass dominated by Sphagnum fuscum (Schimp.) Klinggr.. *Mires and Peat,* 21: 1–16.
7. Maksimova V., Klavina L., Bikovens O., Zicmanis A., Purmalis O. (2013) Structural Characterization and Chemical Classification of Some Bryophytes Found in Latvia. *Chemistry & Biodiversity,* 10: 1284-1294.
8. Marshall T.J., Holmes J.W., Rose C.W. (eds.) (1996) *Soil physics*, Cambridge University Press, Cambridge. pp. 453.
9. Méndez A., Barriga S., Guerrero F., Gascó G. (2011) Thermal analysis of growing media obtained from mixtures of paper mill waste materials and sewage sludge. *Journal of Thermal Analysis and Calorimetry*, 104: 213–221.
10. Michel J.-C., Jackson B.E., Fonteno W.C. (2017) Classification of organic substrates' wettability from contact angle measurements and hydration efficiency tests. *Acta Horticulturae,* 1168: 199–206.
11. Paine R.T. (1971) The measurement and application of the calorie to ecological problems. *Annual Review of Ecology and Systematics*, 2: 145–164.
12. Rovira P., Kurz-Besson C., Coûteaux M.-M., Vallejo V.R. (2008) Changes in litter properties during decomposition: A study by differential thermogravimetry and scanning calorimetry. *Soil Biology and Biochemistry*, 40: 172–185.
13. Taskila S., Särkelä R., Tanskanen J. (2016) Valuable applications for peat moss. *Biomass Conversion and Biorefinery,* 6: 115–126.
14. Thompson D.K., Waddington J.M. (2008) Sphagnum under pressure: towards an ecohydrological approach to examining Sphagnum productivity. *Ecohydrology,* 1: 299–308.
15. Worrall F., Moody C.S., Clay G.D, Burt T.P., Rose R. (2017) The flux of organic matter through a peatland ecosystem: The role of cellulose, lignin, and their control of the ecosystem oxidation state, *Journal of Geophysical Research: Biogeosciences,* 122: 1655–1671.
16. Worrall F., Moody C.S., Clay G.D., Burt T.P., Kettridge N., Rose R. (2018) Thermodynamic control of the carbon budget of a peatland. *Journal of Geophysical Research: Biogeosciences*, 123: 1863–1878.
17. Yoshikawa K., Overduin P.P., Harden J.W. (2004) Moisture Content Measurements of Moss (Sphagnum spp.) using Commercial Sensors. *Permafrost and Periglacial Processes*, 15: 309–318.

ID 62381

SUNDEW AND OTHER HIGH VALUE MIRE PLANTS FOR PALUDICULTURE ON SPHAGNUM MOSS BIOMASS HARVESTING AREAS IN WESTERN FINLAND

*Leila Korpela[1], Emmi Poikulainen[2], Jenni Tienaho[1], Tytti Sarjala[1], Niko Silvan[1]

[1] Natural Resources Institute Finland (Luke), Finland
[2] Tampere University of Applied Science, Finland

leila.korpela@luke.fi

In our pilot project (2016-2019) "Sundew farming for pharmaceutical purposes on low-productive, drained peatlands in Northern Satakunta, Finland", we found that areas, where the top living Sphagnum moss layer of 30 cm above the peat layer has been recently harvested for growing media purposes, are favorable for sundew propagation. The seeding of the sundew (Drosera rotundifolia) is not necessary there because of the sundew seedbank in the area and the lack of competition by the other mire plants before they take over the area.

We produced sundew biomass also vegetatively in the lab aiming to accelerate the biomass production process. We compared the bioactive properties of naturally grown plants and vegetatively grown sundew biomass. To evaluate the antioxidative power of the ethanol extracts of sundew, ORAC and FRAP were measured. Antibacterial effects were tested using four recombinant bioluminescent whole-cell biosensors. We analyzed the bioactive compounds such as naphtoquinones (7-methyljuglone) from the sundew extracts by HPLC-method. It was shown that the antioxidative and antimicrobial properties were better in field grown sundew but they might not be addressed to the naphthoquinone components of the ethanol extracts.

Sundew inventories on the natural and disturbed peatlands in Northern Satakunta, during two summers showed that in Sphagnum harvesting areas sundew is quite abundant and cloudberry and heather are spreading there naturally in a few years.

The shoots of Calluna vulgaris and leaves of Rubus chamaemorus are potential interesting high value raw materials for cosmetics. The biomass production of these plant species in the Sphagnum harvesting areas will be evaluated during the "Innoherb" project and a sequential growing method (paludiculture cascade model) in Sphagnum harvesting areas will be established. In "Innoherb" project we are aiming at novel value chains for underutilized herbs growing in low productive areas to be utilized in high value products like cosmetics.

ID 62709

WOUND HEALING IN PETS USING A COMBINATION OF PEAT DERIVED HUMIC SUBSTANCES AND PROPOLIS

*Lilia Stepchenko, Vladislav Chumak, Anastasiia Kalynychenko, Alisa Lisna

Dnipro State Agrarian and Economic University, Ukraine

stepchenko2@gmail.com

The rapid healing of skin lesions after injuries requires preventing bacterial growth at the wound site and avoiding the formation of antibiotic-resistant strains, maintaining optimal conditions for each phase of the wound healing process, and stimulating the epithelium reproduction. Such requirements are met by the veterinary preparation of peat that contains humic substances with the addition of propolis and vitamin E - "Humifarm", developed in the research laboratory named after Professor L.A. Khristeva of the Dnipro State Agrarian and Economic University.

The effectiveness of the combination was evaluated by the postoperative wounds healing rate in dogs and cats in veterinary clinics in Dnipro, Ukraine. The wound healing rate was judged by the degree of skin edema, dynamics of wound granulation, and time for the wound epithelization. Blood was collected from animals before treatment and after wound healing, biochemical and haematological parameters that characterized animals homeostasis. In the control group, was used a standard wound healing ointment - Levomekol (Kharkiv, Ukraine).

When Humifarm was included in the treatment protocol for postoperative wounds in animals, it was found that wound healing activation by primary intention showed up at the stage of granulation appearance and remains until complete healing.

It is the antioxidant ability and chelating properties of humic substances derived from peat, that restore the function of fibroblasts and activate the formation of granulation tissue by maintaining hydrophilicity and epithelial cells reproduction during the wound healing.

In addition, in the remodeling phase, the epithelization of the wound in experimental group, occurred without the formation of scar tissue. Perhaps this phenomenon is ensured by limiting the excessive fibroblasts function in the formation of collagen in the subcutaneous tissue matrix due to the participation of humic substances.

The duration of the healing process in the experimental group when using Humifarm ointment compared with Levomekol decreased in cats by 25%, and in dogs by 30%.

ID 62427

EFFECT OF NUTRIENT-RICH ASHES (WOOD ASH, OIL SHALE ASH) ON THE RE-VEGETATION OF PUHATU CUTAWAY PEATLAND IN ESTONIA

*Katri Ots[1], Tea Tullus[1], Mari Tilk[2], Mall Orru[3]

[1] Institute of Forestry and Rural Engineering, Estonian University of Life Sciences, Tartu Estonia

[2] Tallinn Botanic Garden, Tallinn, Estonia

[3] Department of Geology, Tallinn University of Technology, Tallinn, Estonia

katri.ots@emu.ee

SUMMARY

Vegetation on abandoned peatlands fails to recover for a very long period of time because the original vegetation has been destroyed and conditions for the germination of seeds and growth of plants are unfavourable. The conditions of abandoned peat production fields in Estonia vary largely; however, in general, the re-vegetation is poor: only up to 20% of the area of cutaway peat fields is covered by plants.

Earlier studies show that treating peat with nutrient-rich ashes (wood ash etc.) significantly increases the content of different nutrients in the substrate, whereby accelerating the process of re-vegetation. The aim of the current study was to analyse the effect of fertilisation with wood ash and a mixture of wood ash and oil shale ash on the formation of ground vegetation (vascular plants and bryophytes) on Puhatu cutaway peatland.

Wood ash and/or oil shale ash (0.8–1.8 kg ash per square) were applied on the peatland manually in June 2011. An inventory of ground vegetation was made in summer of 2019. The results showed that the re-vegetation process was significantly accelerated by ash application: eight years after the treatment, vegetation was still absent from the unfertilized reference area, whereas the average cover of vascular plant and bryophyte layers varied between 10.1–67.3% and 3.3–58.8% in different treatment areas. Altogether, 23 vascular plant and 3 bryophyte species were recorded in the treatment areas, including a protected species *Epipactis palustris*. The results of Multi-Response Permutation Procedures (MRPP) indicated compositional differences between treatments. The higher number of vascular plant indicator species were observed in the experimental area treated with a higher wood ash amount (WA15). It can be concluded that fertilisation with wood ash and a mixture of wood ash and oil shale ash has ensured rapid formation of ground vegetation on Puhatu cutaway peatland.

Keywords: *nutrient-rich ashes, re-vegetation, vascular plants, bryophytes, cutaway peatland*

INTRODUCTION

Residual peatlands may stay non-vegetated for years after peat extraction because the conditions for the germination of seeds and growth of plants are extreme (late spring frosts, high temperature in summer, low content of nutrients, etc.) (Wind-Mulder et al., 1996). Re-vegetation of cutaway peatlands depends on different factors: the size of abandoned fields (Lode, 1999), water regime and time since the last peat harvesting (Orru et al., 2016), chemical characteristics of peat, viable diaspores in peat (Salonen, 1987), distance from the nearest seed banks (Triisberg et al., 2011), etc.
The study in Czech Republic in a cut-over peat bog by Lanta and others (2004) shows that spontaneous re-vegetation is a slow process as the cover of *Sphagnum* mosses was very low (only 1–2%) and the re-vegetation by vascular plants was clearly limited by extreme abiotic conditions (Lanta et al., 2004). The conditions of the vacuum-mined fields in Estonia vary largely; however, in general the re-vegetation is poor: only up to 20% of the area of the cut-away peat fields is covered by plants (Orru et al., 2016). Different studies show that the re-vegetation of the ca 10,000 ha large abandoned peat mining area in Estonia is mainly the result of a natural process (Paal et al., 2011; Triisberg et al., 2013; Karofeld et al., 2016).
Earlier studies have indicated that treating peat with mixed nutrient-rich wood ash and oil shale ash increased significantly the content of different nutrients in the substrate, which are important for the optimal growth and biomass formation of plants (Kikamägi et al., 2014; Ots et al., 2017). Knowledge about the biomass dynamics of the ground vegetation in these areas is very modest. The main objective of the current study was to analyse the effect of wood and oil shale ash application on the coverage, composition and richness of vascular plant and bryophyte layers on Puhatu cutaway peatland and to identify the characteristic species of vascular plants and bryophytes for each experimental area.

MATERIAL AND METHODS

The experimental area of Puhatu is located on a cutaway peat-milling area in Ida-Viru County (North-East Estonia) (59°19.368′N, 27°34.024′E). The area of the abandoned field at Puhatu is 1,359.80 ha (Ramst et al., 2006). The thickness of well-decomposed peat varies in the range of 0.94 to 1.8 m.
The experimental field consisted of five blocks, and each of them was divided into three plots of 10 m × 20 m. In June 2011, 5 treatments in 3 replications were established:

(1) wood ash 15 t ha^{-1} (WA15);
(2) wood ash 10 t ha^{-1} (WA10);
(3) wood ash 10 t ha^{-1} + oil shale ash 8 t ha^{-1} (WA10+OSA8);
(4) oil shale ash 8 t ha^{-1} (OSA8);
(5) Control (unfertilised).

Ash was applied on the non-vegetated cutaway Puhatu peatland manually in June 2011 using a square system (1 m^2 area around the planted seedlings of silver birch, Scots pine or Norway spruce). The ash application amount per hectare, based on the dry weight of ash, was calculated. The amount of ash applied was 0.8–1.8 kg per square.
Chemical analyses of the upper peat layer (0–20 cm) were scrutinised on the ash-treated area and control area in 2019, respectively: pH_{KCl} (4.2–6.7 and 4.1), N (2.4–3.0% and 2.9%), P (13–159 mg kg^{-1} and 13 mg kg^{-1}), K (122–625 mg kg^{-1} and 55–65 mg kg^{-1}), Ca (6181–12 566 mg kg^{-1} and 6263–6658 mg kg^{-1}) and Mg (515–1080 mg kg-1 and 470–511 mg kg^{-1}).
Inventory of the bottom (bryophytes) and field layer (vascular plants) vegetation (the total cover of vascular plant layer, total cover of bryophyte layer and the cover of each vascular plant species) was carried out in July–August 2019 by visually estimating the percentage coverage of each species in 77 systematically placed square (1 m × 1 m) plots, using the scale of 1–100%.
Differences in the species composition between treatment areas were tested with Multi-Response Permutation Procedures (MRPP). Indicator Species Analysis (ISA) was applied to find characteristic

species for different treatments. MRPP and ISA were performed with PC-ORD7 (McCune & Mefford, 2016).

RESULTS

The results showed that the re-vegetation process was significantly accelerated by ash application: eight years after the treatment, vegetation was still absent from the unfertilised reference area, whereas the average cover of vascular plant and bryophyte layers varied between 10.1–67.3% and 3.3–58.8% in different treatment areas (Figure 1). The highest cover of the vascular plant layer was observed on WA15 and the highest cover of the bryophyte layer on WA10+OSA8 (Figure 1).

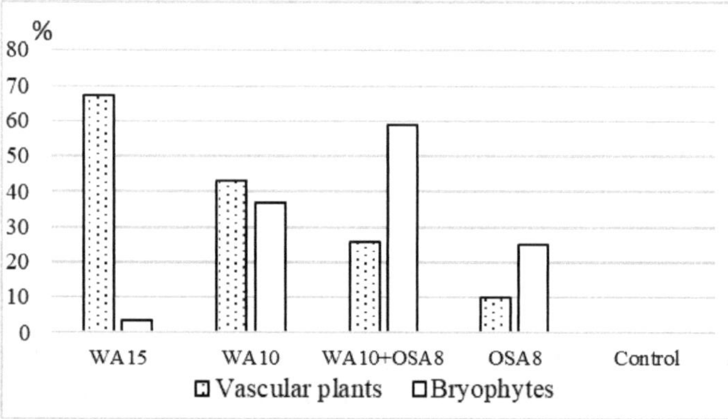

Figure 1. The mean cover (%) of the vascular plant and bryophyte layer per square of different treatments in 2019 (on the left) and re-vegetation of experimental squares 3 months after treatment with wood ash (10 t ha^{-1}) in 2011 (on the right). WA – wood ash, OSA – oil shale ash, 8, 10 or 15 – tons of ash per hectare.

Altogether, 23 vascular plant and 3 bryophyte species were recorded in the treatment areas, including a locally protected species *Epipactis palustris*. The number of vascular plant species recorded on different experimental areas was variable (Figure 2), as well as the mean species richness of vascular plants per square (Svp). The highest Svp was recorded in WA15 (3.8±0.3) and the lowest in OSA8 (2.0±0.3). Frequent vascular plant species on the ash-treated Puhatu cutaway peatland were: *Pyrola rotundifolia* (WA15, WA10 and WA10+OSA8), *Orthilia secunda* and *Epilobium angustifolium* (WA15 and WA10) and *Trichophorum alpinum* (OSA8 and WA10+OSA8). Among bryophytes, pioneer moss species *Ceratodon purpureus* was observed in WA15, WA10 and WA10+OSA8, *Polytrichum strictum* in WA15 and WA10 and *Barbula convulata* only in one treatment (OSA8).

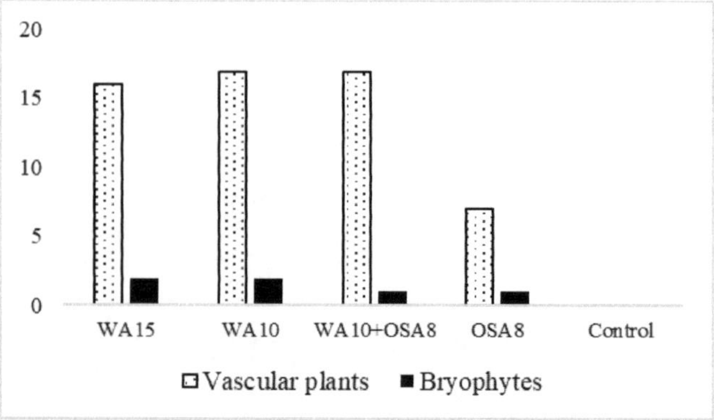

Figure 2. Total number of species recorded on ash-treated areas and on the control area in 2019.

The results of MRPP indicated compositional differences between treatments. All treatments differed significantly ($p<0.001$), with an exception of WA10 vs. WA10+OSA8. Three vascular plant indicator species were observed in the experimental area treated with a higher amount of wood ash (WA15): *Orthilia secunda*, *Pyrola rotundifolia* and *Tussilago farfara*. Two characteristic species of vascular plants and bryophytes were found in the experimental areas: *Epilobium angustifolium* and *Juncus effusus* in WA10, *Eriophorum vaginatum* and *Barbula convulata* in OSA8. Only one characteristic species was found in the experimental area WA10+OSA8 – *Ceratodon purpureus*.

DISCUSSION

During research on natural re-vegetation processes of cutaway peatlands, 106 vascular plant species, 48 lichen and moss species, among them 9 *Sphagnum* spp. were determined (Orru et al., 2016). In this study, a total of 23 species of vascular plants and 3 species of bryophytes were distinguished on the ash-treated area of Puhatu cutaway peatland. 74% of the total number of vascular species were observed on WA10 and WA10+OSA8, two bryophyte species were found on WA15 and WA10; the control area was not re-vegetated. The mean species richness of vascular plants per square recorded in WA15 was 1.9 times higher than in OSA8, where the lowest richness of plant species was observed.

Pioneer species are important for creating a stable surface and for offering protection against drying, frost and wind for less viable species (Lanta et al., 2004; Ferland & Rochefort, 1997). In Estonian disturbed raised bogs species such as *Epilobium angustifolium*, *Carex spp*, *Epilobium palustre*, *Agrostis capillaris*, *Tussilago farfara*, *Calamagrostis epigeios*, *Eriophorum vaginatum* and *Calluna vulgaris* have been pointed out as viable pioneer species with *Polytrichum strictum* being the most common bryophyte species (Kristian & Roosaluste, 1988). The main vascular plant and bryophyte species of naturally recovered cutaway peatlands in Estonia are *Eriphorum vaginatum* and *Polytrichum strictum* (Orru et al., 2016), which considerably help preserve humidity (Boudreau & Rochefort, 1998) and act like nurse plants (Groeneveld et al., 2007). *Polytrichum strictum* was also the most common bryophyte in the current study.

The results of the current study were similar to the results obtained by Näsi et al. 2005 who found that the re-vegetation of a cutaway peatland was significantly accelerated by ash application (Näsi et al., 2005). Vegetation characteristics changed following ash treatments with high ash doses favouring grasses and low ash doses promoting mosses (Ferm et al., 1992). The study results showed also that smaller amounts of wood ash and oil shale ash influenced positively the development of the bryophyte layer.

The results of the effect of oil shale ash are quite unique because only few experiments describe the influence of oil shale ash on the re-vegetation of peatlands. In Rae bog in north-eastern Estonia, plants which cannot tolerate oligotrophic conditions (*Agrostis canina*, *Epipactis palustris*, etc.) occurred two to three years after fertilisation with oil shale ash (5–30 t ha^{-1}) (Valk, 2005). Treating nutrient-poor peat soil with oil shale ash was especially favourable for the growth of *Eriophorum vaginatum* and *Epilobium angustifolium* (Valk, 2005). The growth of *Epilobium angustifolium* on Puhatu cutaway peatland was also affected positively by treatment with wood ash (10 and 15 t ha^{-1}).

Rapid establishment of vegetation may have a major impact on restricting undesirable environmental effects, such as post peat harvesting erosion and leaching of nutrients and solid matter to watercourses (Näsi et al., 2005). Litter composed by the ground vegetation contributes to the sustainable circulation of mineral nutrients and thus promotes also tree growth. The cover of plants and bryophytes varied widely between differently treated areas: the cover of vascular plants was 6.7 times higher on WA15 compared with the results on OSA8 as a lower re-vegetated area. The difference between the higher (WA10+OSA8) and lower (WA15) cover of bryophytes ranges up to 17.8 times, depending on the cover of the vascular plant layer. Näsi et al. (2005) also observed that three years after the fertilisation the coverage of mosses on the sample plot treated with wood ash (7.9 t ha^{-1}) was approximately 5 times greater than on the unfertilised plot. During eight years after mixing of the ash to the upper layer of peat there were no species observed on the unfertilised area, however a small fire-favouring moss species *Ceratodon purpureus* dominated in the bottom layer of the sites fertilised with wood ash (Näsi, et al., 2005). In our experimental area, especially on the mixed ash treatment (WA10+OSA8), the coverage of this moss could reach up to 100%.

CONCLUSION

The long time since the last mining is the main reason why the upper layer of residual peat has been mineralised. Removing peat layers changes rapidly the chemical characteristics of peat, however, treating of the residual peat layer with nutrient-rich wastes (wood ash and oil shale ash) increases the content of different macroelements, especially the amount of phosphorus and potassium. The re-vegetation of abandoned peatlands improves the conditions of peat moisture and stops wind erosion of mineralised peat. This study highlighted that after mixing wood ash and oil shale ash to the upper layer of peat, the rapid growth and development of the vascular plant and bryophyte layer started and the biodiversity of cutaway peatlands significantly increased: a total of 23 vascular plant and 3 bryophyte species were recorded on the treatment areas, including the protected species *Epipactis palustris*. It can be concluded that fertilisation with wood ash and a mixture of wood ash and oil shale ash has ensured rapid formation of the ground vegetation layer on Puhatu cutaway peatland. Re-vegetation by using nutrient-rich ashes (wood ash, oil shale ash, etc.) could be one possible way for the ecological restoration of abandoned peat mining areas.

ACKNOWLEDGEMENTS

This work was supported by the Institutional Research Funding IUT21-04 of the Estonian Ministry of Education and Research, by the Environmental Investment Centre (Project No. 16363), by Eesti Energia AS and by the State Forest Management Centre.

REFERENCES

Boudreau S, Rochefort L. (1998) *Restoration of post-mined peatlands: effect of vascular pioneer species on Sphagnum establishment.* Duluth, Minnesota, International Peat Society: 39–43.
Ferland C, Rochefort L. (1997) Restoration techniques for *Sphagnum*-dominated. *Canadian Journal of Botany*; 75(7): 1110–1118.
Ferm A, Hokkanen T, Moilanen M, Issakainen J. (1992) Effects of wood bark ash on the growth and nutrition of a Scots pine afforestation in central Finland. *Plant and Soil*; 147: 305–316.
Groeneveld E, Massé A, Rochefort L. (2007) *Polytrichum strictum* as a nurse-plant in peatland restoration. *Restoration Ecology*; 15: 709–719.
Karofeld E, Müür M, Vellak K. (2016) Factors affecting re-vegetation dynamics of experimentally restored extracted peatland in Estonia. *Restoration Ecology*; 23(14): 13706–13717.
Kikamägi K, Ots K, Kuznetsova T, Pototski A. (2014) The growth and nutrients status of conifers on ash-treated cutaway peatland. *Trees*; 28: 53–64.
Kristian R, Roosaluste E. (1988) Secondari succession in disturbed raised bogs. *Dynamics and ecology of wetlands and lakes in Estonia.* Tallinn, Academy of Sciences of the Estonian SSR: 145–154.
Lanta V, Doležal J, Šamata J. (2004) Vegetation patterns in a cut-away peatland in relation to abiotic and biotic factors: a case study from the Šumava Mts., Czech Republic. *Suo*; 55(2): 33–43.
Lode E. (1999) Restoration of mires – the question of ethics, aesthetics and environmental awareness! *Turvas*; 1–3: 5–12. (In Estonian).
McCune, B., Mefford, M.J., 2016. PC-ORD. Multivariate analysis of ecological data. Version 7. MjM Software Design, Gleneden Beach, Oregon, U.S.A.
Näsi N, Kubin E, Tillman-Sutela E. (2005) *Revegetation of a cut-away peatland is accelerated by ash-fertilization.* Nove Mesto, TNM Print: 42–46.
Orru M, Ots K, Orru H. (2016) Re-vegetation processes in cutaway peat production fields in Estonia in relation to peat quality and water regime. *Environmental Monitoring and Assessment*;188: 655–666.
Ots K, Tilk M, Aguraijuja K. (2017) The effect of oil shale ash and mixtures of wood ash and oil shale ash on the above- and belowground biomass formation of Silver birch and Scots pine seedlings on a cutaway peatland. *Ecological Engineering*; 108: 296–306.
Paal J. (Ed). (2011) Cutover peatlands, their use and rehabilitation. Tartu, 159 p. (In Estonian).
Ramst R, Orru M, Salo V, Halliste L. (2006) Revision of Estonian cutaway peatlands. The second stage: Ida-Viru, Lääne-Viru, Jõgeva, Järva and Tartu counties. Tallinn, Geological Survey of Estonia: 204 p. (In Estonian).
Salonen V. (1987) Relationship between the Seed Rain and the Establishment of Vegetation in Two Areas Abandoned after Peat Harvesting. *Holarctic Ecology*; 10(3): 171–174.
Triisberg T, Karofeld E, Paal J. (2011) Re-vegetation of block-cut and milled peatlands: an Estonian example. *Mires and Peat*; 8: 1–14.
Triisberg T, Karofeld E, Paal J. (2013) Factors affecting the re-vegetation of abandoned extracted peatlands in Estonia: a synthesis from field and greenhouse studies. *Estonian Journal of Ecology*; 62: 192–211.
Valk U. 2005. *Estonian bogs*. Tartu, OÜ Halo Kirjastus: 314 p.
Wind-Mulder H.L, Rochefort L, Vitt D.H. (1996) Water and peat chemistry comparisons of natural and post-harvested peatlands across Canada and their relevance to peatland restoration. *The Journal of Ecotechnology*; 7: 161–181.

ID 62544

THE EFFECT ON THE BIODIVERSITY OF NATURALLY OCCURRING VASCULAR PLANTS SPECIES IN CUT-AWAY PEATLAND UNDER DIFFERENT DOSES OF WOOD-ASH FERTILIZER.

*Austra Zuševica, Santa Neimane

Latvian State Forest Research Institute "Silava", Latvia

zusevicaaustra@gmail.com

Previous studies in cut-away peatlands show the positive effect of ash fertilizer on soil fertility and naturally occurring plant species amount and composition. Besides, it is the wood-ash that has the most rapid and effective impact on naturally occurring vascular plant species and the formation of vegetation. Vascular plants, by decaying and growing anew, provide soil fertility and reduce mineral leaching in the long term. In three year term, we studied how three different doses of wood-ash - 5, 10 and 15 tons per hectare, impact the biodiversity of vascular plants, and how the distance from drainage ditch influence it. The vegetation cover and species richness was estimated in the field of study, where three sample groups of different doses of wood-ash fertilizer and one control group were established. Each group was divided into five parts, wherein four parts four different coniferous and deciduous tree species were planted each in its own and one part where no tree species were planted. In each part, three sampling plots were set up to determine distance from a drainage ditch. All sample groups were established in three repetitions. Results show that both wood-ash fertilizer and the distance from the drainage ditch have an important impact on plant biodiversity. Compared to the control group, there was a much higher variety and frequency of vascular species in the wood-ash groups, but there was no difference between a low and high dose of fertilizer. In all groups, the higher variety of species was in the sampling plot which was closest to the drainage ditch. vascular plant species variety was not affected by the planted tree species. Harvesting of peatland changes the ecosystem and, without further management, has a negative impact on habitat restoration capacity.

ID 62702

BACTERIAL AND ARCHAEAL DIVERSITY AND ACCUMULATION OF METHYL MERCURY IN THE SEDIMENTS OF DRAINED FORESTS

*Krišs Bitenieks, Arta Bārdule, Zane Lībiete, Dainis Ruņģis, Zane Kalvīte

Latvian State Forest Research Institute Silava, Latvia

kriss.bitenieks@gmail.com

Methylmercury is biogeochemical pollutant, especially in aquatic systems. Its production is mostly microbial driven in anoxic environments. Results from the project "Water management in Baltic forests" (WAMBAF) indicates a concerning levels of mercury in different habitats, including drained peatlands. Knowledge about the correlations and interactions of soil microbial community composition and function with the production, cycling and dispersal of various substances (e.g. CH_4 and MeHg) is required in order to assess the impact of land use and management regimes, as well as to provide a baseline for future mitigation efforts. Here we present the first results of this observational study.

Sediments and water were sampled in eight different sites, each representing a different management impact level (e.g. ditch cleaning, beaver dam removal, intact peatland lake outlet streams). Samplings were done four times during the period of one year. DNA was extracted using DNeasy PowerSoil Kit and sequenced with Illumina MiSeq (16S rDNA V4-V5). hgcA (Hg methylation), mcrA (methane production), dsrA (sulfate reducing bacteria) and merA (Hg reduction) genes will be quantified with qPCR.

Mean Hg concentration in sediments and surface water in the research sites was 42.5 µg kg-1 (SD=68.6 µg kg-1) and below 0.1 ng L-1, respectively. Mean MeHg concentration in sediments and surface water was 6.4 µg kg-1 (SD=12.1 µg kg-1) and 0.4 ng L (SD=0.7 ng L-1), respectively. Environmental variables such as conductivity and total amount of sulphate, nitrogen and carbon highly correlated with mercury and methylmercury.

We observed mixed environmental effects (correlations) on sediment bacterial and archaeal communities but no significant effect on sampling period. Communities were highly distinct between the management systems indicating a possible site effect. Gammaproteobacteria, Deltaproteobacteria were relatively common in most samples.

As methylmercury in aquatic systems is the net result of methylation and demethylation processes, futher developement of methods are needed for better modeling of fluctuations of methylmercury in environment.

ID 62705

ALKALINE SPRING FENS IN ESTONIA – DISTRIBUTION AND VEGETATION

*Mati Ilomets, Laimdota Truus, Raimo Pajula, Kairi Sepp

Tallinn University, Estonia

Ilomets@tlu.ee

Spring fens develop around source discharge area from saturated soil or deeper rock layers. The discharging water is characterised by high mineral content. High Ca and Mg content makes phosphorus immobilized and hardly available to plants. This together with low temperature and lack of nutrients creates specific harsh growth conditions for plants. High Ca content promotes precipitation of tufa or traventine, the concentration centres of which are often shoots of mosses and vascular plants.

Alkaline spring fens with tufa formation are rare type of soligenous wetlands in the whole world. In Estonia, there is likely about 800 spring fens with mean area about 1 ha (from 30 to 0.2 ha). Regions where spring fens are more common are SE-Estonia, western part of the island Saaremaa (W-Estonia) and Sakala Upland (Central Estonia).

We analysed hydrology (depth to water level, pH, EC), topmost peat (Ca, Mg, Fe, K, Na , N, P content) and plant cover on some 80 alkaline spring fens during the three-year project (2011-2013). 130 vascular plant species and more than 80 species of mosses were identified. These are typical fen species in most cases with some exceptional, spring-associated mosses. Plant communities can be highly species diverse but are mostly species poor and with low coverage. The Redundancy Analyses divided the studied spring fens into three main groups: West-Estonian (mainly on Saaremaa), SE-Estonian and on Sakala Upland. The species composition of the first two is well differentiated but in the Sakala Upland plant plant species of the two first are distributed. Mineral content was higher in pore water in SE-Estonia and WE-Estonia; it was weakly related to plant species composition. Available phosphorus for plants was higher in SE-Estonia while N/P relation was highest in W-Estonia and N-Estonia.
It will be discussed about the regional differences of alkaline spring fens especially in the context of water and peat properties.

ID 64207

THE POTENTIAL OF AND CHALLENGES FOR BIODIVERSITY CONSERVATION IN TROPICAL PEATLANDS IN INDONESIA, AS ILLUSTRATED IN SEBANGAU, CENTRAL KALIMANTAN

*Juliarta Bramansa Ottay[1], Mark E. Harrison[2,3], Yusurum Jagau[4], Yunsiska Ermiasi[1], Bernat Ripoll Capill[2], Pau Brugues Sintes[2], Frank van Veen[5], Simon J. Husson[2]

[1] Yayasan Borneo Nature Indonesia, Indonesia
[2] Borneo Nature Foundation International, Indonesia
[3] School of Geography, Geology and the Environment, University of Leicester, UK
[4] Centre for the International Cooperation in Sustainable Management of Tropical Peatlands, University of Palangka Raya, Indonesia
[5] Centre for Ecology and Conservation, College of Life and Environmental Sciences, University of Exeter, UK

The importance of Indonesia's tropical peat-swamp forests (TPSF) for biodiversity is becoming increasingly recognized, yet unfortunately these ecosystems are also becoming increasingly threatened owing to a variety of human disturbances. Here, we highlight both the potential for biodiversity conservation in Indonesian TPSF and assess the challenges facing conservation of these ecosystems, based on information and experiences from Sebangau, Central Kalimantan. Records collected from Sebangau since 1993 by many observers indicate that at least 215 tree, 92 non-tree flora, 73 ant, 66 butterfly, 297 spider, 66 dragon/damselfly, 55 fish, 11 amphibian, 46 reptile, 172 bird and 65 mammal taxa are found here. Of these, 46 species are globally threatened and 59 are currently protected in Indonesia; 22 vertebrate species are Borneo endemics. Many of these species are forest dependent, and the entire community is expected to be important for maintaining the resilience of the TPSF ecosystem and the environmental services that it provides. With this urgent conservation need in mind, we assess key challenges towards and solutions for TPSF conservation and restoration goals in Sebangau, based on a recent multi-stakeholder workshop discussion and literature evaluation, plus our own experiences in Sebangau. Numerous political, economic, legal, social, logistical and research challenges towards conservation in Sebangau are identified, which relate to the 3Rs adopted by the Indonesian Peatland Restoration Agency (Rewetting, Revegetation and Revitalisation), plus a fourth R that is essential to incorporate into TPSF conservation planning: Reducing Fires. These challenges have potential to impact on activities under all 4Rs, with those relating to Rewetting and Reducing Fire being particularly important, and many are inter-dependent and mutually-reinforcing. This understanding of the diverse nature of Sebangau's flora and fauna, and the challenges facing conservation of these, is informing ongoing conservation and restoration efforts involving our organisations and multiple other stakeholders in the region.

ID 73541

MICROBIAL COMMUNITIES AND BIOGEOCHEMICAL FUNCTIONING ACROSS PEATLANDS IN THE ATHABASCA OIL SANDS REGION OF CANADA: IMPLICATIONS FOR RECLAMATION AND MANAGEMENT

*Shaun Allingham[1], Felix Nwaishi[2], Louis J Lamit[3], Roxanne Anderson[4], David R Elliot[1]

[1] Environmental Sustainability Research Centre, University of Derby, UK
[2] Department of Geography and Environmental Management, University of Waterloo, Canada
[3] Department of Biology, Syracuse University, Syracuse, USA
[4] Environmental Research Institute, University of the Highlands and Islands, UK

s.allingham@derby.ac.uk

Peatlands are essential for multiple ecosystem functions and play an important role in global biogeochemical cycles. Knowledge of the environmental drivers of soil microbial community structure and functioning can provide insights to enable effective and evidence-based management. However, it remains largely unknown how microbial diversity contributes to the functioning of belowground processes. Addressing this gap in knowledge will provide insights into the understanding of microbial-mediated processes in peatlands that are undergoing restoration or reclamation.We assessed the relationship between prokaryotic and fungal community structures via DNA sequencing, evaluated soil function by measuring respiration on a range of substrates from three natural fen types (a tree rich fen, a poor fen and a hypersaline fen). Study sites were within the Athabasca Oil Sands region of Canada, and on a reclaimed constructed fen within nearby (~15km) post-mining landscapes. Overall microbial aerobic respiration was significantly higher in the reclaimed fen, but the microbial communities were different. Relative abundance of fungi and prokaryotes was highest in the tree rich fen and microbial community composition was significantly different between fens. Redundancy analysis revealed that pore water pH, plant richness and soil ammonium (NH4) were the main factors that affected functional activity (as determined by substrate utilization capacity). Plant richness, pore water pH and extractable NH4 were the main factors structuring fungal communities, while pore water pH, conductivity, temperature and NH4 were the main factors structuring prokaryotic communities. Further studies are necessary to assess microbe-driven processes in the long term, and future models of reclaimed peatlands should consider the dynamic interaction between communities and ecosystem functionality for which this study forms a useful baseline.

ID 62769

SPRING FEN COMMUNITY IS DETERMINED BY THE CHEMICAL COMPOSITION OF THE INFLUX WATER

*Martin Küttim[1], Marko Vainu[1], Oliver Koit[1], Siim Tarros[2], Joonas Pärn[2], Elve Lode[1], Pamela Abreldaal1, Karin Sisask1, Jaanus Terasmaa1

[1] Tallinn University, Institute of Ecology, Estonia
[2] Geological Survey of Estonia, Estonia

kyttim@tlu.ee

Spring fens are ecologically important groundwater dependent terrestrial ecosystems that harbour species-rich plant communities, accumulate atmospheric carbon to organic sediments, and are significant freshwater reservoirs. Though rich in species, the composition of vegetation is highly dependent on the quantity and quality of the water influx. Therefore, water level draw-down and shifts in nutrient load in the recharge might cause alterations in the community and endanger the spring fen ecosystem.

Matsi spring fen in Southern Estonia receives its water both from Quaternary aquifer system and the underlying Middle-Devonian aquifer that constitute the Middle-Devonian groundwater body in the Gauja-Koiva river basin. In order to find a causal link between the plant community composition and the hydrochemistry of these waters, we determined the influx pathways of the water from both aquifers to the fen, measured the nutrient contents of these waters, and identified all the vascular plant and moss species of the community with their spatial organization in the fen.

While the confined Middle-Devonian aquifer opened from the springs in the core of the fen, the Quaternary waters flowed into the fen from the edge of it. The analyses revealed an increased concentrations of nitrogen and phosphorus within the Quaternary water, possibly originating from agricultural activities, whilst these amounts remained considerably lower in Middle-Devonian waters. Consequently, the plant communities were characteristic to spring fens in the centre of the fen, but became gradually more altered at the edge of it, where the effect was amplified by a ditch.

Our study thus demonstrates important consequences of elevated nutrient concentrations for the spring fen plant communities, and demonstrates the sensitivity of the ecosystem to alterations in the quantity and quality of water recharge.

ID 62613

SOIL ORGANIC MATTER STATUS AND BIOLOGICAL ACTIVITY OF DISAPPEARING RYTEBŁOTA PEAT BOG IN NORTHERN POLAND

*Maciej Markiewicz[1], Łukasz Mendyk[2], Sławomir S. Gonet[1], Magdalena Banach-Szott[3]

[1] Nicolaus Copernicus University in Toruń, Poland
[2] Poznań University of Life Sciences, Poland
[3] University of Science and Technology in Bydgoszcz, Poland

mawicz@umk.pl

The aim of the study was to determine the quantitative and qualitative characteristic of soil organic matter and biological activity of drained Rytebłota peatbog of Brodnica Lake District in Northern Poland.

About 100 years ago the peat bog (area about 40 ha) was drained with a network of ditches in order to new grassland areas. No further maintenance of the channels resulted in variable ground water level during the season.

Four soil pits were prepared. One of them was located at the top of a small mineral hill consisting of sandy, kame-like material, rich in calcium carbonate. Other soils were located on a biogenic plain in the immediate vicinity of the hill. The following properties were determined in soil material: loss on ignition, the content of organic carbon and hot water soluble carbon, total nitrogen, carbonates, hydrolytic acidity, degree of humification and fractional composition of organic matter. Additionally spectral analysis UV-VIS, HPLC and elemental composition were made of extracted humic acids. Soil activity was measured on the basis of total soil CO_2 emission in closed chambers.

Studied soils were characterized by a great variability of the morphology, properties of soil organic matter and biological activity. It is the result of both, specific localization (shallow kettle depression with mineral islands surrounded by the soils developed from lake chalk) and human activities (drainage).

The original soil cover has been transformed under the influence of drainage of the peatland. Nowadays, the mursh-forming processes dominates the evolution of the soil cover of the study area. The results are: e.g. decrease of TOC content, decrease of the C:N ratio, decrease of HWDOC content, increase of humic substances content (HS) and the lower photometric coefficients (A2/A4, A4/A6, A2/A6).

ID 61525

CLIMATE CONTROL ON THE HUMMOCK MORPHOLOGY AND VERTICAL GROWTH OF HUMMOCK *SPHAGNA* IN MIRES OF NORTHERN JAPAN

*Tomotsugu Yazaki[1], Kazuo Yabe[2],

[1]School of Agriculture, Meiji University, Kawasaki, Japan

[2] School of the Art, Sapporo City University, Sapporo, Japan

yazakitm@meiji.ac.jp

SUMMARY

Effects of climate control on peatland morphology and carbon balance are attracting attention. In Hokkaido Island,northern Japan, shapes of *Sphagnum* hummocks are different among regions. Flat and low hummocks are distributed in mires of the western region along the Sea of Japan having warm and drier summer and deep snowcover in winter. Cylindrical and tall hummocks are distributed in mires of the eastern region along the PacificOcean having cooler and humid summer and shallow snowcover in winter. Conical and intermediate-sized hummocks are distributed in mires of southeastern region along the Pacific Ocean. The processes how different shape of hummocks are formed remains unclear. We monitored meteorological and hydrochemical condition, liner growth of hummock *Sphagna*, and hummock height changes in four mires for two consecutive years: Utasai, Sarobetsu, Utonai, and Fuhrengawa. for *Sphagnum papillosum*, *S. subfulvum*, and *S. fuscum*. We hypothesized that summer desiccation and winter snow load affect *Sphagnum* growth and hummock-height changes. Monitoredhummocks that were experimentally subjected to enhanced desiccation by vascular-plants trimming (T), snow- load free by snow shelter (S), vascular-plants trimming and snow shelter (S×T) and control (C). We compared the *Sphagnum* growth and hummock height at each hummock and discussed climatic control on hummock morphology. Linear growths of the same species were higher at mires having high temperatures. Linear growth was lower at T hummocks in most mires, suggesting that summer desiccation restricts *Sphagnum* growth, and inturn restricts hummock height. The hummocks in deep snow-covered region were weighed down by snow load, but the growth was higher at snow-loaded hummocks (C and T). These results suggest that summer desiccation and winter snow load control the *Sphagnum* production and hummock morphology.

Keywords: *linear growth, snow load, vascular-plant trimming, water availability*

INTRODUCTION

Peatlands are attracted attention not only from the perspective of biodiversity, but also in many ecosystem functions such as water sources supply, nutrient regulation, climate regulation, and global warming control. *Sphagnum* spp. is a major peat-forming plants in boreal peatlands (Rydin and Jeglum 2013). Therefore, it is important to understand their ecology in mires in relations with various ecosystem functions. It is well known thata hydrometeorological environment control both the primary production of plants and the decomposition of dead plant. Therefore, understanding relationships between hydrometeorological environment and *Sphagnum* growth is important in considering the current state of the peatland mires and future changes under global-warming conditions.

Boreal peatlands are widely distributed in lowlands of North America and Eurasia in mid to high latitude (mostly45–65°N (Wieder et al. 2006). Hokkaido Island, northern Japan (approximately 42–45°N) has a relatively warm climate: mean annual air temperature in lowland ranges from +5 to 10°C, which is near the southern limit of climatogenious peatland. The climate of summer and winter is different within the island, despite wholly humid oceanic climate. According to previous studies on the relationship between the climate morphology of *Sphagnum*hummocks (Yabe and Uemura, 2001), the hummock is flat and low in the western (area along the Sea of Japan) region because the summer *Sphagnum* growth is restricted due to dry climate, but is tall and cylindrical shapes (pronounced microtopography) in the eastern regions without suppressing the summer *Sphagnum* growth because of cool and moist condition, and intermediate shape in the southwestern regions facing to the Pacific Ocean. Another study demonstrated the relation between hydro-meteorological condition and *Sphagnum* growth or microtopography showed that accelerated summer desiccation by trimming of accompanied plants, restricts the *Sphagnum* growth, while winter snow loads enhanced the growth in the following growing season (Yazaki and Yabe, 2012). These results are obtained in a bog with a direr summer and a snowy winter condition. No studies demonstrated whether summer and winter conditions commonly regulate the *Sphagnum* growth in mires with different climatic conditions.

In this study, we measured the growth of three *Sphagnum* species and the seasonal changes of hummock shapes in four mires with different climate within the Hokkaido Island for two years, and considered how the growth of *Sphagnum* is regulated by the hydrometeorological conditions. Here, the following two hypotheses were established based on the results from Yazaki and Yabe (2012), that moist summer climate and heavy winter snowload promote *Sphagnum* growth. This hypothesis was examined from the measurement results of 4 mires in Hokkaido Island, Japan.

MATERIALS AND METHODS

Site description

The field study was carried out in Hokkaido Island, northern Japan (Fig 1). The Hokkaido Island measures 400km from north to south, and 500 km from east to west. It experiences a humid oceanic climate with precipitation of 800–1900 mm (JMA (Japan Meteorological Agency), 2020), despite the most humid season is different among regions (Table 1). In western regions facing to the Sea of Japan, it experiences warmer and drier summer and snowy winter. In southwestern and eastern regions facing to the Pacific Ocean, on the other hand, it experiences cool and moist summer and shallow snow-covered winter (Yabe and Uemura, 2001)

Following four sites were selected from the eight study sites in which the relation of hummock shape and climatic variable were discussed by Yabe and Uemura (2001) as to the different climate was chosen.

(1) Sarobetsu (45°16′N, 141°50′E, 4 m asl.)

The site is the ombrotrophic bog area, where flat and low hummocks (10–20 cm height from the base) coveredby *Sphagnum fuscum*, *S. papillosum*, and *S. magellanicum* were dominated. Inter-hummock spaces are flat and unsubmerged, where *Sasa cernua*, *Eriophorum vaginatum*, *Gale belgica*, and *Carex middendorffii* dominate.

(2) Utasai (42°38′N, 140°21′E, 97m asl.)
The site is located near the center of a bog where flat and low hummocks (10–20 cm height from the base) covered by Sphagnum papillosum are found in the ombrotrophic area (Yazaki and Yabe, 2012). The ground surface of inter-hummock spaces is flat and higher than the groundwater table, where *Moliniopsis japonica*, *Carex middendorffii*, *Vaccinium oxycoccus*, *Empetrum nigrum*, and *Ilex crenata* dominate.

(3) Utonai (42°45′N, 141°56′E, 2 m asl.)
In the minerotrophic area, *Sphagnum subfulvum* forms moderately raised and conical hummocks (the height is 20–30 cm from the base). *Carex lasiocarpa*, *Carex limosa*, and *Phragmites australis* grow in hollows with shallow water. The surface water was supplied by the spring water near the study site.

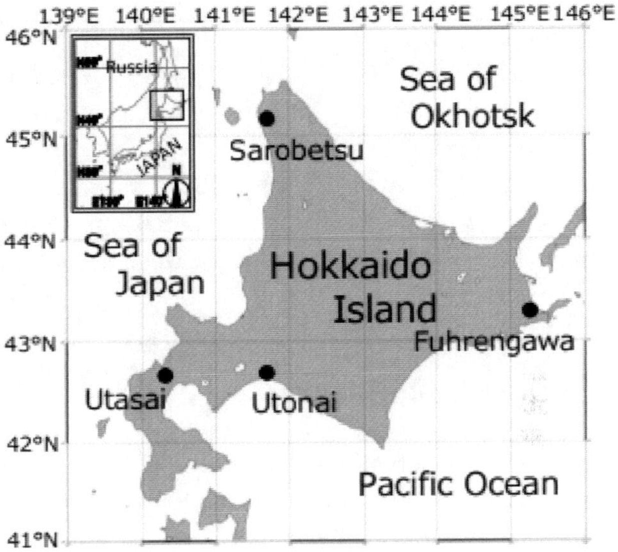

Fig. 1 Map of the study sites in Hokkaido Island.

(4) Fuhrengawa (43°28′N, 145°9′E, 3 m asl.)
In the minerotrophic area, *Sphagnum fuscum*, *S. subfulvum*, and *S. papillosum* form hummocks in the minerotrophic area (Yazaki et al., 2006). Hummocks of *S. fuscum* were extremely raised and cylindrical (the height is approximately 40 cm from the base). *Carex lasiocarpa*, *Carex limosa*, and *Phragmites australis* frequently grow in shallow water in hollows.

Field measurement
In four sites, the change in hummock shapes and vertical growth of hummock *Sphagna* were measured at an interval of approximately 35 days during growing season (April to October in 2002 and 2003. Simultaneously, water level in each site were monitored using a self-recording water gauge. Data of meteorological variables suchas air temperature, relative humidity, duration of sunshine, precipitation, and thickness of snowcover were obtainedfrom the nearest meteorological station managed by Japan Meteorological Agency (JMA, 2020). For measurements of hummock shapes and *Sphagnum* shoot elongation, in order to examine effects of summer desiccation and winter snow load on the *Sphagnum* growth and hummock shape, field tests of vascular plants trimming and snow pressure removal were carried out in all four sites.

We selected 4 hummock with typical size in October or November 2001, and another 4 hummocks in October or November 2002. The 4 hummocks selected in each year were allocated to 4 different treatment: no treatment(control), snow-load-free (S), plant trimming (T), and a combination of snow-load-free and plant trimming (S&T).Hummocks that received S and S&T treatments were covered with snow shelters that were made of wood (180 cm × 90 cm, 50 cm in height with sideboards) to prevent snow entering the shelter from October or December to the following April of both 2001–2002 and 2002–2003. The aboveground part of the vascular plants around the measuring points of the T and S&T treatment hummocks were clear-cut using scissors, to enhance water loss of *Sphagnum* through exposure to wind and sunlight. Vascular-plant trimming was carried out each time of the measurement. Details of the measurement and calculation are explained in Yazaki and Yabe (2012)

Table 1 Climate of the study sites from the nearest meteorological station (average of 1981-2010, JAM 2020)

Regions	**northern**	**western**	**southwestern**	**eastern**
site	Sarobetsu	Utasai	Utonai	Fuhrengawa
Air temperure (°C)				
annual	6.1	7.4	7.6	5.3
summer (Jun–Aug)	16.9	18.0	17.2	14.4
Precipitation (mm)				
annual	1,072.5	1,464.8	1,197.9	1,208.5
summer (Jun–Aug)	265.4	348.6	468.7	380.7
winter (Dec–Feb)	235.4	367.7	125.7	128.3
Max snowcover thickness (m)	0.99	1.34	0.28	0.46

RESULTS AND DISCUSSION

In two years of observation, the air temperature was lower than that in the normal year (1981–2010 average). In 2003, the amount of precipitation and water level condition were different among regions. A drier condition withless precipitation were continued in early summer (May to July) in the northern and western region facing to the Sea of Japan (Sarobetsu and Utasai). Water level in these sites declined lower than –30 cm from the hollow surface.Contrarily, wet conditions due to frequent heavy rain were observed in the southwestern and eastern sites facing to the Pacific Ocean (Utonai and Fuhrengawa). In all sites, the snow-cover thickness in the previous winter was similar to the normal condition.

The annual (May to October) shoot growths of *Sphagnum* in Control (no snow load, no plant trimming) was 5.7–16.2 mm for *Sphagnum subfulvum*, 8.4–41.3 mm for *S. papillosum*, and 8.2–21.3 mm for *S. fuscum* (Fig. 2). The annual growth of *S. papillosum* was different among site: the growth is larger in southwestern warmest site (Utasai) than the other two sites.

The result of a three-way ANOVA showed that accompanied vascular plant removal affected in all species. Snow-load removal, on the other hand, affect the linear growth only of *S. papillosum* (Fig.2; Table 2).

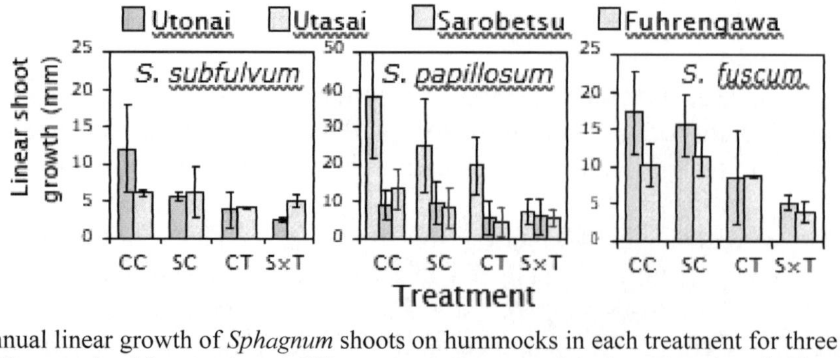

Fig. 2. Annual linear growth of *Sphagnum* shoots on hummocks in each treatment for three *Sphagnum* species. CC: control, SC: snow-load free treatment, CT: accompanying vascular plant trimming, S×T: combination of snow-load free and accompanying vascular plant trimming. Values are the mean linear growth within a hummock. Error bars indicate the standard deviation (n = 2 years)

Table. 2 Results of three-way ANOVA showing the effects of site, snow load, and plant trimming on the Sphagnum

Species factors	S. subfulvum df	F-value	P		S. papillosum df	F-value	P		S. fuscum df	F-value	P	
site	1	0.232	0.643		2	44.046	<0.001	**	1	2.896	0.127	
snow load	1	1.635	0.237		1	9.63	0.009	**	1	1.393	0.272	
trimming	1	7.577	0.025	*	1	37.31	<0.001	**	1	14.761	0.005	**
site:snow load	1	2.952	0.124		2	7.072	0.009	**	1	0.038	0.850	
site:trimming	1	2.545	0.149		2	9.133	0.004	**	1	1.996	0.195	
snow load: trimming	1	1.336	0.281		1	0.637	0.440		1	1.055	0.334	
site:snow load:trimming	1	0.618	0.455		2	0.482	0.629		1	0.35	0.571	
residuals	8				12				8			

asterisks denote significant effect: * at $P<0.05$, ** at $P<0.01$

Total linear growth during snow-free season of *Sphagnum* ranged from 5.7 to 41.3 mm, which is within the rangereported in temperate and boreal peatland (eg. Krebs et al., 2016; Laine et al., 2011; Kuttim et al., 2020), althoughprior data of linear *S. subfulvum* were not found.

Removal of accompanied vascular plants promoted *Sphagnum* desiccation. It is reported that a die-off due to heatwaves are apparent especially in places where it is exposed to sunlight (Bragazza 2008). The shade of accompanying vascular plant keeps the surface wet from solar radiation and wind and facilitates the *Sphagnum* survival and growth when water level is low.

The snow load in winter weighed the ground surface down in most hummocks and make *Sphagnum* surface near the ground water table and enhance water availability of *Sphagnum* shoots by moving them near the ground watertable expect in the Utonai, where the snow-cover thickness is low. Increased winter snow cover has been reportedto promote growth in the following year by increasing the dry bulk density of the surface of the *Sphagnum* (Dorrepaal et al. 2004; Yazaki and Yabe 2012).

CONCLUSION

Linear growths of hummock-forming *Sphagna* were interregionally different being influenced by the climatic condition. Summer desiccation restricted the growth, but winter snow load enhanced the growth of the followinggrowing season. These controls would determine the interregional difference of hummock shapes. Since meteorological (climate) condition control the *Sphagnum* growth and hummock shape, climate change should affect the carbon sink function of peatland near the southern limit of climatogeneous peatlands.

REFERENCES

1. Bragazza L. (2008). A climatic threshold triggers the die-off of peat mosses during an extreme heat wave. *Global ChangeBiology*; 14: 2688–2695.
2. Dorrepaal E, Aerts R, Cornelissen JH, Callaghan TV, Van Logtestijn RS. (2004) Summer warming and increased winter snowcover affect *Sphagnum fuscum* growth, structure and production in a sub-arctic bog. *Global Change Biology*; 10: 93–104.
3. JMA (Japan Meteorological Agency) (2020) AMeDAS data. http://www.data.jma.go.jp/obd/stats/etrn/index.php. Accessed on26 Mar 2020 (in Japanese).
4. Krebs M, Gaudig G, Joosten H. (2016) Record growth of *Sphagnum papillosum* in Georgia (Transcaucasus): rain frequency,temperature and microhabitat as key drivers in natural bogs. *Mires & Peat*; 18(4): 1–16.
5. Küttim, M., Küttim, L., Ilomets, M., & Laine, A. M. (2020). Controls of *Sphagnum* growth and the role of winter. *EcologicalResearch*; 35: 219–234.
6. Laine AM, Juurola E, Hajek T, Tuittila ES. (2011) *Sphagnum* growth and ecophysiology during mire succession. *Oecologia*;167: 1115–1125.
7. Rydin H., Jeglum JK (ed.). (2013) The biology of peatlands, 2nd edition. Oxford University Press, New York, United Statesof America, 382pp.
8. Wieder RK, Vitt DH, Benscoter BW, 2006. Peatland and the boreal forest, *In*: Boreal Peatland Ecosystem, edited by WiederRK, and Vitt DH, Springer, Verlag Berlin Heidelberg, 1–8.
9. Yabe K, Uemura S. (2001) Variation in size and shape of *Sphagnum* hummocks in relation to climatic conditions in Hokkaido Island, northern Japan. *Canadian Journal of Botany*; 79: 1318–1326.
10. Yazaki T, Urano S, Yabe K (2006) Water balance and water movement in unsaturated zones of *Sphagnum* hummocks inFuhrengawa Mire, Hokkaido, Japan. *Journal of Hydrology*; 319: 312–327.
11. Yazaki T, Yabe K (2012) Effects of snow-load and shading by vascular plants on the vertical growth of hummocks formed by *Sphagnum papillosum* in a mire of northern Japan. *Plant Ecology*; 213: 1055–1067.

ID 62704

CONTROLS ON PEATLAND PORE WATER CHEMISTRY IN SUURSOO-LEIDISSOO MIRE NW ESTONIA

*Galina Kapanen, Raimo Pajula, Mati Ilomets, Laimdota Truus, Martin Küttim, Kairi Sepp

Institute of Ecology Tallinn University, Estonia

galya@tlu.ee

Hydrochemistry of minerotrophic fens is importantly dependent on the groundwater chemistry. Result of drainage the share of groundwater in the water balance is diminished. Therefore, the restoration success depends importantly on the pre-restoration situation.

We studied the hydrochemistry of a large alkaline sedge fen (over 3000 ha) in the Suursoo-Leidissoo mire area, Estonia (over 20 000 hectares), sparsely ditched over 100 years ago.

Spatial and seasonal variability in pore water chemistry was investigated. There, we established and sampled for the pore water eighteen transects, which are located cross to ditches drained with the different intensity. The water sampling was done in fall 2018 and during 2019. For 2019 the seasonal dynamics of water chemistry were analyzed as samples were collected in spring, summer and autumn. Among others water pH, electrical conductivity, water anions and cations, total organic carbon (TOC) content were analyzed.

In our presentation we introduce some first result. The pore water chemistry data exhibited considerable variability. Factor analysis differentiated peatland water chemistry along three major axes of chemical variation, interpreted as axes of organic carbon concentration, mineral concentration, and deposition influence.

ID 62781

QUALITATIVE COMPOSITION OF WATER-SOLUBLE ORGANIC COMPOUNDS RELEASED TO GROUNDWATERS FROM MOUNTAIN PEATLANDS – CASE STUDY FROM WESTERN BIESZCZADY MTS. (SE POLAND)

*Mateusz Stolarczyk, Magdalena Gus-Stolarczyk,

Jagiellonian University, Institute of Geography and Spatial Management, Poland

stolarczykmateusz25@gmail.com

From the point of view of maintaining environmental sustainability, wetlands are particularly important ecosystems due to carbon accumulation in the form of decomposed organic matter and the retention of both biogenic elements and water. Peatlands are undergoing transformation due to changes in natural conditions (hydrological, microclimatic, geomorphological), as well as a result of human activity, including exploitation, drainage works, deforestation and afforestation. This leads to many irreversible changes in the peat deposit, increased rate of mineralization of organic compounds, which causes both quantitative and qualitative changes in the molecular composition of organic matter, as a result of which dissolved organic compounds are released into ground and surface waters.

The main aim of the study was to determine the seasonal variability of the release of organic compounds (water-soluble carbon compounds) into ground and surface waters from organic soils of ombrogenic peatlands. Furthermore, the qualitative chemical composition of these organic compounds was considered.

The research was carried out in 2016-2017 in two peatlands - Tarnawa Niżna II (degraded) and Litmirz (natural) in the Western Bieszczady Mts. (SE Poland). Samples for analysis were taken from 10 research plots (5 from degraded site and 5 from natural site). Each of them has been characterized by making and describing a soil profile and seasonal sampling from uppermost part of the soils. In addition to basic chemical analyzes, an organic carbon concentration and qualitative chemical composition (via FTIR spectrometry) were also carried out in peat and groundwater samples.

The results indicate the presence of secondary humification processes of organic matter related to, among others with fluctuations in groundwater levels and drainage. Measurements of dissolved organic carbon concentration qualitative composition made for groundwater sampling points at the studied area showed differences depending on the condition of the organic soils.

ID 61477

MAPPING OF FORMER PEAT FIELDS AND CUTAWAY PEATLANDS FOR TARGETING GREENHOUSE GAS MITIGATION

Jyrki Lehtinen[1], Miia Saarimaa[2] *Mira Isoniemi[3]

[1] Finnish Forest Centre, Savonlinna, Finland

[2] Finnish Forest Centre, Oulu, Finland

[3] Finnish Forest Centre, Kokkola, Finland

mira.isoniemi@metsakeskus.fi

SUMMARY

Peatlands released from peat production or from agriculture are a marked source of greenhouse gas emissions. Their area covers about 300 000 ha in Finland. Targeting afforestation measures on these soils wouldreduce their CO2 emissions significantly. Mapping the location of potential afforestation sites scattered over the country is needed in order to be able to guide greenhouse gas mitigation measures to these sites. For locating these areas, new methods and tools that utilizing georeferenced data sets are needed.

In this project, open source data of forest resources, peat production areas, agricultural areas and the depth ofpeat layer was combined for identifying potential afforestation areas. A geographical information system was used with selection criteria for analyzing the data and mapping afforestation sites. This method produces regional maps of potential afforestation sites which can be used to contact land owners for information on options available for greenhouse gas mitigation.

Keywords: *afforestation, GIS, peatland, climate change*

INTRODUCTION

About 2 500–3 000 ha of peatlands is released from peat production (Soimakallio et al. 2020) and about 3 000 ha from agriculture annually in Finland (MISA-project 2019). It is estimated, that by far about 44 000 ha have been abandoned from peat production (Soimakallio et al. 2020) and based on the estimation made by Natural Resources institute Finland, the area of abandoned agriculture land covers about 150 000 ha in Finland (VMI12). Without measures these areas can remain non-vegetated for up to decades. Peatlands released from peat production or from agriculture are a marked source of environmental loading to water courses and greenhouse gas emissions.

Afforestation is one of the most important after-uses of peat production areas. There is plenty of nitrogen in remaining peat, but due to a lack of phosphorus and potassium, afforestation is rarely successful without fertilization or land tillage. Wood ash is an excellent fertilizer for peat production areas that have been abandoned as it contains phosphorus and potassium but not nitrogen. Ash can increase the growth of peatland forests for up to 30 years without harmful environmental impacts.

Also abandoned former peat fields may also be harnessed to carbon sequestration. Since 1969, there have been almost 300 000 ha afforested fields in Finland (Ydinkohtia joutoalueiden metsitystuesta 2.3.2021). Peat fields are also significant source of greenhouse gas emissions after the end of cultivation. In addition to carbon, peat releases nitrous oxide, which is much stronger greenhouse gas compared to carbon.

Climate change is one of the greatest challenges facing the entire world. Targeting afforestation measures on suitable sites could reduce their CO2 emissions significantly. Identification of potential afforestation sites nationally is needed in order to be able to guide greenhouse gas mitigation measures especially to these sites. For locating these areas, new methods and tools that utilizing georeferenced data sets are needed.

Landowners together with forestry and agricultural operators need information on suitable sites that could potentially be afforested and about the measures that could be used. The aim of this project is to develop geographical information system (GIS) -based methods for searching the most potential sites for afforestation and to develop methods for targeting the measures. This project provides information that can be used to increase the carbon sinks in Finland by afforestation of former peat fields and cutaway peatlands in economically, socially and environmentally sustainable way.

MATERIALS AND METHODS

Identifying potential afforestation sites has been utilized by combining data from different environmental GIS- databases. The mapping of cutaway peatlands was utilized by using national Terrain database maintained and constantly updated by The National Land Survey of Finland. Data representing organic material in soil extraction area were used to identify peat production areas. We compared data from two different timing; namely years 2010 and 2019 and based on change detection analysis, we were able to find the areas that have been released from peat production. Areas shifted to agricultural use were removed from the selection. In addition, the areas classified as peat production areas in the Terrain database in the year 2019, were manually verified by using aerial photographs.

The mapping of potential afforestation sites of former peat fields was utilized by using Land Parcel Identification data maintained by the Finnish Food Authority and separate agricultural parcel data, which was exploited to estimate the use of each parcel annually from the year 2007 onwards. Land Parcel Identification data contains permanent information on the exterior borders of the parcel, even if it would no longer be used in cultivation. The data was processed further so, that parcels whose cultivation data ended in 2017 at the latest were filtered. These parcels were therefore no longer eligible for agricultural use and it can be assumed that they are no longer intensively cultivated.

Furthermore, data on conservation areas, seaside meadow lands, the traditional biotopes, nationally valuable landscapes, built heritage and cultural environments, targets that were received support from the Act on the Financing of Sustainable Forestry and forest mask produced by the Finnish Forest Centre were taken into account so, that potential afforestation sites were targeted outside of these areas. The reliability of the developed method was tested initially by field inventories.

Finally, we produced regional statistics of potential afforestation sites. This information can be used to make counseling activities to land-owners.

RESULTS

Our preliminary results demonstrate that totally ca. 93 000 ha of fields has been abandoned from agriculture (classified as meadows 45 500 ha and as fields 47 500 ha) (Figure 1a). Of these, about 31 000 ha are located in peatlands, where peat depth is at least 30 cm. Totally, the amount of potential afforestation sites covers 3.9% of current arable land in Finland. Moreover, after the year 2010, ca. 25 155 ha of peat production areas have been abandoned from peat extraction (Figure 1b).
The results of this study at municipality scale have been published in webpages of Finnish Forest Centre (in Finnish only, link in References).

DISCUSSION

The method worked well as the analyses have produced novel information on potential afforestation sites in national extent at municipality scale. However, a large amount of uncertainties was identified especially with the parcel data. For example, the Land Parcel Identification data maintained by the Finnish Food Authority doesnot give direct information on the suitability of the field for afforestation, as it gives only information on applying agricultural aids.
Field inventories we found to be very important and they gave as information on the usefulness and reliability ofthe results. This underlines the fact, that our GIS-based method can be used to identify potential afforestation sites in rather coarse scale, but it does not give recommendations considering the measures that should be made. Field investigations are necessary, when afforestation measures are planned in practice.

CONCLUSION

We can conclude that it is possible to produce useful and cost-effective GIS-based methods and tools for identification of potential afforestation sites at municipality scale. The results achieved in this project may help in increasing the awareness of the possibilities of reducing greenhouse gas emissions. Moreover, awareness of the possibilities of increasing carbon sinks can be improved based on the results of this study.

ACKNOWLEDGEMENTS

This project was funded by The European Agricultural Fund for Rural Development (Reference number 97940).

REFERENCES

1. Soimakallio, Sampo; Sankelo, Paula; Kopsakangas-Savolainen, Maria; Sederholm, Camilla; Auvinen, Karoliina; Heinonen, Tero; Johansson, Annika; Judl, Jachym; Karhinen, Santtu; Lehtoranta, Suvi; Rasanen, Satu; Savolainen, Hannu (2020). Turveraportti: Turpeen rooli ja sen kaytosta luopumisen vaikutukset Suomessa. Sitra 2020. 182 p.
2. MISA-project 2019, https://tietokayttoon.fi/julkaisut/raportti?pubid=URN:ISBN:978-952-287-618-8
3. VMI12, https://stat.luke.fi/en/metsa
4. Ydinkohtia joutoalueiden metsitystuesta 2.3.2021, https://mmm.fi/documents/1410837/22015134/Ydinkohtia%2Bjoutoalueiden%2Bmetsitystuesta.pdf/5097ca86-ed77-5b8c-9571-6f342ae3f191/Ydinkohtia%2Bjoutoalueiden%2Bmetsitystuesta.pdf?t=1608216550090
5. Results of the study https://www.slideshare.net/Metsakeskus/potentiaalisten-metsityskohteiden-kartoitus- suonpohjilla-ja-peltoheitoilla

Figure 1. Examples of potential afforestation sites: a) field abandoned from agriculture, and b) field abandonedfrom peat production.

ID 62352

CARBON ACCUMULATION AND BIOMASS FORMATION IN AFFORESTED CUTAWAY PEATLANDS

*Katri Ots, Karin Aguraijuja

Estonian University of Life Sciences, Estonia

katri.ots@emu.ee

In Estonia, drained and extracted peatlands are some of the largest source of CO_2 emission. The hypothesis of this research is that application of nutrient-rich ashes in abandoned peat-milling fields promotes afforestation in these areas and the emission of greenhouse gases will decrease because plants with stimulated growth linking carbon effectively Earlier studies show that treating peat with different ashes (wood ash, oil shale ash) significantly increases the content of different nutrients in the substrate, which are important for stimulating the growth and biomass formation of plants. It is very important to find relationships between rapid biomass production and C storage dynamics, because this is one of the main key questions of greenhouse gas emission from cutaway peatlands.

Peatlands in different parts of Estonia vary to a great extent and therefore, the effect of biofuel ashes on tree biomass formation also differs by areas. The use of wood ash significantly increases the height growth and total above-ground biomass formation of Scots pine, Norway spruce and especially silver birch. Measurement results of CO_2 emitted from peat show that an average of 0.05–0.15 g m^2 of CO_2 per hour was emitted in the reference area (no ash applied) and in areas treated with wood ash (10 and 15 t ha^{-1}) in Puhatu (NE Estonia), but the most intense soil respiration was observed during autumn months on Puhatu cutaway peatland in a silver birch experimental area (0.15–0.30 g m^2 per hour) where wood ash mixed with oil shale ash had been applied. On average, 46–51% of carbon accumulated in different tree fractions.

The greater CO_2 emission in areas treated with ashes is compensated for by considerably more active tree biomass formation, as a result of which wood sequesters more carbon than is emitted in the course of soil respiration.

ID 62419

4000 YEARS PEATLAND CLIMATE RESPONSES IN MURMANSK REGION DURING THE PAST 4000 YEARS

Olivia Kuuri-Riutta

University of Helsinki, Finland

olivia.kuuri-riutta@helsinki.fi

During the past decades temperatures have risen significantly all over the world due to anthropogenic greenhouse gas emissions. The global warming has been predicted to affect northern ecosystems, such as peatlands. Currently northern peatlands form a carbon storage and their net impact on climate is cooling, although an individual peatland might be a net carbon source and therefore have a warming impact. Changing temperature and moisture conditions are predicted to change the carbon cycle in peatlands and therefore their climate impacts.

In this study, I investigated the past changes in the vegetation and carbon dynamics of a subarctic peatland using plant macrofossils. My study site is located in Lovozero, Kola Peninsula. Based on the vegetation changes I describe how the peatland has interacted with climate during the past 4000 years. I also predict how this change is likely to continue due to the global warming.

My results show a shift from a sedge-dominated fen into a Sphagnum-dominated bog. These changes indicate drier conditions and may be a result of increased evapotranspiration caused by warming temperatures. Overall, this study gives support to the predictions according to which the current global warming is weakening the carbon sink in peatlands due to drying and may even turn them into net carbon sources, activating a significant warming feedback mechanism.

ID 62518

POST-FIRE CO2 AND CH4 EMISSIONS FROM FIRE DEGRADED TROPICAL PEAT SWAMP FORESTS IN BRUNEI

Massimo Lupascu1, *Hasan Akhtar1, Thomas E. L. Smith2, Rahayu S. Sukri3

1 National University of Singapore, Singapore
2 London School of Economics, UK
3 Universiti Brunei Darussalam

hasanakhtar@u.nus.edu

Tropical peat swamp forests (PSF) in Southeast Asia are one of the most carbon (C) dense ecosystem in the world storing 3% of global soil C on 0.25% of the total land area. However, these have been extensively drained and exploited for multiple land-uses, leading to frequent fires in the region. Fire burns the modern C rich peat layers and alters physico-chemical characteristics as well as hydrology, which may result in converting these ecosystems into a prolonged source of C as emissions to the atmosphere exceeds photosynthesis. Therefore, to further our understanding of long-term impacts of fire on C cycling, we investigated C emissions in intact and burnt sites in Brunei Darussalam, which has experienced 7 fires over last 40 years. We quantified the magnitude and patterns of C emissions (CO_2, CH4 and Dissolved Organic C) and soil-water quality characteristics along with continuous monitoring of soil temperature and water table level from June 2017 to January 2019. We also used natural tracers (14C) to investigate the age and sources of C contributing to ecosystem-respiration (Reco) and CH4.

We found major differences in physico-chemical parameter and hydrology, which in turn affected C dynamics, especially CH4. Prolonged higher water table and changes in Electrical Conductivity, pH and Dissolved Oxygen in burnt sites have created optimum methanogenesis conditions, where CH4 emissions was approximately twice (7.8±2.2 mgCH4m-2hr-1) compared to intact site (4.0±2.0 mgCH4m-2hr-1). However, the patterns for Reco did not show significant difference between burnt (432±83 mgCO_2m-2hr-1) and intact site (359±76 mgCO_2m-2hr-1). Furthermore, radiocarbon (14C) signature was overall modern for CO_2 and CH4 fluxes in both transects, implying a microbial preference for more labile C fraction in peat porewater. With frequent fires and more flooding in future, these fire-degraded tropical PSFs may remain a hot spot of C emissions, as suggested by our findings.

Key words: *Tropical peat swamp forests, Fire, CO_2, CH4, Radiocarbon*

ID 62660

FINE ROOT PRODUCTION IN BOREAL PEATLAND FORESTS: EFFECTS OF TREE SPECIES, CLIMATE AND SITE NUTRIENT REGIME

*Wei He[1], Päivi Mäkiranta[2], Paavo Ojanen[1], Petra Strakova[1], Rabbil Bhuiyan[1], Raija Laiho[1]

[1] University of Helsinki, Finland
[2] Natural Resources Institute Finland (Luke), Finland

wei.he@helsinki.fi

Fine roots are an important component of ecosystem C cycling in boreal forests and peatlands. Due to arduous and time-consuming nature of fine root production determinations, there is an urgent need to develop an indirect method that can estimate fine root production using easily measurable stand factors.

We studied fine root production by ingrowth cores for cover a wide geographic range as well as different tree stand structures and development stages, and soil nutrient regimes and water table, and develop models for estimating. Stand basal areas of pine, spruce and deciduous trees give a reasonable model. The residual of this model don't seem to correlate with the temperature sum. Division of sites to nutrient poor and rich categories does not significantly improve this model.

ID 62947

PEATLANDS IN THE NATIONALLY DETERMINED CONTRIBUTIONS: AN OVERVIEW OF CASES AND OPPORTUNITIES

Tatiana Minayeva[1], *Arthur Neher[2]

[1] Germany/ Centre for Conservation and Restoration of Peatland Ecosystems RAS, Russia
[2] Wetlands International, The Netherlands

Arthur.Neher@wetlands.org

The Nationally Determined Contributions (NDC) is the mechanism for the implementation of the Paris Agreement. This national reporting requires documentation of the reduction of greenhouse gas emissions from all sources in the country, at best described qualitatively. Emissions coming from land use and land-use change is one such source. The current rough estimation of land-use induced emissions make up a quarter of all emissions globally and could be even more significant as far as the converted wetlands, peatlands and permafrost areas are not adequately assessed yet. National-level activities aimed at peatland conservation, management and restoration could result in a substantial reduction of GHG emissions and enhance the adaptation capacities of ecosystems and communities. The national reporting is based on the evaluation of the projects aimed both climate change mitigation and adaptation. The framework for monitoring, reporting and verification (MRV) of the activities demands clear numerical indicators. Many countries avoid including peatland management activities in their NDCs as they cannot provide adequate reporting, mostly lacking baseline data and quantitative indicators for MRV. The authors have carried out an analysis of the existing NDCs that include peatlands and wetlands. The issues preventing a full national reporting in many countries include the following: availability of peatlands inventory and mapping; the land-use change mapping with differentiation of the land-use practices; the availability of the data on the emission factors; and the numeric characteristics of the adaptation services of peatland ecosystems, especially regarding to water regime and climate regulation. The opportunities for the reporting within the NDC framework are discussed based on the experience of peatland restoration projects implemented by Wetlands International in Russia, Indonesia, Mongolia.

ID 72583

SUSTAINABLE WATER MANAGEMENT CONTRIBUTION TO MINIMIZE PEATLAND'S FIRE IN INDONESIA

*Nurul Ihsan Fawzi, Ika Zahara Qurani

Tay Juhana Foundation, Indonesia

ihsan@tayjuhanafoundation.org

Conventionally, agriculture in peatland needs to drain peatland in order for crops to grow, but the result is usually over-drained and makes it vulnerable to fires. Indonesia experiences fires almost every year with million hectares of peatland being burned. In this research, we analysed the contribution of the water management system, which has existed for > 30 years, on fires occurring on Sungai Kampar – Gaung Peatland Hydrological Unit in Pulau Burung District of Riau Province. The used data was hydrological monitoring, fires hotspot from MODIS satellite images, and fire management in the region. The result shows the water management system known as "Water Management Trinity" in the district has successfully maintained a water table at range 30 – 70 cm, which is the lowest level occurred at dry season. Despite a high water table, 1,704 hotspots were detected in two decades monitoring (2000 – 2020). Fieldwork found that the hotspot happened in a short period because of rapid fire-fighting response and high soil moisture that prevented fire spread-away. The burnt area is dominated by scrub or abandoned land, and compounded by communities burning's habit. In recent years, the hotpots were reduced due to the land turned into productive coconut smallholder plantation and burn-free farming practice. In this research we conclude that water management in peatland agriculture has been minimizing the risk of peatland's fires - alongside with improvement local people capacity and activity in managing peatland without burning.

ID 72683

FUNCTIONAL TRAIT LINKAGES BETWEEN FLAMMABILITY AND DECOMPOSABILITY FOR TROPICAL FRESHWATER AND PEAT SWAMP FOREST SPECIES

*Nur Estya Binte Rahman, Stuart William Smith, Kwek Yan Chong, Pei Yun Teo, Shi Yu Phua, Daniel Wei Jie Lee, Cheryl Yang Aw, Yuti Ariani Fatimah, Janice, Teresa Ser Huay Lee, David Albert Wardle

Nanyang Technological University, Singapore

First two authors contributed equally to the development of the study

nur.estya@ntu.edu.sg

Wet tropical freshwater and peat swamp forest ecosystems represent globally significant stores of terrestrial carbon. Increased anthropogenic disturbances in these ecosystems is predicted to lead to significant losses of plant and soil carbon stores through decomposition and fire. Although recent theoretical and experimental work has begun to investigate how decomposition and flammability may be coupled (or decoupled) among species in a handful of ecosystem types, wet tropical swamp ecosystems are notably missing from the literature. To address this knowledge gap, we conducted litter decomposition and flammability experiments using tree species leaf litter from the Nee Soon freshwater swamp forest, Singapore. We collected leaf litter from 22 tree species including wetland specialists found in peat and freshwater swamps of South East Asia. We measured annual leaf litter decomposition using litterbags with different mesh sizes to partition the contribution of soil microbes and fauna. We calculated leaf litter (1) ignitability (i.e., the time to smoking, pyrolysis (incandescence or glow) and/or flaming), (2) combustibility (i.e., cumulative heat release and maximum flaming temperature) and (3) sustainability (i.e., flaming and smouldering duration) by burning leaves and monitoring timing of flammability and changes in temperature. Finally, we collected morphological, physiological and chemical leaf traits (e.g., surface area to volume ratio, rate of water loss, lignin and phenolic content) for each species to assess their ability to predict flammability and decomposability across wetland swamp species in South East Asia. We expect results from our study to improve predictions on decomposition and fire dynamics of freshwater and peat ecosystems in this region.

ID 72783

THE EFFECT OF TEMPERATURE INCREASES AND WATER-TABLE DRAW-DOWN ON THE EMISSION OF GREENHOUSE GASSES FROM A RAISED BOG

Nazia Tabassum

Natural Resource Management, Norwegian University of Science and Technology (NTNU), Norway

naziat@stud.ntnu.no

Increased air temperature and evapotranspiration due to climate change may increase the emission of greenhouse gases (GHGs) i.e., methane (CH4) and carbon-dioxide (CO2) from peat soils that can add up to the positive global warming feedback causing climate change. The current study experimentally investigates a raised bog's CH4 and CO2 emission responses at increased temperature and reduced water-levels. 16 semi-intact peat core samples differentiated by high water and low water levels and 3 intact background core samples with no change in water-levels-were incubated at three different climate room temperatures i.e., 4°C, 17°C and 25°C, for a total period of 28 days. In order to estimate flux, CH4 and CO2 concentrations from headspace gas samples were measured by gas chromatography with a standard concentration of 10 ppm. At 4°C, intact cores on average produced higher CH4 flux (49.57+/- 9.08 µmol CH4 m−2 h−1) compared to the semi-intact cores. Low water level cores at 17°C produced higher CH4 and CO2 flux (4.28+/-1.43 µmol CH4 m−2 h−1 and 44.89 µmol CO2 m−2 h−1) than their high-water level counterparts. At 25°C CH4 and CO2 fluxes have further increased but the emission of low water-table cores remained higher than high water-table cores. Compared to the range of emission at high temperatures found by other studies, the CH4 and CO2 fluxes obtained here were low. Although no significant trend of change could be detected in the emission of CH4 and CO2, variability in flux responses was explained from methodological standpoints i.e., intactness and structural homogeneity of the experimental cores, period of incubation, flux measurement technique, depth-wise delineation of oxic-anoxic zones, and the effect of temperature and water-level on methanogenesis. The study found substantial inconsistency among literature investigating peatlands' depth-wise GHG emissions, therefore, evaluations of flux estimation methods are highly recommended for obtaining reliable emission data.

ID 72879

SUSTAINABLE WATER MANAGEMENT CONTRIBUTION TO MINIMIZE PEATLAND'S FIRE IN INDONESIA

*Nurul Ihsan Fawzi, Ika Zahara Qurani

Tay Juhana Foundation, Indonesia

ihsan@tayjuhanafoundation.org

Conventionally, agriculture in peatland needs to drain peatland in order for crops to grow, but the result is usually over-drained and makes it vulnerable to fires. Indonesia experiences fires almost every year with million hectares of peatland being burned. In this research, we analysed the contribution of the water management system, which has existed for > 30 years, on fires occurring on Sungai Kampar – Gaung Peatland Hydrological Unit in Pulau Burung District of Riau Province. The used data was hydrological monitoring, fires hotspot from MODIS satellite images, and fire management in the region. The result shows the water management system known as "Water Management Trinity" in the district has successfully maintained a water table at range 30 – 70 cm, which is the lowest level occurred at dry season. Despite a high water table, 1,704 hotspots were detected in two decades monitoring (2000 – 2020). Fieldwork found that the hotspot happened in a short period because of rapid fire-fighting response and high soil moisture that prevented fire spread-away. The burnt area is dominated by scrub or abandoned land, and compounded by communities burning's habit. In recent years, the hotpots were reduced due to the land turned into productive coconut smallholder plantation and burn-free farming practice. In this research we conclude that water management in peatland agriculture has been minimizing the risk of peatland's fires - alongside with improvement local people capacity and activity in managing peatland without burning.

ID 61436

THE LAW OF THE FLOW OF WATER BY DARCY IS A SPECIAL CASE IN THE LAW OF FALL

Volker Schweikle

Member of the DGMT (german society for mires and peat) and editor of their yearly reports in the TELMA,

volker.schweikle@gmail.com

SUMMARY

Replacing the since 1960 antiquated hydraulic head h_p or H/m by the pressure p/Pa in the pressure-volume-based Darcy gives for the water conductivity $k_{f,s} = k_{DV}$ the unit $m^3 \cdot s \cdot 10^{-4} \cdot kg^{-1}$, with $k_{DV} = \frac{r^2}{8} \cdot \eta^{-1} = k_{D0} \cdot \eta^{-1}$ and $f(\eta = f(T))$ with η = 0,028 $mPa \cdot s \cdot °C^{-1}$ (viscosity η and permeability k_{D0}/m^2). In the pressure-mass-based Darcy is the unit of $k_{Dm}/s \cdot 10^{-1}$. The units of k_{DV} or k_{Dm}, respectively, represent neither an area nor a time! It is impossible to derive the transmissivity $\sum_{i=0}^{n} k_n \cdot s$ from the laws of Darcy and Hagen-Poiseuille (s is the distance of the flow of water). With the use of the potential $\Psi/J \cdot m^{-3}$ in the law of Darcy a balance of the units is impossible, but in the law of fall, which includes the law of Darcy. The law of fall including friction and slope is represented by

$$\frac{1}{2} m \cdot \Delta v^2 = s \cdot m \cdot g \left((1 - \mu_z \cos \alpha) \left(1 - \frac{\mu_F}{\mu_M} \right) \right)$$

with mass m/kg, velocity of flow $v/m \cdot s^{-1}$, distance of flow s/m, acceleration of the earth $g/\approx 10\ m \cdot s^{-2}$, inclination α/°, friction μ/- with $_z$ by load (μ_z has to be 1 if $\cos \alpha = 0°$), $_M$ = matrix and $_F$ = fluid.

In the range of the term $\left((1 - \mu_z \cos \alpha) \left(1 - \frac{\mu_F}{\mu_M} \right) \right) > 0$ and about < 0,05, the flow is paraboloid streaming and the law of Darcy with $v \sim h_{pot}$ (height of the potential energy h_{pot}/m). I point out, that in the law of Darcy the term of force with $h_p \cdot \rho \cdot g \cdot s^{-1}$ or $\sin \alpha \cdot \rho \cdot g$ may be used generally to describe the flow of water in matrices of peat and soil, and if > 0,05 the flow is hyperboloid bolting and the law of fall with $v^2 \sim h_{pot}$ is the law of choice. The boundary 0,05 is a modification of the number of Froude; including friction and inclination.

***Keywords**: Froude number, modern units of coefficients of proportionality ($k_{f,s}$), flow patterns*

INTRODUCTION

Due to the introduction of the "Système International d'Unités (SI-Units) from 1960 and the introduction of a national convention of parameters based upon the SI in Germany to avoid physical substitutes like "hydraulic head" instead of pressure gradient, it was necessary to standardize physical symbols in teaching profession. Further interests were how units of the coefficient of proportionality (= hydraulic conductivity k_{fs}) will change and is it possible to work out similarities or differences between physical laws in hydraulics. – According to agreements of physicists parameters are written italic and units steep, both separated by a slash, for example *mass*/unit (*m*/kg).

MATERIALS AND METHODS

The material are the equations of hydraulics by Darcy (Hartge & Horn, 2014; Schweikle 2012, 2017, 2019) and by Hagen-Poiseuille and the law of fall by Galilei/Newton (Kuchling 2014, Zanke 2014).

The methods are:

combining and comparing the laws of (1) Darcy and Hagen-Poiseuille and (2) Darcy and the law of fall.

RESULTS

(1) Darcy and Hagen-Poiseuille

Darcy: $\frac{V}{A \cdot t} = k_{DV} \frac{\Delta p}{s}$ Hagen-Poiseuille: $\frac{V}{t} = \frac{\pi \cdot r^4 \cdot \Delta p}{8 \cdot \eta \cdot s}$ or $\frac{V}{\pi \cdot r^2 \cdot t} = \frac{V}{A \cdot t} = \frac{r^2}{8\,\eta} \frac{\Delta p}{s}$,

with the volume of water V/m³, the time t/s, the cross section of a tube or a specimen of peat A/m², the radius of a tube r/m, a pressure difference Δp/Pa, the distance of water flow s/m, the viscosity of water η/mPa·s. with $\eta = \mathrm{f}(T)$ or $\frac{0{,}028\ \mathrm{mPa \cdot s}}{°\mathrm{C}}$.

Equating the parameters of yield $\frac{V}{A \cdot t}$ and of pressure $\frac{\Delta p}{s}$ results in

$k_{DV} = \frac{r^2}{8} \frac{1}{\eta}$ resp.. $k_{DV} = k_{D0} \cdot \frac{1}{\eta} / \frac{\mathrm{m^2 \cdot m \cdot s}}{10^4 \cdot \mathrm{kg}}$, with the permeability k_{D0}/m² (Schweikle 2012, 2017).

k_{DV} replaces the former $k_{f,s}$.

(1a) Darcy,volume-pressure-based, written as $\frac{V}{A \cdot t} = k_{DV} \frac{\Delta p}{s} = k_{DV} \frac{h_p \cdot \rho \cdot g}{s} = k_{DV} \cdot \sin \alpha \cdot \rho \cdot g$ with the hydraulic head h_p/m, the density of water $\rho/10^3$ kg·m⁻³, the acceleration of the earth g/ about 10 m·s⁻² and the slope $\sin \alpha$ is indicated by "+" = downhill and "– =" uphill. A negative volume means, that water has been lifted upwards by capillary or artesian force/ flows downwards by gravitational force and "+" or "–" do not represent mathematical operators, but directions.

Calculation of $k_{DV} = \frac{r^2}{8} \frac{1}{\eta} / \frac{\mathrm{m^2 \cdot m \cdot s}}{10^4 \cdot \mathrm{kg}}$ yields the same units like in (1) above.

Darcy, mass-pressure-based, written as $\frac{m}{A \cdot t} = \frac{r^2}{8} \frac{\rho}{\eta} \cdot \frac{m \cdot g}{A \cdot s}$ gives for $\frac{r^2}{8} \frac{\rho}{\eta} / \frac{\mathrm{s}}{10}$ with s = f(t)

The first result is, that neither $\frac{r^2}{8}$/m² nor $\frac{t}{10}$/s represent neither an area nor a time!

A disadvantage of the mass-pressure-based Darcy is the lack of a direction of the force.

(1b) Transmissivity

Assuming $q \sim (k_{\mathrm{DV}} \cdot s^{-1})$ or $\frac{k_{DV}}{s} \cdot h_{\mathrm{p}} \cdot \rho \cdot g$ results, that the pressure term loses his direction or his characteristic of being a vector. People believing in transmissivity should prove that the specific resistance for the flow of water in a tube or a peat matrix should be $\rho_{\mu} \sim \frac{8 \cdot \eta \cdot \pi}{s} / \frac{8 \cdot 10^4 \cdot \mathrm{kg}}{\mathrm{m} \cdot \mathrm{s}^2}$ (Kuchling 2014).

(2) Darcy and the law of falling bodies

The volume-pressure-based law of flow of Darcy has the form

$$q = \frac{V}{A \cdot t} = v = k_{\mathrm{DV}} \cdot \frac{\Delta p}{s} = \frac{r^2}{8} \cdot \frac{1}{\eta} \cdot \frac{h_{\mathrm{p}} \cdot \rho \cdot g}{s} = k_{\mathrm{DO}} \cdot \frac{1}{\eta} \cdot \sin\alpha \cdot \rho \cdot g$$

and the law of falling bodies expanded by the volume of peat soil $V_{\mathrm{bo}}/\mathrm{m}^3$ has the form

$$\frac{1}{2 \cdot V_{\mathrm{bo}}} \cdot m \cdot v^2 = \frac{m \cdot g \cdot s(1-\mu_{\mathrm{f,m}})(1-\cos\alpha)}{V_{\mathrm{bo}}} \quad \text{or } v^2 = 2g \cdot s \cdot (1-\mu_{\mathrm{f,m}})(1-\cos\alpha).$$

The potential $\psi/\mathrm{J} \cdot \mathrm{m}^{-3} = \frac{W}{V_{\mathrm{bo}}} = \frac{m \cdot g \cdot h_{\mathrm{pot}}}{V_{\mathrm{bo}}}$

Transplanting the potential without the elements in brackets in the law of Darcy yields $v = k_{\mathrm{DV}} \cdot \sin\alpha \cdot \frac{\rho \cdot g \cdot h_{\mathrm{pot}}}{V_{\mathrm{bo}}}$ and balancing the units gives (height of the potential energy $h_{\mathrm{pot}}/\mathrm{m}$).

$\frac{\mathrm{m}}{\mathrm{s}} = \frac{\mathrm{m}^3 \cdot \mathrm{s}}{10^4 \cdot \mathrm{kg}} \cdot \sin\alpha \cdot \frac{10^3\ \mathrm{kg} \cdot 10\mathrm{m} \cdot \mathrm{m}}{\mathrm{m}^3 \cdot \mathrm{s}^2 \cdot \mathrm{m}^3}$ or, with $\sin\alpha$ with values between -1 and $+1$, yields $\mathrm{m}^2 = -1$ to $+1$. The use of the potential in the law of Darcy is therefore absolutely wrong.

The law of fall includes the law of Darcy. The law of fall including friction and slope is represented by

$$\frac{1}{2} m \cdot \Delta v^2 = s \cdot m \cdot g \left((1-\mu_z \cos\alpha) \left(1-\frac{\mu_{\mathrm{F}}}{\mu_{\mathrm{M}}}\right) \right)$$

with mass m/kg, velocity of flow $v/\mathrm{m} \cdot \mathrm{s}^{-1}$, distance of flow s/m, acceleration of the earth $g/\approx 10\ \mathrm{m} \cdot \mathrm{s}^{-2}$, inclination $\alpha/°$, friction μ/- with $_{\mathrm{Z}}$ by load (μ_z has to be 1 if $\cos\alpha = 0°$), $_{\mathrm{M}}$ = matrix and $_{\mathrm{F}}$ = fluid. Scientists teaching hydraulics (Zanke 2014) think the μ_z to be unnecessary.

In the range of the term $\left((1-\mu_z \cos\alpha) \left(1-\frac{\mu_{\mathrm{F}}}{\mu_{\mathrm{M}}}\right) \right) > 0$ and about $< 0{,}05$, the flow is paraboloid streaming and $v \sim h_{pot}$ and the law of Darcy will be valid. I point out, that in the law of Darcy the term of force with $h_{\mathrm{P}} \cdot \rho \cdot g \cdot s^{-1}$ or $\sin\alpha \cdot \rho \cdot g$ may be used generally to describe the flow of water in matrices of peat and soil. If > 0,05 the flow is hyperboloid bolting and the law of fall with $v^2 \sim h_{\mathrm{pot}}$ is the law of choice. The boundary 0,05 is not a fixed boundary but a smooth one and a modification of the number of Froude; including friction and inclination.

In case of artesian flow, the above law of fall should be expanded by the law of throw.

DISCUSSION

The results are in general clear, but the Froude number will be discussed:

The law of Darcy is a linear equation $x = \rho \cdot g \cdot k_{DV} \cdot y$ with $x = v$ and $y = \sin\alpha$.
The law of fall of bodies is a square equation $x^2 = 2g \cdot s\,(1 - \mu_{f,m})(1 - \cos\alpha)\,y$ with $x^2 = v^2$ and $y = s(1 - \cos\alpha)$, (a parable in the 2. main situation). Comparing both equations shows, that the Froude number depends on the length of the flow s, the inclination $\cos\alpha$ and the friction $\frac{\mu_F}{\mu_M}$ (dependent on temperature and polarity of the fluid and the electrostatical character of the matrix. Mathematically there is no way to transform the mathematical equations, except the data overlap due to a high variance and h_{pot} is $\sim \approx v$.

CONCLUSIONS

The permeability k_{D0}/m^2 does not represent an area but a friction between water and matrix and k_{D0} cannot derived from the geometric quality of any tubes or matrices, which change additional their geometry by shrinking and swelling.
Probably the viscosity of water in pores with $r \leq 2$ µm increases due to the very small relation of the volumes of
the inner circle to the outer ring around the inner circle, by developing large crystal-like structures of water-dipoles which remain stable due to a reduced amount of choppy (force of Brown) single dipoles from the center of the pores (Fischer 2012).

REFERENCES

Hartge K.-H., Horn R. (2014, 4th ed.) Einführung in die Bodenphysik. Schweizerbart (Stuttgart).

Fischer L. (2012) Water is lumpy. Spektrum der Wissenschaft (Heidelberg) l.c. Science 336, p. 897-901; (2012).

Kuchling H. (2014, 4th ed.) Taschenbuch der Physik. Fachbuchverlag Leipzig im Carl Hanser Verlag (München).

Schweikle V. (2012): Der Einfluss der Temperatur auf $k_{f,s}$ (=k_{DV}) im Strömungsgesetz von Darcy. *Telma* 42: 77 – 80; Hannover.

Schweikle V. (2017) Grundlagen der Wasserbewegung nach Darcy in Moor und Torf. *Telma* 47: 129 – 138; Hannover.

Schweikle V. (2019) Allgemeine und spezielle Strömungsgesetze mit ihren Proportionalitätskoeffizienten in Torfen. *Telma* 49: 101–108; Hannover.

Stahr K., Kandeler E., Hermann L., Streck Th.(2016; 4. Auflage) Bodenkunde und Standortlehre; – UTB (Stuttgart).

Zanke U. C. E. (2014, 9th ed.) Hydraulik; in Lecher, Lühr, Zanke (editors) Taschenbuch der Wasserwirtschaft. Springer (Wiesbaden).

ID 61783

STUDYING THE HYDROLOGY OF ESTONIAN MIRES: GPR PROFILING ANDFINDING POSSIBLE RELATIONS BETWEEN HYDRAULIC CONDUCTIVITY AND EASIER TO MEASURE PARAMETERS OF PEAT

*Raul Paat[1], Marko Kohv[1], Argo Jõeleht[1]

[1]Institute of Ecology and Earth Sciences, University of Tartu, Tartu, Estonia

raul.paat@ut.ee

SUMMARY

Mires are water sensitive habitats where even the small changes in water level can affect its conditions. One important characteristic in understanding the hydrology of peatland is the hydraulic conductivity of peat. Hydraulic conductivity measurements in peat are very time-consuming and need special equipment. Finding a relation between hydraulic conductivity and parameters that are easier to determine in laboratory or *in situ*, such as bulk density, degree of decomposition, depth of peat, ash content and botanic composition can provide a simpler way to estimate hydraulic conductivity. The lateral extent and continuity of the peat layers and relief of the underlying mineral soil can be determined with ground penetrating radar (GPR). We designed an extensive network of GPR profiles with coring sites and with *in situ* hydraulic conductivity measurements in northeastern Estonian mires. The hydraulic conductivity was measured *in situ* using BAT-geosystems permeameters in highly decomposed peats and conventional piezometer slug-tests in less decomposed part of the peatland. Botanical composition and degree of decomposition on von Post scale were described at the field and each layer was subsampled for laboratory analysis. We measured the dry bulk density, ash content in the laboratory and compared those with *in situ* hydraulic conductivity measurements. Results show that different peat layers can be distinguished from the radar profiles. There is also an indication that the hydraulic conductivity depends on the combination of different parameters.

Keywords: mires, hydraulic conductivity, ground penetrating radar, dry bulk density, degree of decomposition

INTRODUCTION

Mires are one of the most important soil carbon sinks in the northern hemisphere where the amount of stored carbon is estimated to be approximately 1055 Gt (Nichols & Peteet, 2019). They are also acting as a natural habitat for many rare plant and animal species. Carbon dioxide and other greenhouse gas emissions from peat are strongly related to the water table in mires (Moore & Knowles, 1989). Mire vegetation is also strongly related to the waterregime and plant communities living there are greatly affected by even small shifts of the water level.
The hydrology of mires is very complex and cannot be taken unequivocally. Conventional acrotelm/catotelm conceptual model (Ingram, 1978) is not always useful and peat properties such as hydraulic conductivity, dry bulkdensity, degree of decomposition and botanical content can vary even on a microscale level laterally and vertically (Baird et al., 2016). Carrying out singular hydraulic conductivity tests in different microforms is very time- consuming and thus cannot be used to study the hydraulic conductivity of peat at great extents, so more general and easier methods are needed to characterize the hydrology of different peatlands on a larger scale. The purpose of this work is to study the hydrology of the mires in North-Eastern Estonia by finding connections between the hydraulic conductivity and other peat properties, such as bulk density, degree of decomposition, ash content and botanical composition and relate those findings with the data seen from the GPR profiles.

MATERIALS AND METHODS

The peat samples were collected from the mires in northeastern Estonia with a Russian type peat corer. The samples were taken so that every significant peat layer in the cross-section would be represented. Botanical composition along with the degree of decomposition on von Post scale was determined in situ. The gathered samples were takeninto the laboratory where peat properties, such as dry bulk density and ash content were measured (Chambers et al., 2011). A sled mounted Ground Penetrating Radar (Zond 12e; Radar Systems Inc) working at 300 MHz frequency was used to study the lateral extent and thickness of different peat layers. The acquired data were post processed and topographically corrected using Prism 2 software. Peat core descriptions were used during interpretation of radar profiles. The hydraulic conductivity of peat was measured with permeameters (Torstensson, 1984) in less permeable peat layers and using PVC piezometers (slug-test method) in the more conductive peat horizons. The hydraulic conductivity was calculated using a method that is combining Hvorslev, 1951 falling head test theory with the Boyle's-Mariotte's law (Torstensson, 1984) in the case of the permeameter tests and by applying Hvorslev, 1951 formula in case of the slug-tests. The hydraulic conductivity tests were conducted at thesame depth with taken peat samples. The relations between the hydraulic conductivity (K) and other physical properties of peat were analyzed statistically and a generalized linear model was fitted to the dataset to evaluate the possibility of predicting K values from the more easily measured peat parameters.

RESULTS AND DISCUSSION

As the variation of hydraulic conductivity over all measurements is very high, ranging from 2.0×10^{-10} to 6.05×10^{-4} m/s, it shows nonlinear relationships with the other measured parameters. To better study the relationships and to fit a general linear model, the K values were log(10)-transformed. As depth of the measurements showed non-linearity with the log10(K) values, the variable was also log(10)- transformed for the modeling process. All the independent variables significantly improved the overall performance of the model according to the F-tests ($p<0.05$ in all cases). The model fitted with all the possible variables also showed the lowest AIC- score over all the othervariable combinations modeled, making it the preferred choice. The results of the final simple generalized linear model are shown in Table 1 and summarized with Equation 1, where BD is the dry bulk density (g/cm^3); VP is the von Post score as a descriptor of the degree of decomposition; log10depth is the transformed depth of measurementbelow peat surface; AC is the ash content of the sample as percentage (%) of the whole dry sample; omb or tr arethe categorical values decoded 0 or 1 depending on the botanical composition of the peat sample. The predictive performance of the model is pictured with Figure 1.

$$\log_{10} K = -4.115 - 17.200BD - 0.188VP - 1.729 \log_{10} depth + 0.033AC + 0.305omb - 0.321tr$$

(1)

The proposed model can explain 66% of the variation in log10K values (adjusted R^2=0.664). The dry bulk density(g/cm^{-3}) has the highest relative effect on the log10K values according to the standardized regression coefficients (-0.728), followed by log10depth (-0.585) and von Post score (-0.521). Ash content and the hydraulic phase of the mire, through which the botanical composition of the peat is characterized, have the least relative effect on the log10K values (standardized coefficient values: 0.214, 0.305 and -0.321 respectively, see Table 1). This kind of a generalizable predictive model can describe the hydraulic conductivity of peat relatively well and could be used to calculate a basic estimation of the K based on the more easily determined physical properties of the peat.

Table 1. Results of the general linear model.

Descriptor	**Category**	**Coefficient**	**Standard Error**	**Standardized coefficient**	**t**	**Significance**
Intercept		-4.115	0.336	-	12.241	<0.001
Dry bulk density (g/cm^3)		-17.200	2.941	-0.728	-5.848	<0.001
Von Post score		-0.188	0.040	-0.521	-4.664	<0.001
Log10depth (m)		-1.729	0.266	-0.585	-6.509	<0.001
Ash content (%)		0.033	0.015	0.214	2.190	0.030
Phase	minerotrophic	-	-	-	-	-
	ombotrophic	0.305	0.235	0.305	1.296	0.196
	transitional	-0.321	0.269	-0.321	-1.193	0.235

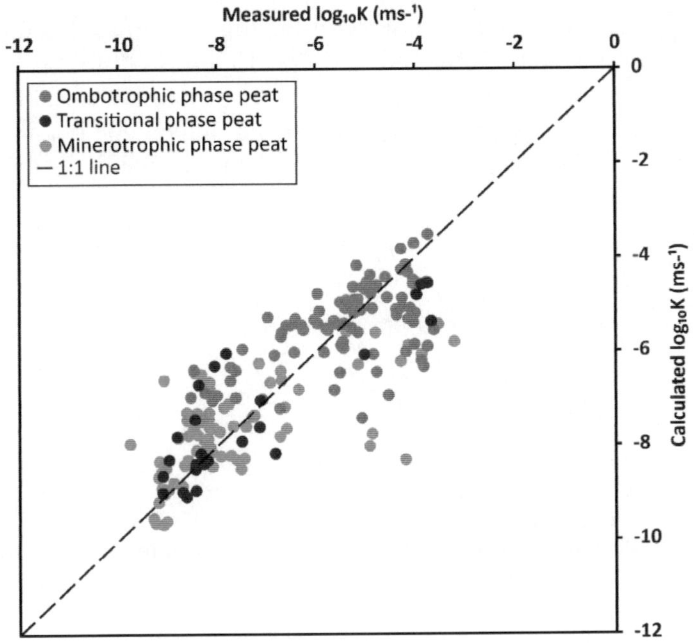

Figure 1. Performance of the general linear model (table 1).

At least three layers can be distinguished from most of the GPR profiles (Figure 2). The clearest seen reflector is marking the boundary between the underlying mineral sediments and peat column. The fen stage peat, consistingmostly of sedges and reeds, is also well detectable on the profiles. This highly decomposed layer shows faint to no distinct reflectors on the profile with increasing depth from the surface. The bog stage peat, consisting mainlyof sphagnum mosses, can be differentiated from the profiles as a layer with reflectors showing mostly no distinguishable layer surfaces. One additional layer with clearer and distinct reflections can be seen on the profiles. These reflectors coincide with the highly amorphous peat layer that mostly consists of decomposed tree stumps

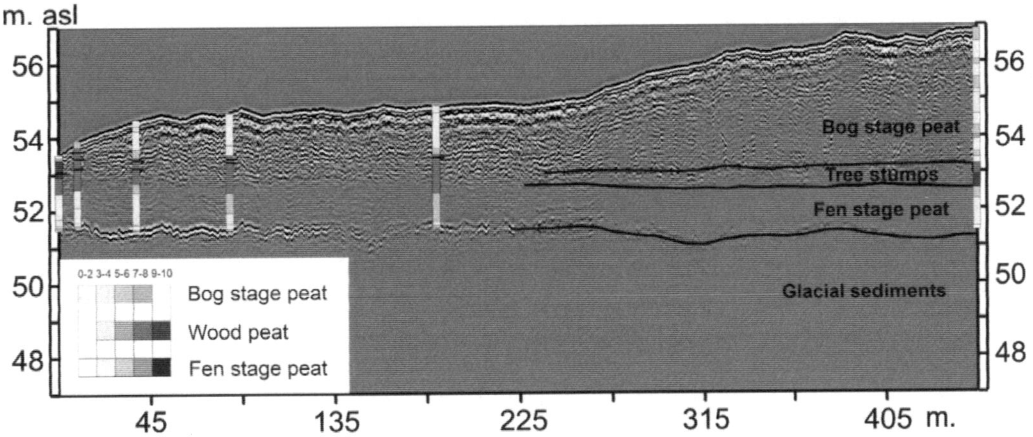

Figure 2. Ground penetrating radar profile of the Selisoo bog with boreholes and von Post scores.

CONCLUSION

Physical properties such as dry bulk density, degree of decomposition, $\log_{10}$depth, ash content and botanical composition can explain an adequate amount of variability of the log(10)- transformed hydraulic conductivity of the peat. The resulting model coupled with the findings of the GPR profiling can offer an easy and less time- consuming way to gain basic knowledge about the hydraulic functioning of the peatland. This kind of approach could be implemented to gain necessary data for any future hydrological or hydrogeological modeling of the peatlands in the northeastern Estonia.

ACKNOWLEDGEMENTS

This project was funded by the Estonian Environmental Investment Centre (project number: 14533).

REFERENCES

Baird, A. J., Milner, A. M., Blundell, A., Swindles, G. T., & Morris, P. J. (2016). Microform-scale variations in peatland permeability and their ecohydrological implications. *Journal of Ecology*, *104*(2), 531–544.

Chambers, F. M., Beilman, D. W., & Yu, Z. (2011). Methods for determining peat humification and for quantifying peat bulk density , organic matter and carbon content for palaeostudies of climate and peatlandcarbon dynamics. *Mires and Peat*, *7*(September 2016), 1–10.

Hvorslev, M. J. (1951). Time Lag and Soil Permeability in Ground-Water Observations. *WaterwaysExperimental Station Bulletin 36*, 1–50

Ingram, H. A. P. (1978). SOIL LAYERS IN MIRES: FUNCTION AND TERMINOLOGY. *Journal of SoilScience*, *29*(2), 224–227. https://doi.org/10.1111/j.1365-2389.1978.tb02053.x

Moore, T. R., & Knowles, R. (1989). The influence of water table levels on methane and carbon dioxideemissions from peatland soils. *Canadian Journal of Soil Science*, *69*(1), 33–38.

Nichols, J. E., & Peteet, D. M. (2019). Rapid expansion of northern peatlands and doubled estimate ofcarbon storage. *Nature Geoscience*, *12*(11), 917–921.

Torstensson, B.-A. (1984). A New System for Ground Water Monitoring. *Groundwater Monitoring &Remediation*, *4*(4), 131–138.

ID 62570

EXPORT OF SUSPENDED SOLIDS AND NUTRIENTS FROM SMALL FORESTED CATCHMENT AREAS ON DRAINED PEAT SOILS

*Zane Kalvite[1], Ivars Klavins[1], Laura Voitina[2], Zane Libiete[1], Aigars Indriksons[3]

[1] Latvian State Forest Research Institute 'Silava', University of Latvia, Latvia
[2] University of Latvia, Latvia
[3] Latvia University of Life Sciences and Technologies, Latvia

zane.kalvite@silava.lv

Studies on the interactions of forests and aquatic ecosystems in Latvian forest science have always been important, and forest management impact on water quality recently has gained special attention. Various forestry activities may affect water ecosystems, posing a risk of erosion and increased runoff of suspended solids and nutrients, for example, from clearfelling areas, road reconstruction and drainage system maintenance sites. Drainage systems, acting as water transportation channels, may facilitate leaching of suspended solids and nutrients, therefore, to ensure sustainable interaction between forestry and water management and plan adequate mitigation measures, scientifically sound information is required.

Runoff data and measurements of physical and chemical parameters from five catchments on drained peat soils were used to calculate export of suspended solids and nutrients. The study area is located in the central part of Latvia, Veseta river watershed in experimental forests of Forest Research Station Kalsnava where the discharge is measured on main ditches of the drainage system with V-notch weirs since 1968. The total area of the studied catchments is 455 ha (area of individual catchments varies from 29.6 to 131.3 ha), forest cover exceeds 90%. First time drainage in the area was carried out during the 1960s. In 2016 the drainage system maintenance was carried out.

Yearly export of nutrients and suspended solids was calculated for different time periods (1997-2001, 2015-2016 and 2019-2020) depending on availability of water chemical, physical and runoff data. Yearly export of N-NH4+ varied 0.032-14.130 kg·yr/ha; N-NO3- – 0.000-27.483 kg·yr/ha; P-PO43- – 0.000-0.614 kg·yr/ha. Calculations were also performed for Cl, Na, DOC, S-SO42-, TN, TSS and base cations. Export of biogenic elements and suspended solids in periods of observations has been affected by volume of runoff due to changes in precipitation and drainage system maintenance.

ID 62745

DOES A PEAT PRODUCTION PLAY A MAJOR ROLE IN LAKE SEDIMENTATION – SEDIMENTATION PATTERNS OF 62 FINNISH LAKES

*Tuija Vähäkuopus, Tommi Kauppila, Jari Mäkinen, Antti Ojala, Samu Valpola

Geological Survey of Finland, Finland

tuija.vahakuopus@gtk.fi

Peat extraction activities and the related drainage of the peatlands are known to result in an increase in water flow from the peat production sites, stronger peakedness of the hydrograph, and in the export of suspended solids and dissolved organic matter. This has caused concerns of the impacts of peat extraction in the receiving water bodies and it is often assumed that peat extraction would cause excessive increase of organic matter sedimentation in downstream lake basins, resulting in thick sediment deposits and significant changes in sediment quality.

Attempts have been made to separate the effects of peat extraction and peatland forest drainage in the lacustrine environment in Finland. More robust and generalizable results on the effects of peat extraction on lacustrine sedimentation can be obtained by increasing the number of study sites.

Geological Survey of Finland conducted a lake sediment research project assessing the possible impact of environmental loading of peat production compared to other land uses in lakes and waterways. Altogether 62 lakes were selected for further studies. The study aimed at identifying and selecting basins from two lake groups; the first group of lakes receives waters from peat production areas (impacted lakes) while the other lake group has other land uses than peat extraction in their catchment (reference lakes).

The aims of the study were to investigate i) between-group differences in the rate of recent sedimentation, ii) between-group differences in sediment chemical composition, and to iii) characterize the common lake and catchment properties that have an effect on the sediment quality in these basins. In addition, the results will provide general information on the properties of lacustrine sediments and sedimentation patterns in peatland-rich regions in western Finland, which are typically intensively drained for forestry, agriculture, and peat extraction.

ID 62767

SURFACE WATER QUALITY AND PEAT PRODUCTION: MITIGATING EFFECT OF SEDIMENTARY PONDS

*Marge Uppin[1], Anna-Helena Purre[1,2]

[1] STEIGER Engineering LLC, Tallinn, Estonia
[2] School of Natural Sciences and Health, Tallinn University, Tallinn, Estonia

marge@steiger.ee

SUMMARY

Surface water quality impacted by the drainage from peatlands with anthropogenic impacts such as peat milling or forestry are one of the main concerns related to peat production. In Estonia, about 20 000 ha are covered by active milled peatlands, making up 0,5 % of land area, so milled peatlands make up significant area of drainage basins of many rivers. To reduce the impact of peatland drainage to quality of surface water, several mitigation measures such as sedimentary ponds or constructed treatment wetland for water cleaning can be used. We aimed at determining the impact of active milled peatlands on surface water quality, and assessing the overall effect of mitigating measures on the drainage water quality.

During water quality monitoring conducted by peat production companies in 2014 - 2020, pH, suspended solids (SS), total nitrogen (N_{tot}) and total phosphorus (P_{tot}) concentrations, biological oxygen demand (BOD_7), and chemical oxygen demand (COD) was determined from the outflows of 30 peat production areas in Estonia. Sampling was done 1 – 4 separate times on 104 points dividing into near-natural recipient (without peat production), peat production without mitigation measures, peat production with mitigation measures, and water from recipient and peat production area.

Drainage water quality met generally the requirements of legislation. Mitigation measures such as sedimentary ponds significantly reduce the amount of BOD_7, SS and P_{tot} in drainage water from peat production sites. Drainage water from milled peatlands have higher COD and N_{tot} than natural recipient, however there was no mitigating effect of sedimentary ponds. Although drainage water from peat production areas corresponds to requirements in Estonia, application of mitigation measures such as sedimentary ponds can further reduce the concentrations of SS and P_{tot} in outflow. These indicators are the main water quality concerns related to peat production in Estonia.

***Keywords**: peat excavation, water quality, wastewater, nutrition load, leaching*

INTRODUCTION

Surface water quality impacted by the drainage from peatlands with anthropogenic impacts such as peat milling or forestry are one of the main concerns related to peat production. In Estonia, about 20 000 ha are covered by active milled peatlands, making up 0.5 % of land area. So, milled peatlands make up significant area of drainage basins of many rivers. To quantify and mitigate those impacts several drainage water quality indicators such as amount of suspended solids (SS), chemical oxygen demand (COD), biochemical oxygen demand (BOD_7), contents of total nitrogen (N_{tot}) and phosphorus (P_{tot}), and pH are monitored in drainage water outflows of peat production sites. In addition, if there can be expected any impact from the drainage water on the recipient water body, peat producers also monitor the water quality of the recipient water body to which the drainage waters are led.

There is little leaching of nutrients or erosion of SS (both organic and mineral particulates) in undisturbed peatlands, because of microbial immobilisation and plant uptake. Drainage decreases water level and increases the oxygen content of the soil, which increases the decomposition of organic matter and mineralization. Decomposition results in leaching of nutrients that were previously immobilised in partly decomposed plants (Kløve, 2001). SS, mainly composed of plant detritus, is transported with drainage water issuing from a peat excavation area mostly as a result of erosion or to a minor extent through wind action or the effects of machinery used on the site. Besides presented as a SS, organic matter is washed out of a peat excavation area and carried out by drainage ditches as dissolved substances. The acidity of the runoff water from natural mires vary according to its nutrient concentration, for example *Sphagnum* mires may even have a pH less than 4. The ditching of a peat excavation area results in increasing discharge, which increase the acidity of the outflow water at first by comparison with the natural state. After few years the pH of the runoff water will rise (Svahnbäck, 2007). Thus, peat excavation may cause elevated nutrient, organic matter, and SS concentrations in downstream waters. The environmental changes caused by peatland drainage include eutrophication of waterbody and SS settling in downstream, affecting aquatic and benthic communities (Kløve, 2001).

To reduce the impact of peatland drainage to quality of surface water, several mitigation measures such as sedimentary ponds or constructed wetland can be used for cleaning the water. According to the main regulations concerning the water quality in Estonia – Water Act and Minister of Environment regulation no 61, the set maximum limits for drainage water from the peat production sites are SS 40 mg/l, BOD_7 15 mg/l, P_{tot} 1 mg/l and N_{tot} 45 mg/l. Additionally, pH must be monitored, and COD can be monitored, while there are no limits set for these indicators in legislation From 2019, also monitoring of oil products (maximum limit 5 mg/l) is required on all peat production sites. As before enforcement of this change in legislation in 2020, monitoring of oil products has been done only occasionally on few sites, this variable was currently not included in this study. There are no set limits for water quality monitoring of recipient water bodies, and in recipient water bodies BOD_5 instead of BOD_7 is monitored.

The purpose of the study is to determine the impact of active milled peatlands on surface water quality in Estonia and assess the overall effect of mitigating measures on the drainage water quality.

MATERIALS AND METHODS

During water quality monitoring conducted by peat production companies in 2014 - 2020, pH, suspended solids (SS), total N and P concentrations, biochemical oxygen demand (BOD_7 in drainage water and BOD_5 in recipient water), and chemical oxygen demand (COD) was determined from the outflows of 30 peat production areas in Estonia (figure 1). Sampling points divided into near-natural recipient (without peat production), peat production outflows without mitigation measures, peat production outflows with mitigation measures, and mixed water from the recipient and the peat production area. Study sites were chosen so that at least four years of water quality data was available for all sites, whereas for half of the sites data was available for all of the years and sampling periods. Sampling was generally done two times per year (usually II (spring, S) and III (autumn, A) quarter) per sampling point, or at least once a year in case of recipient monitoring. Water sampling is done during the peat production period (generally May-September in Estonia). Total of 66 up to 124 sampling points were analyzed during each of the sampling times each year. If the water level was very low and there was no water outflow, water quality sampling was generally not done.

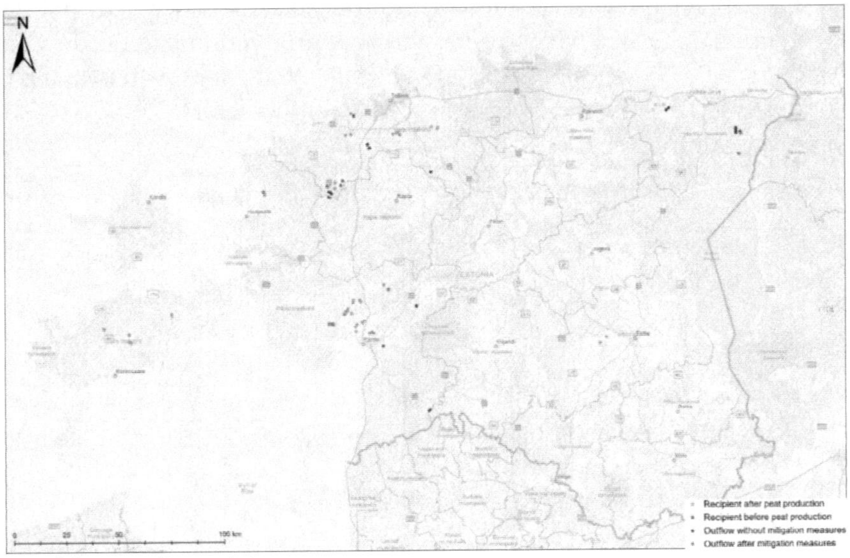

Figure 1. Locations of the sampling points.

According to regulation no 49 of Minister of Environment "Sampling methods", sampling must be done by person accredited to sampling of surface water and sewage water. In study sites, sampling has been done by accredited experts outside of the peat production company or by accredited person inside the company. Samples were transported to the accredited laboratory in Estonia in cool and dark box. All analysis results have been also reported to the Environmental Board. Sampling in some sites and years, and all of the data analysis was done by the authors of this study. For data analysis, IBM SPSS ver 23 was used, where non-parametric data analysis methods (Mann-Whitney tests, Spearman correlation coefficients) were applied.

RESULTS

Water quality in the outflows of the peat production site generally met the requirements set in the Estonian legislation. Most problematic variable not meeting the requirements was concentration of SS. No problems occurred with amount of nutrients in the drainage waters (table 1). There has been no clear direction of the temporal trend in percent of samples meeting the water quality criteria, while SS levels have weakly increased and pH levels decreased over the study period (table 2).

Table 1. Percent of drainage water samples not fulfilling the water quality criteria requirements set in Minister of Environment regulation no 61. There are no set limits for those criteria requirements in natural waters, so the data from natural waters is not shown.

	SS	BOD_7	N_{tot}	P_{tot}
Peat production site with settling	2 %	0%	0 %	0 %
Peat production site without settling	4 %	1 %	0 %	0 %

Application of mitigation measures generally decreased ($Z > 4$; $p < 0.01$) the amount of pollution indicators (SS, BOD_7, P_{tot}, COD), while this was not the so for N_{tot} ($Z = 0.2$; $p > 0.05$) and pH ($Z = 0.4$; $p > 0.05$; figure 2). Surface water before the peat production site outflow (natural waters) had similar ($Z < 1.3$; $p > 0.05$) levels of SS, BOD_5, N_{tot} P_{tot} and pH as waters in the recipient water body after peat production, while later had significantly higher COD ($Z= 3$; $p < 0.01$) than before the outflow from the peat production site.

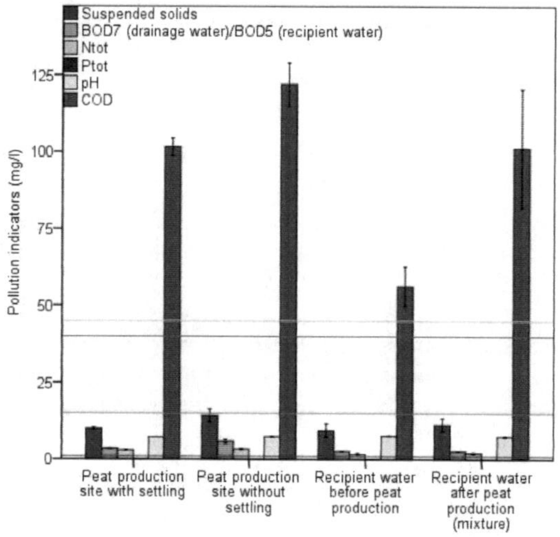

Figure 2. Water quality criteria related to peat production in studied sites. Average values are brought out with standard errors. Lines with different colours indicate the set limits for respective water quality criteria in Minister of Environment regulation no 61

Effect of different mitigation measures (different number (1-3) of settling ponds on one outflow, artificial water purification wetlands) on water quality was analysed. Settling the drainage water in one or two settling ponds reduced significantly ($Z > 2.6$; $p < 0.05$) the concentrations of SS, BOD_7, P_{tot} and COD in comparison with unsettled drainage waters. While by using three settling ponds resulted in increased levels of N_{tot} ($Z=3.1$; $p < 0.01$), but decreased the level of P_{tot} ($Z = 3.6$; $p < 0.01$), and had no effect on other criteria of water quality ($Z < 1.5$; $p > 0.05$). In few larger peat production sites also artificial wetlands have been built for drainage water purification, which significantly lowers the concentrations of all water quality indicators (SS, BOD_7, N_{tot}, P_{tot}, COD; $Z > 2.8$; $p < 0.01$) except pH ($Z = 1$; $p > 0.05$).

All concentrations of different water quality variables correlated statistically significantly with each other (table 2). Amount of SS had stronger correlations with BOD_7 and P_{tot}. COD had stronger correlations with BOD_7, N_{tot}, P_{tot} and pH. Although all other water quality variables correlated positively with other quality variables, pH had negative correlations with all other water quality variables, indicating that with higher pH of the drainage water, the water quality tends to improve.

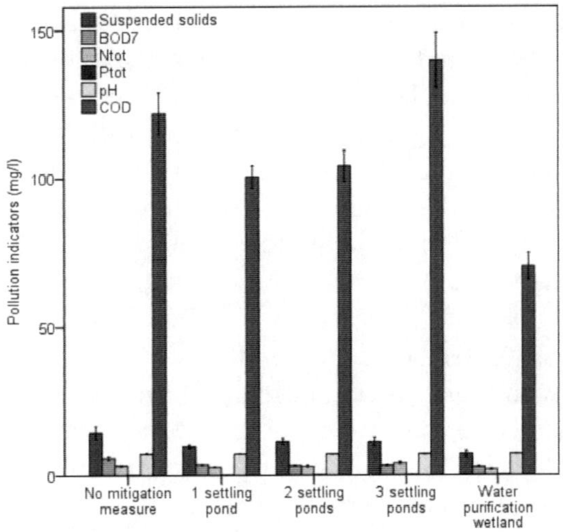

Figure 3. Water quality criteria in outflows of peat production sites with different mitigation measures. Average values are brought out with standard errors.

Table 2. Spearman correlation coefficients between sampling time and water quality variables.

	Sampling time	SS	BOD_5/ BOD7	N_{tot}	P_{tot}	pH	COD
Suspended solids	0.14*	–					
BOD_5/BOD_7	-0.06	0.26*	–				
N_{tot}	-0.03	0.12*	0.18*	–			
P_{tot}	-0.03	0.32*	0.29*	0.18*	–		
pH	-0.15*	-0.12*	-0.11*	-0.15*	-0.11*	–	
COD	-0.01	0.25*	0.31*	0.29*	0.32*	-0.32*	–

Statistical significance of the correlation coefficient is shown with the asterisk (*), indicating that the correlation coefficient is significant on level $p < 0.01$.

DISCUSSION

Peat production causes nutrient and suspended solids load to the watercourse. However, N and P loading to surface water is rather small in Estonia, the main concern related to peat excavation is suspended solids (both organic and mineral particulate) and organic matter load to surface water. Load of solids is highest in the spring during the snow melting, and during heavy rains in summer and autumn, mostly because of erosion (Gregory et al. 2007). Our study generally supports the previous results related with correlations between the water quality indicators. Tuukkanen et al. (2016) reported strong and positive correlations between concentration of SS and P_{tot}, which is confirmed by the results of this study. Therefore, it can be expected that the P_{tot} loads are generally transported via SS, and by reducing the amount of SS (e.g. by settling ponds or longer ditch network as proposed by Gregory et al. 1984) can reduce also the phosphorus load on the surface water quality. No such strong correlation between the P_{tot} and SS was found in study by Kløve (2001). The differences between studies could be the result of different peat botanical composition and therefore peat chemo-physical properties in production sites. In the study by Svahnbäck (2007) significant positive correlation between P_{tot} and SS was found in case of *Carex* peat and correlation was insignificant on *Sphagnum* peat. Our study also supports the results of Tuukkanen et al. (2016) about the negative correlations between pH, and COD and N_{tot}, although correlations in this study are somewhat weaker than reported by Tuukkanen et al. (2016). Similar correlations, although statistically insignificant have been reported before by Svahnbäck (2007).

Most common way reduce the SS load (and therefore also P_{tot}) is to establish sedimentation ponds before leading the drainage water out from the peat production area to recipient. Besides reducing the SS load, total P content, COD and BOD_7 values decrease after treatment in sedimentary pond, as these are related to organic particulate of SS. However, sedimentary pond has no effect on pH values and total N content in water. To ensure the efficiency of the sedimentation pond, it must be regularly maintained. The larger nutrient and SS load reducing effect of mitigation measures such as sedimentation ponds on SS and P_{tot} concentrations than N_{tot} is reported before by Kløve (2000). Suspended solids settle to the bottom of the pond and need to be removed once a year to prevent reducing the storage capacity of the pond. Otherwise, the drainage water residence time in pond is insufficient for settling and results in increased SS load to the recipient. Insufficient settling times and higher erosion has been reported before by St-Hilaire et al. (2006) in Canadian peat excavation site in climatic conditions with higher precipitation (818 mm/a) than in Estonia (573- 761 mm/a). Constructed treatment wetlands are found to be more effective than sedimentary ponds for drainage water treatment (similarly to Kløve, 2000), having also effective by reducing total N content in water. However, the use of wetlands is restricted, as it needs large area to establish. Also, sedimentary ponds and constructed wetlands are reported to be inefficient (or even increase SS loads) in e.g. forestry-drained peatlands, where these mitigation measures cannot be constructed into thick peat layer, with sufficient dimensions, and maintained as often as necessary (Nieminen et al. 2018). Assessing the effect of peat excavation on drainage water depends also on water sampling methods and quality. It is recommended that water samples must be representative, not taken at extreme weather condition (incl flooding). Also, water sampling during the minimum water level should be avoided, as during the sampling ditch bottom sediments may end up in the sampling container, which maybe cause of some of the exceedances reported in this study.

CONCLUSION

Our results show that generally drainage water quality meets the national requirements, or even stays significantly below the set limits. Occasional exceeding of the limits are probably result of not applying the mitigation measures (settling ponds, artificial water purification wetlands), not applying and managing these properly (settling ponds have to be cleaned at least once a year and engineered taking into account the size of the peat production site), or incorrect sampling methods (e.g. sampling from stagnant water). The settling ponds have effect on reducing the amount of suspended solids, biochemical and chemical oxygen demand and total P content, whereas having no significant effect on total N content or pH. Use of artificial water purification wetlands lower the concentrations of all studied criteria but have no effect on pH. Therefore, if high nitrogen concentrations are problematic, water purification wetlands should be preferred instead of settling ponds.

ACKNOWLEDGEMENTS

Authors thank peat producers AS Tootsi Turvas, AS Jiffy Products Estonia, OÜ KEKKILÄ-BVB EESTI, Biolan Baltic OÜ, ASB Greenworld Eesti OÜ, MV Turvas OÜ and AS Torf for allowing to use their monitoring data in this study.

REFERENCES

1. Gregory J.D, Skaggs R.W, Broadhead R.G, Culbreath R.H, Bailey J.R, Foutz T.L. (1984) Hydrologic and water quality impacts of peat mining in North Carolina. Water Resources Research Institute of the University of North Carolina.
2. Minister of Environment. Regulation no 49 from 03.10.2019. Proovivõtumeetodid. In force from 11.10.2019.
3. Minister of Environment. Regulation no 61 from 08.11.2019. Nõuded reovee puhastamise ning heit-, sademe-, kaevandus-, karjääri- ja jahutusvee suublasse juhtimise kohta, nõuetele vastavuse hindamise meetmed ning saasteainesisalduse piirväärtused[1]. In force from 15.11.2019.
4. Water Act. Passed 30.01.2019 by Riigikogu. In force from 01.01.2021.
5. Kløve B. (2000) Retention of suspended solids and sediment bound nutrients from peat harvesting sites with peak runoff control, constructed floodplains and sedimentation ponds. *Boreal Environment Research*; 5: 81-94.
6. Kløve B. (2001) Characteristics of nitrogen and phosphorus loads in peat mining wastewater. *Water Resources*; 35: 2353-2362.
7. Nieminen M, Piirainen S, Sikström U, Löfgren S, Marttila H, Sarkkola S, Laurén A, Finér L. (2018) Ditch network maintenance in peat-dominated boreal forests: Review and analysis of water quality management options. *Ambio*; 47: 535-545.
8. St-Hilaire A, Courtenay S.C, Diaz-Delgado C, Pavey B, Ouarda T.B.M.J, Boghen A, Bobée B. (2006) Suspended Sediment Concentrations Downstream of a Harvested Peat Bog: Analysis and Preliminary Modelling of Exceedances Using Logistic Regression. *Canadian Water Resources Journal*; 31: 139-156.
9. Svahnbäck L. (2007) Precipitation-induced runoff and leaching from milled peat mining mires by peat types: a comparative method for estimating the loading of water bodies during peat production. Department of Geology, University of Helsinki.
10. Tuukkanen T, Kløve B, Marttila H, Heikkinen K, Karppinen A. (2016) Processes and site characteristics controlling nutrient and sediment runoff loads from peat harvesting sites. *14th International Peat Congress*. Extended abstract No. 312.

ID 72812

SMALL-SCALE SPATIAL VARIABILITY OF HYDRO-PHYSICAL PROPERTIES OF NATURAL AND DEGRADED PEAT SOILS

*Miaorun Wang, Haojie Liu, Bernd Lennartz

Faculty of Agricultural and Environmental Sciences, University of Rostock, Germany

miaorun.wang@uni-rostock.de

The spatial variability of soil properties plays an important role in water and carbon cycles in peatlands. The objective of this study was to analyze the spatial variation of hydro-physical properties of peat soils and to establish pedotransfer functions (PTFs) to estimate the hydraulic properties of peat using readily available soil properties. We selected three study sites, each representing a different state of peat degradation (natural, degraded and extremely degraded). At each site, 72 undisturbed soil cores were collected from 5 m by 5 m grid cells in an area of 35 m by 40 m. The saturated hydraulic conductivity (Ks), soil water retention curves, total porosity, macroporosity (pore diameter > 50 μm), bulk density and soil organic matter content (SOM) were determined for all sampling locations. The Van Genuchten (VG) model parameters (θs, α and n) were optimized using the RETC software package. A strong positive correlation between macroporosity and Ks was observed irrespective of the degradation stage of the peat. However, the relationships between macroporosity and Ks differed between the natural and the drained peatlands. Adding macroporosity to the PTFs substantially improves the prediction of Ks and VG parameters. Results showed that the soil hydro-physical properties (e.g., Ks and VG model parameters) exhibit different levels of spatial heterogeneity depending on the peat degradation stage. The geostatistical analysis suggests that the spatial dependence of soil hydro-physical properties varies depending on the considered property as well as land management (e.g., drainage). Bulk density and SOM are spatially dependent, whereas Ks and macroporosity are spatially independent if the peat is severely degraded. Overall, the peat degradation stage plays an important role and should be generally considered in the spatial analysis of peatlands. The obtained semivariograms may serve as a basis for 2D and 3D hydrological modelling and peatland restoration studies.

ID 72858

LANDSCAPE-LEVEL EVALUATION OF WATER STORAGE AND ITS SEASONAL VARIATION IN A TROPICAL PEATLAND, WEST KALIMANTAN, INDONESIA

*Niken Andika Putri[1], Tsuyoshi Kato[1]

[1]PT. Mayangkara Tanaman Industri/PT. Wana Subur Lesatri, Jakarta, Indonesia

niken@wanasl.com

SUMMARY

Tropical peatlands are important carbon reservoirs and play an essential role in regulating the water balance. The ecosystem services provided by tropical peatlands, such as carbon storage and watershed protection functions, have attracted attention in conservation and rehabilitation. However, general knowledge on tropical peatlands water storage capacity is little known due to in situ measurements' technical difficulties. This study aims to estimate the volume of water stored in a tropical peatland at the landscape level. The study was conducted in the two forest plantation areas and adjacent protection forest with 125,010 ha. Firstly, topographic and peat depth surveys were conducted across the landscape by applying a high-accuracy survey protocol. The groundwater levels (GWLs) and rainfall were measured automatically and manually in the study areas. In total, there were 868 and 30 monitoring points for GWLs and rainfall, respectively. The analysis was done using GWLs and rainfall data from January to December 2020. The mean annual precipitation is 3786 mm, with 3884 mm in areas relatively close to the coast and 3688 mm inland, with a tendency for precipitation to decrease in inland areas. The result showed that the water storage capacity of the study area is about 5.6 billion m^3. Despite the seasonality of precipitation and changes in local precipitation patterns, no significant changes were observed in the monthly water storage volume determined from the GWLs. The reason for the absence of significant seasonal changes in water storage in the landscape was suggested to be the use of stock-based water management for peatland management.

Keywords: *landscape, groundwater level, rainfall, tropical peatland, water management*

INTRODUCTION

Tropical peatlands are distributed over in the Amazon, Congo Basin, Southeast Asia, and Papua New Guinea. Many studies have been done to recognize the importance of tropical peatlands as a terrestrial carbon pool. However, other vital roles of tropical peatlands are not being studied as much as carbon storage function. Tropical peatlands play roles in the regional and local water cycle, influencing groundwater recharge and river base flow(Bourgault et al. 2014). The hydrological function of tropical peatlands is assumed to be identically important as the carbon storage function. Unfortunately, general knowledge on tropical peatlands water storage capacity is less known due to in situ measurements' technical difficulties.

Peat is an organic material with high water content, in which it occupied about 95 % water by weight and 85 % by volume (Lindsay et al. 2019). For that reason, tropical peatlands are essential for water storage and supply. To date, there is increasing attention in the understanding of the forest-water relationship. A study by Ellison et al. (2017) revealed that forest-water interactions have many benefits, such as terrestrial surface cooling, groundwater recharge, flood moderation, water purification, and infiltration. Further, the long-distance forest-water relationships are also essential for rainfall generation and water supply through water moisture recycling (Noordwijk and Ellison 2019). According to van der Ent et al. (2010), approximately 40% of terrestrial precipitation originates from forest evapotranspiration, in which roughly half the evapotranspiration returns as rainfall over land. Although the forests-water relationship is starting to get acknowledged, their interaction in the tropical peatlands remains unclear.

An urgent rethinking of tropical peatlands' hydrological function is required not to underestimate the importance of tropical peatlands. Therefore, this study aims to estimate the volume of water stored in a tropical peatland at the landscape level and compare the volume of water stored in the plantation area and natural forest. To accomplish those goals, several field surveys were conducted across the landscape by applying a high-accuracy survey protocol. Continuous data collection was also conducted from both areas with and without water management.

MATERIALS AND METHODS

The study site is a tropical peatland located in the western coastal plain of West Kalimantan, Indonesia (Figure 1). It includes two forest concessions of approximately 115,000 ha and Mendawak protection forest of approximately 20000 ha under state control. This study focused on peat of 125,010 ha, and therefore, mineral soil was excluded from further analysis. The climate of the study area is humid tropical, with the dry season usually occurred July to August. The mean annual rainfall in the study area for 2020 was 3786 mm. The two forest concessions are planted with about 20000 ha of *Acacia crassicarpa,* as the main commercial species. Meanwhile, the Mendawak protection forest is a natural forest formed on a huge peat dome with a depth of more than 10 m. The concession areas have been equipped with well-designed and planned water management through several field surveys prior to the operation of the forest plantation.

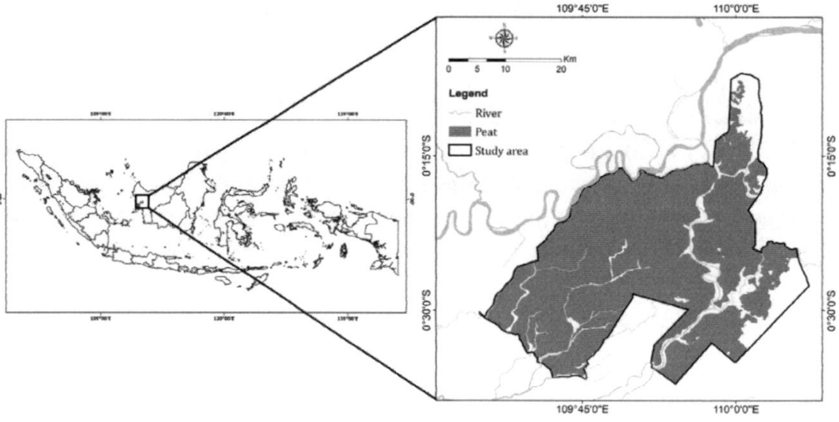

Figure 1. Location of the study area

The topographic survey was conducted manually using theodolite across the landscape with total grid lines of 1800 km and spaced at every 25 to 50 m for measurements. At last, the contour map was created with intervals of 0.5 m. The peat survey was conducted to obtain peat depth dan peat properties information. Peat depth survey was carried out by peat auguring in 900 points along with the transects of 144.2 km long. Meanwhile, the peat characteristics survey was conducted by sampling as many as 144 peat samples taken at 48 points with different elevations using ring samplers. The peat samples were then analysed to determine the peat porosity values.

The groundwater levels (GWLs) and rainfall were measured both manually and automatically in the study areas. In total, there were 868 GWLs monitoring points. The manual method was conducted using Dipwell, while automatic measurement used a data logger. Meanwhile, rainfall was measured automatically using a rain gauge in 30 monitoring points. In addition to manual and automatic measurements, the real-time monitoring system was also applied for GWLs and rainfall monitoring using SESAME II (Sensory data Transmission Services II by Midori Engineering). The system record GWLs and rainfall data every hour which can be checked on the web in real-time. The analysis was then done using GWLs and rainfall data from January to December 2020.

For water storage calcaulation, the areas were divided into three classes of peat depths which are <3 m, 3–7 m, and >7 m considering the variance of peat properties. Next, peat bottom elevation was obtained by subtracting the surface elevation with peat depth. Further, the groundwater table (GWT) was subtracted by peat bottom elevation using a cut-and-fill tool provided by the GIS software (ArcGIS 10.5) to determine the peat volume. Finally, the volume of water stored was estimated by multiplying each peat depth class' mean porosity by the peat volume.

RESULTS

Surface Elevation, Peat Depth, and Peat Porosity

The surface or ground elevation ranged from 0.5 to 13.7 m with the mean of 6.1 m, whereas the peat depth ranged from 0.6 to 12.0 m with the mean of 5.0 m. Prior to the calculation, the entire areas were divided into three-peat depth classes to avoid overestimating or underestimating the volume of water stored. The class of <3 m, 3–7 m, and >7 m account for 36.6 %, 41.8 %, and 21.6 % of the toal areas, respectively. Meanwhile, each peat depth class's porosity was 87.6%, 92.9%, and 93% for <3 m, 3–7 m, and >7 m class, respectively.

Groundwater Levels Fluctuations and Variation in Rainfall

The mean monthly rainfall in the study site during 2020 ranged from 152 to 400 mm. As can be seen from Figure 3 (a), there is no distinct pattern between dry and wet season appeared in the study area. The annual precipitation is 3786 mm, with 3884 mm in areas relatively close to the coast and 3688 mm inland, with a tendency for precipitation to decrease in inland areas. Figure 3 (b) displayed mean monthly GWLs fluctuations during 2020 in plantation area and natural forest. The result demonstrated that the GWLs in the plantation area tended to be stable, with only slight changes across the year. Meanwhile, significant fluctuations in GWLs were observed in the natural forest following the change in rainfall. However, the water table depth in the plantation area appeared smaller than the natural forest.

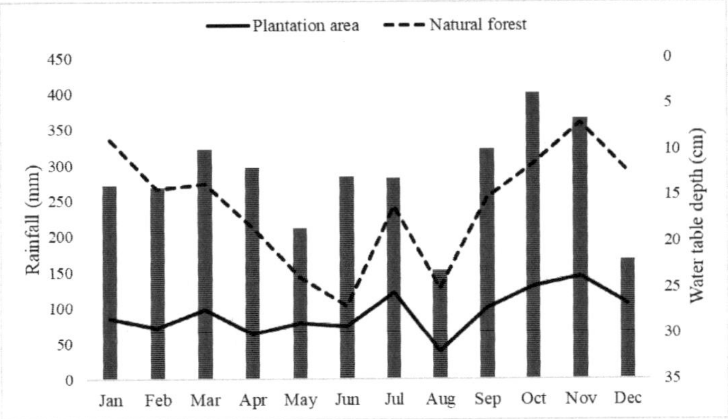

Figure 3. Mean monthly: (a) rainfall from 30 monitoring stations and; (b) groundwater levels from 861 and 7 monitoring points in plantation area and natural forest, respectively

Water Storage and its Seasonal Variation

The estimated volume of monthly water stock at the landscape level is shown in Figure 4 (a). The results showed that the monthly water storage capacity of the study area is about 5.4 to 5.6 billion m^3 or 43000 to 44000 $m^3\ ha^{-1}$. The lowest water stock was found in August, in which case has the lowest rainfall. However, the fluctuations of water storage capacity were not significant compare to the change in rainfall.

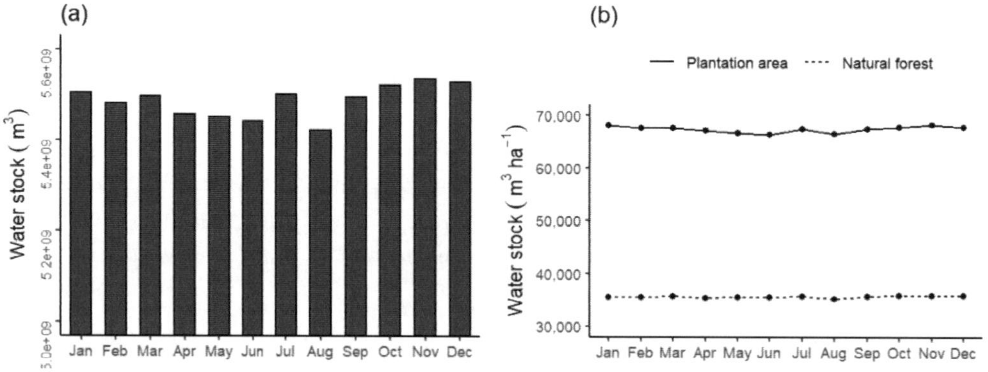

Figure 4. Estimated monthly water stock in the: (a) landscape level and (b) plantation area and natural forest

Water storage capacity was also calculated for both areas with and without water management. As can be seen in Figure 4 (b), the water storage per ha in the plantation area was higher than in the natural forest. The mean monthly water storage of plantation area and natural forest was 35578 m^3 ha^{-1} and 67351 m^3 ha^{-1}, respectively. Despite their high water storage capacity, a slight fluctuation could be observed in the natural forest areas. In comparison, the plantation areas did not show significant changes. Meanwhile, the water storage in peat depth class of <3 m, 3–7 m, and >7 m were 17665, 50436, and 75715 m^3 ha^{-1}, respectively.

DISCUSSION

In this study, we estimated the water storage capacity of tropical peatlands in Indonesia, particularly West Kalimantan. The monthly water storage capacity in the study areas is ranging between 43000 and 44000 m^3 ha^{-1}. These values are four times higher than those reported by previous studies for tropical peatlands in Southeast Brazil (Campos et al. 2012; da Silva et al. 2013; Bispo et al. 2016). Bispo et al. (2016) reported that about 9291 and 10,926 m^3 ha^{-1} of water were stored in two different sites in the Araçuaí River basin in the northeastern Minas Gerais state Brazil. da Silva et al. (2013), in the same state of Minas Gerais, Brazil, reported an average water volume of 9948 m^3 ha^{-1}, while Campos et al. (2012) reported a range between 1039 and 10833 m^3 ha^{-1}.

This difference in result may be due to the difference in the method used to estimated water storage capacity. In the previously mentioned studies, the water stock was measured using the PVC sampler to calculate the total volume of water in the profile. Such a method might be not practical if applied in the area with high variability in topography or peat characteristics. Further, the difference in peat depth can also influence the water storage capacity of tropical peatlands. The average peat depth reported by Campos et al. (2012) was 0.2 – 1.5 m between sections, while da Silva et al. (2013) used an average depth of 1.2 m. Similarly, an average peat depth of 1.1 and 1.3 m was applied by Bispo et al. (2016). In contrast, high variance of peat depth was observed in this study area, where peat depth ranging between 0.6 and 12.0 m with an average of 5.0 m. However, despite its high variance, the peat depth's spatial variability in the study area had been considered during the water storage calculation by utilising the GIS software. The same reason was also applied when comparing water storage capacity in the plantation area and natural forest.

In general, the fluctuation of water stored in peatlands is higher in the natural forest than in the plantation area. This result indicates the importance of water management in maintaining the high water level despite changes in rainfall. Without water management, the GWLs will be difficult to control and maintain, especially during the dry period. A study in the natural forest without water management showed that the water levels could even drop to more than 100 cm below the peat surface during severe dry season (Unpublished data). Under current climatic conditions, it is likely that the water storage capacity of tropical peatlands will be most impacted as the GWLs may experience drastic variation. Not only is that water stored in the tropical peatlands vital for protecting peatland, but their existence is also thought to be important in mitigating climate change through atmospheric moisture recycling. Soil moisture can also be released into the air contributing to cloud generation and precipitation elsewhere or known as "river in the sky" (Ellison et al. 2019). Ultimately, a transformative shift in thinking is required not only just seen tropical peatlands as a carbon or water storage but also as a regulator of climate.

CONCLUSION

In this study, the water storage and its seasonal variation at the landscape level in a tropical peatland were estimated. The result demonstrates that tropical peatland in the study area holds a massive amount of water, four times higher than previously reported in the Brazilian tropical peatland. The difference in calculation method, peat depth, and peat characteristics influence the volume of water stored in the tropical peatlands. The result also shows the importance of proper water management to maintain high water levels evenly distributed throughout the year.

ACKNOWLEDGEMENTS

This study was supported by Sumitomo Forestry, co., Ltd., Alas Kusuma Group, and The Sustainable Trade Initiative (IDH). We thank the entire staff of WSL-MTI for their efforts in field works, data collection, and continuous supports.

REFERENCES

1. Bispo DFA, Silva AC, Christofaro C, Silva MLN, Barbosa MS, Silva BPC, Barral UM, Fabris JD. (2016) Hydrology and carbon dynamics of tropical peatlands from Southeast Brazil. *Catena;* 143:18–25.
2. Bourgault MA, Larocque M, Roy M. (2014) Simulation of aquifer-peatland-river interactions under climate change. *Hydrol Res;* 425–440. https://doi.org/10.2166/nh.2013.228
3. Campos JR da R, Silva AC, Vidal-Torrado P. (2012) Mapping, organic matter mass and water volume of a peatland in Serra do Espinhaço Meridional. *Rev Bras Ciência do Solo;* 36:723–732.
4. da Silva ML., Silva AC., Silva BPC., Barral UM., Soares PGS., Vidal-Torrado P. (2013) Surface mapping, organic matter and water stocks in peatlands of the Serra do Espinhaço meridional - Brazil. *Rev Bras Cienc do Solo;* 37:1149–1157.
5. Ellison D, Morris CE, Locatelli B, Sheil D, Cohen J, Murdiyarso D, Gutierrez V, Noordwijk M Van, Creed IF, Pokorny J, Gaveau D, Spracklen D V, Bargués A, Ilstedt U, Teuling AJ, Gebreyohannis S, Sands DC, Muys B, Verbist B, Springgay E, Sugandi Y, Sullivan CA. (2017) Trees, forests and water: Cool insights for a hot world. *Glob Environ Chang;* 43:51–61. https://doi.org/10.1016/j.gloenvcha.2017.01.002
6. Ellison D, Wang-Erlandsson L, van Noordwijk M. (2019) Upwind forests: managing moisture recycling for nature-based resilience. *Unasylva;* 70:14–26.
7. Ent RJ Van Der, Savenije HHG, Schaefli B, Dunne SCS. (2010) Origin and fate of atmospheric moisture over continents. *Water Resour Res;* 46:1–12.
8. Lindsay R, Ifo A, Cole L, Montanarella L, Nuutinen M. (2019) Peatlands: the challenge of mapping the world's invisible stores of carbon and water. *Unasylva;* 251:46–57.
9. Noordwijk M Van, Ellison D. (2019) Rainfall recycling needs to be considered indefining limits to the world' s green water resources. *PNAS;* 116:8102–8103. https://doi.org/10.1073/pnas.1903554116

ID 62117

PREDICTION, PREVENTION AND CONTROL OF PEATLAND FIRES IN MALAYSIA AND ASEAN REGION

*Faizal Parish, Nagarajan Rengasamy, Serena Lew

Global Environment Centre, Malaysia

fparish@gec.org.my

Peatland fires are one of the main causes of peatland degradation and greenhouse emissions. Extensive areas of peatlands have burned in Southeast Asia over the last 25 years with estimates ranging from 1 to 4 million ha/fire season. Peatland fires in the region are estimated to have emitted 300-900 tCO_2/ha per fire and up to 2 billion tonnes of CO_2 in a severe fire season. The focus of fire management in the region has shifted over the last 30 years from a focus on fire fighting to fire prediction and prevention. ASEAN Guidelines on peatland fire management adopted in 2015 recommended adoption of the Peatland Fire Management Cycle with focus on four stages, prevention, preparedness, response and recovery as well as recommending that at least 80% of the resources for peatland fire management be spent on prevention. This paper describes recent progress in peatland fire prediction, prevention and monitoring in the region including use of weather prediction, fire danger rating systems (FDRS) and fire warning and alerts. It also details the history of peatland rewetting and water management as part of the fire prevention strategy. It describes in detail the results and lessons learned from a recent review of the Malaysian Peatland Fire Prevention Programme covering the period 2009-2019. Malaysia has 2.56 million ha of peatland of which more than 200,000ha have been identified as fire prone. Fire prevention measures have included blocking of drainage canals constructed for agriculture or logging, constructing tubewells, ponds and pipelines for providing supplementary water supply in dry season to prevent and control fires as well as construction of watch towers for monitoring fire prone areas. The study recommended that the programme be continued and enhanced in the future with greater emphasis on peatland rewetting and active monitoring of fire prone areas, enhanced use of drone and satellite monitoring, FDRS deployment and multi-stakeholder engagement.

ID 72842

PEAT FAILURE IN TROPICAL COASTAL PEATLANDS IN BENGKALIS ISLAND

*Hiroki Kagawa[1], Koichi Yamamoto[1], Ariyo Kanno[1], Atsushi Koyama[2], Motoyuki Suzuki[1], Sigit Sutikno[3], Noerdin Basir[4], Muhammad Haidar[5]

[1] Yamaguchi University, Japan
[2] Miyazaki University, Japan
[3] Riau University, Indonesia
[4] Politeknik Negeri Bengkalis, Indonesia
[5] Geospatial Information Agency, Indonesia

hkagawa@yucivil.onmicrosoft.com

SUMMARY

Tropical coastal peatland has large area in Indonesia and Malaysia. Currently, Bengkalis Island in Riau, Indonesia, an-area of the tropical coastal peatland is facing peat failures (peat mass movements) and coastal erosion of peat coast. Coastal line setback and collapse traces with clear boundaries were found by aerial drone photographs and high resolutions satellite images. The peat failures and coastal erosion effected coastal line setback approximately 90 m for 5 years. I was found that the peat failure in the north coast of Bengkalis Island had similar features to bog burst and bog flow in boreal peatland. We named them tropical coastal bog burst and tropical coastal bog flow, respectively. We defined aspect ratio as dividing collapsed area (m^2) by the distance of aperture. If it is under 1.0 and tension cracks, secondary features of the boreal bog burst, are found, it is called coastal bog burst, On the other hand, when the aspect ratio is over 1.0 and clear boundary trace of collapsed area with peat rafts, we call it coastal bog flow. Mode of the longitudinal tilt angle of coastal bog bursts showed the range between 3.0 degrees 3.9 degrees and coastal bog flows showed it between 1.0 degrees to 1.9 degrees.

Keywords: Peat failure, Tropical coastal peatlands, Coastal bog burst, Coastal bog flow, Coastal erosion

INTRODUCTION

Indonesia has 210,000 km^2 of tropical peatlands (Page *et al.*, 2011). Peat fires and oxidative decomposition, which emit large amounts of carbon dioxide from tropical peatlands, are currently a global problem. Peat fires in Indonesia in 1997 are estimated to have released between 0.81 and 2.57 Gt of carbon into the atmosphere (Page *et al.*, 2002). Tropical peatlands can be broadly divided into inland peatlands and coastal peatlands. Though it is difficult to classify them clearly, but there is an example that peatlands within 80 km from the coast are defined as coastal peatlands (Dommain *et al.*, 2011). Inland peatlands are present in Kalimantan Island. Coastal peatlands, on the other hand, are found in the coastal areas in Kalimantan and Sumatra. In Sumatra Island, 60.1 % of the 64,300 km^2 of coastal peatland is located in Riau Province (Ritung S *et al.*, 2012). In this study, the target area was the northern part of Bengkalis Island, Bengkalis regency, Riau province, Indonesia. Bengkalis Island (Fig. 1) has an area of about 900 km^2, which situates between Malacca straits and Bengkalis straits. Bengkalis Island is almost entirely covered with peat soil and there are four major peat domes (Supardi *et al.*, 1993). Most of the Island's peat swamp forests have already been converted into oil palm plantations, and canals for transportation of bunches of palm oil fruit have been constructed in the plantation areas. Proper management of canal water levels in plantations can not only reduce the risk of desiccation and oxidative decomposition of peat, but also the risk of peat failure (Yamamoto *et al.*, 2014). Coastal erosion is progressing in the northern part of Bengkalis Island. Satellite imagery analysis shows that the coastline retreat is at 34 m/yr for 30 years (Kagawa *et al.*, 2017). There are no mangroves in the focused area of Bengkalis Island, which is U.S. army maps from the 1950s indicate that there were mangroves (U.S. Army Map Service, 1955). Moreover, peat swamp forest that once existed inland are now exposed to the coast and forms 6 meters height peat cliff because of coastal erosion as well as peat failures. Carbon outflow from peat failures is as important as carbon outflow from coastal erosion. As of the 2010s, it is estimated that additional 11 MtC of particulate organic carbon have been discharged into the ocean due to the occurrence of coastal peat failures other than the coastal erosion in northern part of Bengkalis Island (Kagawa *et al.*, 2017). Peat failures in coastal areas of the tropics has been

Fig.1 Target area

reported to form peaty debris fans, and the number of peaty debris fans increases with the amount of rainfall (Yamamoto *et al.*, 2019). In other words, large amount of rainfall increases the risks of peat failures.

The peat failures in boreal peatlands have been studied earlier and classified by their own characteristics. In the classification of peat failures in boreal peatlands, peat failures were classified into bog burst, bog flow, bog slide, peat slide, peaty-debris slide, and peat flow (Dykes and Warburton, 2007). This classification based on shape of raft, ground material, traced frame, shape of tear, mechanism of peat failure, movement speed of peat mass, moisture content of the collapsed slope. Most of the peat failures that have occurred in boreal peatlands in United Kingdom and Ireland have occurred on slopes with thin blanket bogs that are about 2 - 3 m thick (Dykes and Warburton, 2007). Peat failure in high latitudes has been reported to kill fish in rivers (McCahon *et al.*, 1987; Wilson *et al.*, 1996), damage infrastructure (Colhoun *et al.*, 1965), and affect natural drainage of peatlands (Alexander *et al.*, 1986; Coxon *et al.*, 1989).

Facing recent climate change and coastal erosion, the risk of tropical coastal peat failure is expected to be increased. Therefore, for the purpose of tropical coastal peatland management, we attempted to classify tropical coastal peat failure by morphology so that it can be easily applied to assess future disasters in surrounding areas.

MATERIALS AND METHODS

The study methods consisted of field surveys and image analysis. Field surveys included a continuous topographic cross-sectional survey using RTK-GNSS, an aerial photographic survey using UAV, water level observation of groundwater and channel, and climate observation.

Temporal terrain cross-section surveys using RTK-GNSS (Trimble 5700 / 5800) were conducted from August 24, 2013 to September 7, 2016 at approximately one-year intervals. The field survey area was situated along the channel on the east side of oil plantation (Fig.2(a)) in a northerly direction towards the peat failures site.

Aerial photogrammetry using UAV was conducted on December 17, 2014, January 10, 2015, November 22, 2015, March 8, 2016, March 4, 2017, and July 29, 2018. The photogrammetric range is shown in the ortho image in Fig.3. For the shooting on November 22, 2015 and March 8, 2016, a UAV (Arris M650) which equipped a compact digital camera (Ricoh GR), and on March 4, 2017 and July 29, 2018, DJI Phantom 4 was used. The shooting time interval was 2 seconds. Ground control points (GCPs) were set up during the shooting, and surveying was done with RTK-GNSS (Trimble 5700 / 5800). For aerial photographs, SfM-MVS processing was performed using commercially available software (Agisoft Photoscan Professional) to create a digital surface model (DSM).

The groundwater level was observed at ST. G in the oil plantation located about 500 m away from the collapse area. The water level of the cannel was observed at ST. C about 300 m away from the collapse area.

Rainfall data were acquired Selatbaru port (1.565N, 102.231E) and Perapat Tunggal village (1.547N, 102.029E) in Bengkalis Island.

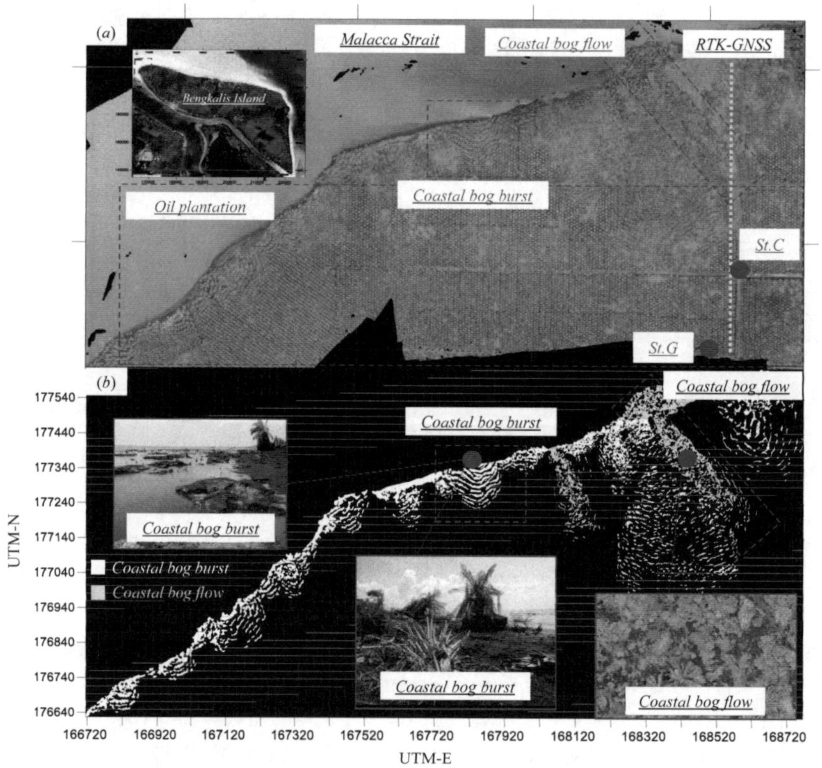

Fig.2 Arial photography of surveyed area on March 4th, 2017(a) and traced surface tears(b)

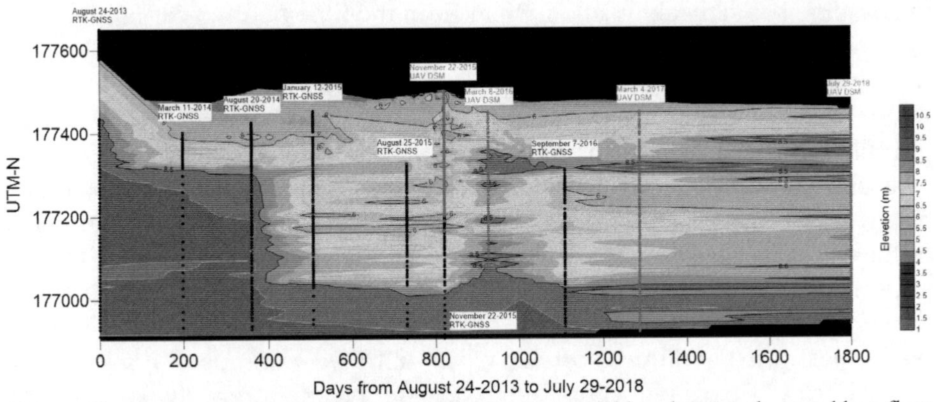

Fig.3 Changes in ground elevation over time due to coastal bog burst and coastal bog flow

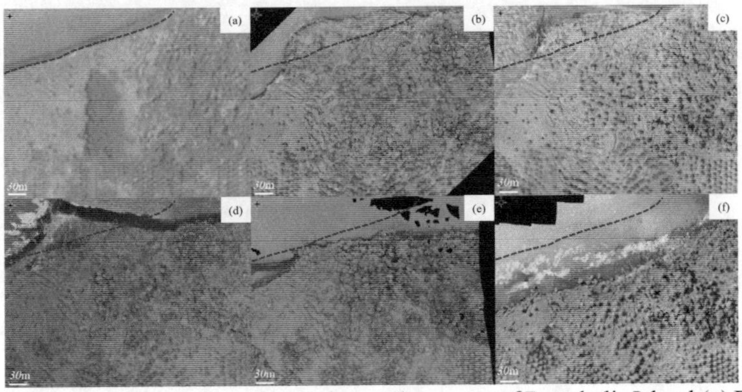

Fig.4 Coastal peat failure and coastal erosion in the northern area of Bengkalis Island.(a) Before peat failure, SPOT-6 imagery on Sep. 18, 2013, (b) After peat failure, UAV imagery on Dec. 17, 2014, (c) Jan. 10, 2015, (d) March 07, 2016, (e) March 4, 2017 and (f) July 29, 2018. The red dotted line indicates the coastline on Sep. 18, 2013.

RESULTS

Fig.2(a) shows the aerial photogrammetry by UAV on Mar. 4, 2017. Highlighted tears of peat failures were drawn in Fig.2(b). Aerial photogrammetry revealed that traces of peat failures were found in all the area of the targeted area, in the northern part of the palm oil plantation on around March 2017. These tears are observed in the upper region of the bog burst in boreal peatland as the tension crack.

Fig.3 shows the temporal longitudinal altitude change of the targeted section because of the peat failure, combined results of RTK-GNSS cross-sectional elevation survey and UAV aerial photogrammetry field survey. At first, there were no peat failure on August 24, 2013. Tension cracks were observed on March 11, 2014, half years after the last measurement. It shows that peat failure in the northern coastal area that brought elevation decrease. By January 10, 2015, there were the massive bog flow which has caused by the collapse of canal in the plantation, still the trace of the first peat failure on 2014 remained. A peaty debris fan was formed by the movement of slurry peat mass at the coast of the focused area. Between September 7, 2016 and March 4, 2017, peat disturbance occurred from inland due to the collapse of the plantation canal again. As a result, same place decreased elevation. Until 29 July 2018, new collapse was not found.

Fig.4 shows the coastal peat failure and coastal erosion in progress. Fig.4 shows (a) Before peat failure, SPOT-6 imagery on Sep. 18, 2013, (b) After peat failure, UAV imagery on Dec. 17, 2014, (c) Jan. 10, 2015, (d) March 07, 2016, (e) March 4, 2017 and (f) After coastal erosion, UAV imagery on July 29, 2018. The red dotted line indicates the coastline on Sep.18, 2013. It can be found that the coastline has setback by about 90 m from the time before peat failure occurred.

DISCUSSION

To classify peat failures, the aspect ratios of the peat failure were calculated for each failure. The aspect ratio was calculated by the area of the peat failure divided with the coastal length of the failure zone. As a result, the characteristic of the peat failure with an aspect ratio under 1.0 was similar that of the concentric tension crack, which is a secondary characteristic of the bog burst in boreal upland peatland. As a characteristic of the peat failure with an aspect ratio over 1.0, there was a peaty debris fans with a clear boundary of collapse traces like bog flow in boreal upland peatland, irregular peat rafts, and traces of slurry peat outflow. Consequently, we decided to call the former peat failure as "Coastal bog burst" and the latter peat failure as "Coastal bog flow". The white area in the Fig.2(b) can be classified as Coastal bog burst, and yellow one is classified as the Coastal bog flow. More moisture or open water was found in the collapse traces of Coastal bog flow than Coastal bog burst. In addition, the tilt angle was calculated for the purpose of adding more features. Coastal bog burst showed mode surface tilt angle from 3.0 degrees 3.9 degrees, Coastal bog flow showed it from 1.0 degrees to 1.9 degrees. Fig.5 shows the mode tilt angles of the longitudinal section of coastal bog burst and coastal bog flow.

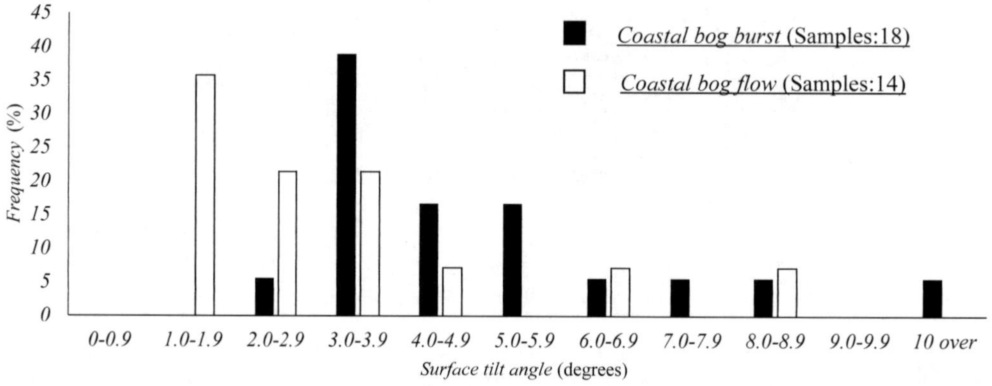

Fig.5 Histograms of mode tilt angles of the longitudinal section of coastal bog burst and coastal bog flow Coastal bog burst showed mode surface tilt angle from 3.0 degrees 3.9 degrees, Coastal bog flow showed it from 1.0 degrees to 1.9 degrees

CONCLUSION

As a result of temporal survey on the tropical peat coast of Bengkalis Island, Riau, Indonesia, we were able to confirm the changes of the peatland ground by the peat failure over time. There was a clear decrease in ground elevation due to the occurrence of peat failures.

As a result of trying to classify the morphology of peat failures, it was thought that it could be classified into "Coastal bog burst" and "Coastal bog flow". Coastal bog burst is a coastal peat failure with an aspect ratio of under 1.0, and a phenomenon the concentric tension crack, which is secondary feature of the collapse like bog burst in boreal upland peatland. Coastal bog flow is a collapse with an aspect ratio of over 1.0, like a bog flow in boreal upland peatland, there was a tidal flat where irregular peat rafts were generated and there was a clear boundary between collapse traces, and traces of slurry-like peat outflow remained. Coastal bog burst was characterized as a steeper slope occurrence in the coastal area compared to coastal bog flow. These coastal peat failures accelerate coastal peat deterioration.

ACKNOWLEDGEMENTS

This study was carried out with the support of MEXT/JSPS KAKENHI Grant number 17H01668.

REFERENCES

1. Alan P. Dykes, Jeff Warburton 2007. Mass movements in peat: Aformal classification scheme, *Geomorphology* 86 (2007) 73 93.
2. Alexander, R.W., Coxon, P., Thorn, R.H., 1986. A bog flow at Straduff Townland, country Sligo. *Proc. R. Ir. Acad.* 86B, 1107-119.
3. Colhoun, E.A., Common, R., Cruikshank, M. M., 1965. Recent bog flows and debris slides in the north of Ireland. *Sci. Proc. R. Dublin Soc.*, Ser. A2, 163-174.
4. Coxon, P., Coxon, C.E., Thorn, R.H., 1989. The Yellow River (County Leitrim, Ireland) Flash flood of June 1986.In: Beven, K., Carling, P. (Eds.), *Floods: Hydrological, Sedimentological and Geomorphological Implications*. Wiley., Chichester, pp.199-217.
5. Dommain, R., Couwunberg, J., Joosten, H. 2011. Development and carbon sequestration of tropical peat domes in south-east Asia:links to post-glacial sea-level changes and Hol-ocene climate variability, *Quaternary Science Reviews*, Vol.30, Issues 7-8, pp.999-1010.
6. Hiroki Kagawa, Koichi Yamamoto, Muhammad Haidar, Ariyo Kanno, Yoshihisa Akamatsu, Motoyuki Suzuki, Sigit Sutikno, Noerdin Basir, Masahiko Sekine 2017. Present Condition of The Coastal Erosion in The Islands in Riau Province, Indonesia, *JSCE Proceedings G (Environment) (Proceedings of Environmental Engineering Research)*, Vol.73, No.7, Ⅲ_213-Ⅲ_219.
7. Koichi Yamamoto, Tsuyoshi Watanabe, Hirohumi Okuyama, Muhammad Haidar, Noerdin Basir, Ariyo Kanno, Masahiko Sekine 2014. Peat Coast Erosion of the Bengkalis Island and its Effect on the Groundwater Discharge, *Japan Society of Civil Engineers Proceedings B2 (Coastal Engineering)*, Vol.70, No.2, Ⅰ_1466- Ⅰ_1470.
8. Koichi Yamamoto, Tomoharu Asakuma, Hiroki Kagawa, Sigit Sutikno, Noerdin Basir, Ariyo Kanno 2019. Occurrence and Disappearance of Temporary Peat Fan by the Land Slide at the Coastal Peat Coast. *Japan Society of Civil Engineers Proceedings B2 (Coastal Engineering)*, Vol.75, No.2, Ⅰ_1249- Ⅰ_1254.
9. McCahon, C.P., Carling, P.A., Pascoe, D., 1987. Chemical and ecological effects of Pennine peat-slide. *Environ. Pollut.* 45, 275-289.
10. Page S, Rieley J, Banks C. 2011. Global and regional importance of the tropical peatland carbon pool. *Glob Change Biol.*;17(2):798-818
11. Ritung S, Wahyunto dan Nugroho. K 2012. Karakteristik dan Sebaran Lahan Gambut di Sumatera, Kalimantan dan Papua Dalam Edi Husen, Anda M, Noor M, Mamat HS, Maswar, Fahmi A, Sulaiman Y(eds) *Pengelolaan Lahan Gambut Berkelanjutan*. Balai Besar Litbang SDLP, Bogor.
12. Supardi and A.D.Subekty, Sandra G. Neuzil 1993. General geology and peat resource of the Siak Kanan and Bengkalis Island peat deposits, Sumatra, Indonesia, *Geological Society of America Special Paper* 286, 45-61.
13. Susan E. Page, Florian Siegert, John O. Rieley, Hans-Dieter V. Boehm, Adi Jaya & Suwido Limin 2002. The amount of carbon released from peat and forest fires in Indonesia during 1997, *Nature* VOL 420 7
14. U.S. Army Map Service 1955. Bengkalis, Series T503, NA48-9.
15. Wilson, P., Griffiths, D., Carter, C., 1996. Characteristics impacts and cause of the Carntogher bog-flow, Sperrin Mountains, Northern Ireland. *Scott, Geogr. Mag.* 112, 39-46

ID 74161

PEATLAND FIRES IN LATVIA – THEIR HISTORY AND IMPACT

*Inese Silamiķele, Laimdota Kalniņa, Māris Klaviņš and Jānis Krūmiņš

University of Latvia, Faculty of Geography and Earth Sciences, Department of Environmental Sciences, Raina blvd. 19, LV 1586 Riga, Latvia

Inese.Silamikele@lu.lv

SUMMARY

It is assumed that bogs and fens in their healthy, natural state are quite fire resistant. However, number of peatland wildfires has increased over the recent decades. Most often wildfires are caused by reckless human activity but can also occur by natural ignition , which can be partly explained by climate change. Air temperatures soar during summer seasons, and are usually accompanied by very low volume of precipitation and strong winds in some cases. Dry and hot spells like this are becoming longer, causing lowering of groundwater level in peatlands. Bog fires can be considered as serious natural phenomena considering their significant dimensions (from local scale fires to regional), increase of frequency of bog fires during last decades is promoted by dryer and warmer climate as well as due to human activities.

It is expected that also in Latvia incidence of fires in bog areas will significantly increase both in pristine mires and peat harvesting sites due to climate change, including increase of average air temperature and prolonged dry periods. Analysis of peat geological sections indicate that even during the Stone Age when human activity was insignificant in the territory of current Latvia periodical burning of peatlands did naturally occur. Studies of peat properties show traces that even before human inhabitation of larger areas the forests and mires were affected by wildfire of natural origin.

The aim of the study is to find records from peatland sections confirming fire events in the past and to determine the impact of the bog fires on the vegetation, peat properties and bog ecosystem functioning.

The results of study provide suggestions for the future management of bog ecosystems and peatlands in the light of climate warming.

***Keywords**:* peatland, bog wildfires, climate change

INTRODUCTION

The boreal zone has been defined in the north-east of Europe. This zone includes areas formed by the retreat of the glacier approximately 14,000 to 16,000 years ago. Due to the movement of the glacier and its melting waters, river and lake beds and other relief forms were formed. The depressions, which were difficult to drain and contained sediments with low permeability, had favorable conditions for the development of peatlands. In the areas freed from the glacier plants from the areas not affected by the glacier were introduced and gradually adapted to the prevailing climatic conditions at that time.

During the last 12,000 years, climatic conditions in the territory of Latvia can be characterized by both warm and humid, as well as cool and relatively drier periods (Kalnina et al., 2015). Presence of humans in the territory of Latvia can be traced since the retreat of the glacier, when they followed reindeer, which moved along the edge of the glacier, where it was wetter and where food could be found (Zagorska, 2012). Whereas, economic activity, which significantly affects the environment is traceable since the Iron Age (Vasks, 2001).

The territory of Latvia belongs to the boreal zone, which is generally characterized by a cool and humid climate, which however is warming as a result of climate change. The Boreal zone covers up to 18.8% of the EU's territory, including Sweden, Finland, Estonia and Lithuania. Approximately 10% of the territory of Latvia (640,000 ha) is occupied by mires, while peat extraction takes place in 25,725 ha (Priede, 2019). 4,6% of the territory are bogs with active peat formation, where the peat layer is more than 30 cm thick. Active peat formation can be observed also in bog forests in the total area of more than 200,000 ha. Other mires are drained for agriculture, forestry or other uses.

It is assumed that the natural development of bogs can be affected by two major natural environmental factors - flood and wildfires. Wildfires in bogs are quite frequent and periodically areas occupied by fire are large and endangers the economic activity, human health and wildlife. The peculiarity of bog wildfires is that not only the above-ground parts of plants are damaged from fire, but layers of peat at different depths can be affected by fire and change properties of substrate. Specifics of how wildfire affects mire is determined by the specific properties of peat as a substrate and combustion material (Huang, Rein 2018). The burning and roasting of peat promote changes in peat structure and composition, which then affect its function in the environment and the possibilities of use. Some of the major changes include the formation of charcoal and tar (Rosenburgh et al., 2013, Ozols et al., 2020.)

Due to the climate change, it is predicted that the frequency of wildfires will increase in Latvian mires. However, Latvia has not yet developed or approbated a methodology on wildfire studies in mires. So far no detailed research has been conducted on wildfires in mires or on their impact on vegetation, peat resources, landscape, etc. in long-term historical retrospective (Suveizda 2016), although such studies are considered relevant worldwide (Marcisz et al., 2019, Noblea at all., 2019).

The aim of this study was to evaluate the impact of wildfire on mire ecosystems and the rate and intensity of mire recovery from wildfire. Carrying out research on mire wildfires in the territory of Latvia is crucial because not all historical data on wildfires have been preserved, which therefore complicates the general understanding of the overall situation, but the information obtained today can be useful for more successful interpretation of peat sediment data.

MATERIALS AND METHODS

To evaluate and monitor bog wildfires, initially it is required to compile all available information on wildfire cases and to analyze the data with scientific methods, which can characterize the distribution of bog wildfires, areas affected by fire, frequency of wildfires and their dependency on climatic and anthropogenic factors, as well as permanent impact on further development of the vegetation and landscape.

During 2019 and 2020 we have studied and examined four bogs with the evidence of past wildfires - Sēmes bog, Saklaura bog, Bažu bog, and Kemeru bog with the aim to characterize peat burning at different time and space scale. In addition, databases on wildfire records and other information resources were analyzed to compare and supplement the research data. During field works peat monoliths were collected for laboratory analysis. The analysis of peat botanical composition allowed to determine peat type and dynamics of plant cover development, while charcoal remains (> 100 μm) in peat composition pointed to wildfire events in the past (Stivrins et al. 2019).

RESULTS

In accordance with the composition of vegetation, mires in Latvia are boreal bogs. Raised bog vegetation predominantly contains sphagnum cover (S. magelancium, S. fuscum, etc.), shrubs

(Calluna vulgaris, Empetrum nigrum, Ledum palustre, Rhynchospora alba, Scheuchzeria palustris), and trees (Pinus sylvestris). At the same time, the raised bog peat also consists of Phragmites, Carex, Eriophorum, Sphagnum etc. remains with low to average decomposition degree.

One of the study sites was Bažu bog in the National Park of Slītere. Bažu purvs occupies 2646 ha and is predominantly raised bog with the peat layer of 0.5 to 4.0 m. Even though it was formed approximately 5,600 BP, the bog dome has not yet developed (Pakalne, Kalniņa, 2005). Data show that since the formation of the mire there has been at least 35 wildfires. The most frequent wildfires occured in the time frame between 5,500 and 4,000 and before 3,000 and 2,000 BP, while during the last 2,000 years the frequency of wildfires in Bažu bog has significantly decreased (Stivrins et al., 2019). Evidence points to wildfire at the beginning of bog formation, where in peat large charcoal content and burnt plant fragments can be observed.

Another one of the study sites was Saklaura bog, where three (1978, 1992, 2018) relatively recent episodes of wildfires can be traced. Above the burnt peat layer with high charcoal content and high peat density, which corresponds to a wildfire in 1978, there is 3 cm of raised bog peat layer containing shrub and sphagnum remains pointing to fast recovery from fire. Above the burnt peat layer, which corresponds to wildfire of 1992, there is another 2 cm of raised bog peat, which is similar in composition to the layer, which formed after the wildfire in 1978 - shrubs and sphagnum, respectively. Vegetation has not yet begun to recover from the last wildfire in 2018 and fresh peat layers are yet to form. Moreover, peat at the surface layer is with the highest natural density (0,085 g/cm^3) when compared to the rest of peat profile. The most damaged from fire were Calluna vulgaris, Rubus chamaemorus, Oxycoccus palustris, Ledum palustre and Betula nana.

Within other studies in many cases microscopic charcoal particles have been identified in peat, which corresponds to 8,000 to 6,000 BP. These peat layers with charcoal are often covered by fen peat. The recurrence of such conditions indirectly point that wildfires can promote paludification and bog development.

During the time period from 2011 to 2018, 46 wildfires were registered. 12 of these wildfires were covering less than 0,1 ha, 12 were covering the area from 0,1 to 0,5 ha, five were from 0,5 to 1,0 ha, 10 with the area of 1,0 to 5,0 ha, 6 of area from 5 to 35 ha, but 2 were covering the area of more than 200 ha. The majority of bog wildfires cover small territories (up to 0,5 ha) as they are typically quickly noticed and extinguished. In comparison, in the same time frame, the average territory of wildfires in forests was approximately 1,3 ha (Suveizda, 2016). During 2018 wildfire in Saklaura bog in five days more than 239 ha of bog burned down, while in the same year the largest wildfire occurred in Stiklu bog, where more than 529 ha of bog burned down.

Wildfires are affecting bog microrelief forms. It has been observed that a high intensity wildfire can promote bog microrelief to level off, while local and low intensity wildfire can in turn cause the development of new microrelief forms (Namateva, 2011).

Most wildfires in Latvia are caused by negligent conduct and they can spread to large areas due to strong wind (>12 m/s); however, the depth affected by fire typically does not exceed several cm. Data shows that in drained bog burnt is only dried peat within the first 2 to 5 cm. We found that if the moisture of burnt peat was less than 7%, then in the depth of 10 cm the moisture of peat was 50%, but in the depth of 20 cm peat was not affected by burning at all.

DISCUSSION

The effect of climate change on the increase in the incidence of wildfires can be correlated with the data from the studies on Holocene climate optimum (6,000 - 7,000 BP). During the Holocene climate optimum, the weather was warmer and drier than at the present day, with the average annual temperature from 2,5 to 3,5°C higher (Seppä, Poska, 2004).

The prevalence of human-caused bog wildfires and their impact on the ecology of the ecosystem differ greatly from natural wildfires in undisturbed bog conditions (Suveizda, 2016). Wildfires caused by lightning are less than 1% of all wildfires in Latvia, while the rest are caused by various human activities. Large wildfires in Latvia were raging during the World War, but in the post-war period many wildfires were recorded in 1963 and 1992. Alas, the fire recording system of the Soviet time was generalized, which did not allow the distinction among types of wildfires and how much of them accounted for wildfires especially in bog. At the same time, bogs affected by wildfires throughout recent history can still be traced in nature by indicative footprints, such as burnt fallen trees and trunks, which can keep track of wildfire for more than 60 years. Amongst other past wildfire indicators are local changes in vegetation, such as denser Calluna vulgaris or Eriophorum vaginatum cover. Moreover, atypical for raised bogs species, such as Chamerion angustifolium, Cirsium arvense, Rumex acetosella and Polygonum can temporarily appear in previously burned areas. Some deep pits, which are now filled with water, in mires may be formed as ground cave ins due to tree trunks and roots burning away during a wildfire.
Drained bogs are typically considered to be the most affected by wildfires, where fire can reach deeper peat layers and spread to larger areas. However, in this study, it was found that the largest wildfires occur in natural bogs due to limited access to extinguish them. We found that if there are no aggravating circumstances, then in drained bogs the fire does not reach deeper than 10 to 15 cm in the peat layer. Nonetheless, large amounts of charcoal particles are released in the air during mire wildfires, which after a certain period of time precipitate on the surface of bog and under certain environmental conditions remain buried within the peat layer allowing tracing past wildfires. The area of coal layer typically correlates with the area of mire and studies in Europe show that the area affected by wildfire typically is 40 km^2 on average. However, bogs in Europe are typically with open type landscapes and specific vegetation, while it cannot always be attributed to bog conditions in Latvia.
Analysing the data used in our study, it could be observed that the majority of wildfires in bogs took place in mid-summer - in July and August. However, in 2015 one wildfire broke out in February, while in 2018, one occured in November, both of which most likely due to human activities.

CONCLUSION

With increasing average temperature and prolonged periods of drought it is expected that the frequency of wildfires in bogs will gradually increase. The risk of major scale wildfires can be reduced and limited by drainage and infiltration ditches, which can delimit areas of mires; however, they cannot completely stop the spread of fire to adjacent areas and drainage can increase the risk of wildfire itself.
Our research has shown that wildfires are affecting the tree cover in bogs the most, affecting its further viability to varying degrees. The further viability of tree cover and of bog vegetation in general depend on the intensity of wildfire and the depth affected by fire. The vegetation on burnt peat soil can recover relatively quickly; however, due to changes in the microrelief and nutrient availability and soil chemistry, different temporal or permanent species can appear.
There are differences between wildfires in natural and drained bogs. In drained bogs the depth affected by fire does not exceed 10-15 cm and the wildfire is typically spread evenly throughout the area. Whereas, wildfires in natural bogs are spread unevenly and the depth affected by fire is strictly dependent on the vegetation cover and bog microrelief. In natural bogs, the areas most affected by wildfires are those with sphagnum moss cover, which is thought to be much drier than other parts of bogs. Wildfires can also change the relief of bog - when tree trunks and roots are burned away it causes ground to cave in and form new water bodies.

In conclusion, it has been found that wildfires affect undisturbed raised bogs the most, whilst transitional mires, fens, quaking bogs and bog forests are affected only fragmentarily due to variations in vegetation cover, groundwater level and other differences at ecosystem level.

ACKNOWLEDGEMENTS

This study was funded by the University of Latvia project "Studies of impact by peatland burning on the environment and bog recovery intensity" with partners JSC 'Latvia's State Forest', The Nature Conservation Agency and Latvian Peat Association.

REFERENCES

1. Kalnina L, Stivrins N, Kuske E, Ozola I, Pujate A, Zeimule S, Grudzinska I, Ratniece V. (2015) Peat stratigraphy and changes in peat formation during the Holocene in Latvia. Quaternary International; 383: 186-195
2. Marcisz K, Lamentowicz L, Gałka M, Colombaroli D, Tinner W. (2019) Responses of vegetation and testate amoeba trait composition to fire disturbances in and around a bog in central European lowlands (northern Poland). *Quaternary Science Reviews*; 208: 129-139
3. Namateva A. (2011) Bog Microlandscapes in Teici, Orlava and Gaini Bogs, Austrumlatvija Lowland, Latvia. *Peatlands International.* International Peat Society, Finland, 56 - 59
4. Noblea A, Crowleb A, Glavesb D J, Palmera S M, Holden J. (2019) Fire temperatures and Sphagnum damage during prescribed burning on peatlands. *Ecological Indicators*; 103: 471-478
5. Ozols V, Silamikele I, Kalnina L, Porshnov D, Grandovska S, Arbidans A, Krumins J, Klavins M. (2020) What happens to peat during bog fires? Thermal transformation processes of peat organic matter and possible impacts of it. *Agronomy Research*; 18, 1
6. Pakalne M, Kalnina L. (2005) Mire ecosystems in Latvia. Steiner, G. M. (ed.). Moo von Sibirien bis Feuerland / Mires from Siberia to Tierra del Fuego. Linz : Biologiezentrum.
7. Priede A. (ed.) 2019. Sustainable and responsible after-use of peat exctraction areas. 256
8. Rosenburgh Alday J G, Harris M P, Allen K A, Connor L, Blackbird S J, Eyre G, Marrs R H. (2013) Changes in peat chemical properties during post-fire succession on blanket bog moorland. *Geoderma*; 211, 98–106
9. Seppä H, Poska A. (2004) Holocene annual mean temperature changes in Estonia and their relationship to solar insolation and atmospheric circulation patterns. *Quaternary Research*; 61: 22-31
10. Stivrins N, Aakala T, Ilvonen L, Pasanen L, Kuuluvainen T, Vasander H, Gałka M, Disbrey H, Liepins J., Holmström L. (2019) Integrating fire-scar, charcoal and fungal spore data to study fire events in the boreal forest of northern Europe. *The Holocene*; 1-11.
11. Suveizda L. (2016) Forest Fires in Latvia from 1990 to 2014. In: Cinate, K. (ed.) Current management practices for specially protected habitats and species in Latvia: Forests, 101-106
12. Vasks A. (ed) (2001) The prehistory of Latvia. Publishers of the institute of the history of Latvia: Riga
13. Zagorska I. (2012) Senie ziemeļbriežu mednieki Latvijā (in latvian, Ancient reindeer hunters in Latvia),"Zinātne"

ID 62343

PEATLANDS AS ARCHIVES OF ATMOSPHERIC METAL DEPOSITION, ŠIJEC PEAT BOG – CASE STUDY FROM SLOVENIA

*Valentina Pezdir[1], Mateja Gosar[1],

[1]*Geological Survey of Slovenia, Ljubljana, Slovenia*

valentina.pezdir@geo-zs.si

SUMMARY

Ombrotrophic peatlands are good archive of historical atmospheric deposition as their only source of water is precipitation. In Slovenia, peatlands represent a smaller area. In three areas (Pokljuka, Pohorje and Jelovica) are peatlands labelled as raised bogs. Our research is focused on Šijec bog on Pokljuka plateau.
First geochemical study on Šijec bog was conducted in 1999, when 5 composite samples of different sections (0–10 cm, 10–20 cm, 20–30 cm, 30–50 cm and 50–70 cm) were taken. Samples were analysed in Bureau Veritas Mineral Laboratories at Vancouver, Canada. The air dried samples were ground to analytical grain size (<0.063 mm) and were analysed following the aqua regia (1 : 1 : 1 HCl : HNO_3 : H_2O) extraction. Concentrations of following 36 elements were determined: Ag, Al, As, Au, B, Ba, Bi, Ca, Cd, Co, Cr, Cu, Fe, Ga, Hg, K, La, Mg, Mn, Mo, Na, Ni, Pb, S, Sb, Se, Sr, Te, Th, Ti, Tl, U, V, W, Zn. Most elements have elevated element concentrations in upper 20 cm of peat. In the peat section 10–20 cm Pb (125.1 mg/kg), Cd (1.46 mg/kg) and Hg (0.171 mg/kg) stand out with higher concentration values. Higher element concentration values in upper section are most probably the result of anthropogenic activities in the valleys surrounding Pokljuka plateau and its wider surroundings. Dust particles originating from these activities were deposited on peat by short and long-range wind transport and precipitation.

***Keywords**: ombrotrophic peatland, geochemistry, atmospheric dust, pollution*

INTRODUCTION

Peatlands are areas covered by peat (Charman, 2002), known also as mires or more broadly as wetlands. Peatlands can be hydromorphologically classified as ombrotrophic peatlands (bogs) that receive water mainly from precipitation (Biester et al., 2014; Clymo, 1987) and minerotrophic peatlands (fens) that receive water from other sources, such as groundwater and surface runoff (Clymo, 1987). Ombrotrophic peatlands are domed peatlands raised above the surrounding soils and above the influence of ground water (Cocozza et al., 2003), therefore groundwater has no influence on the peatland. In peatlands, waterlogged conditions are present, that enable the slow decay of organic matter (Cocozza et al., 2003), which is an important factor in peat accumulation where accumulation rates must be higher than decay rates (Lapen et al., 1996).
Due to anaerobic waterlogged conditions, peatlands act as sinks for atmospheric dust deposition (Smieja-Król et al., 2010). Peatlands are composed of mostly organic material and the inorganic part represents only a small percentage. Even though values of inorganic particles in peat are low, their small changes, specifically increase in trace elements concentration, can be good indicator of predominantly anthropogenic influence. Trace elements concentration are usually higher in upper layers of peat, which reflects the increased anthropogenic atmospheric pollution in last centuries (Smieja-Król et al., 2010), especially noticeable in the vicinity of mining and smelting areas (Nieminen et al., 2002).
In this paper, we present and discuss part of the first results of geochemical studies on ombrotrophic peatlands in Slovenia (peat bog Šijec, Pokljuka plateau) which was conducted in 1999 but not yet presented. In 2019 we started a more detailed geochemical study where we first reviewed our old data of peat element concentrations that will be followed by analysis of multiple new peat cores.

STUDY AREA

In Slovenia, peatlands cover only a very small part of the country. Largest peatland is Ljubljana mire, located in central Slovenia. Smaller peatlands, labelled as raised bogs can be found on Pokljuka plateau and Jelovica in northeastern Slovenia, and on Pohorje in northern Slovenia. Our research is conducted on Šijec bog on Pokljuka plateau (Figure 1).

Šijec bog is located at 1194 meters above sea level and covers approximately 15 ha. Due to its elevation the bog has cooler climate as the Slovenian average. For Slovenian Alps abundant precipitation is common in spring and autumn months. In winter they can be covered with snow for several months.

Šijec bog has relatively flat topography with elevated edges and three highest points along the southern border. The bog has lowest point in its northwestern part where larger depression is apparent. The highest areas are the driest and high pine bushes grow on them. Other areas are covered with Sphagnum mosses and grass. In the central part of the bog, water pools and hollows can be found, surrounded by small drier ridges, covered with smaller pine bushes.

Peat depth is approximately 7 to 9 meters in its deepest points and up to 4 meters on the edges of the Šijec bog (Pezdir et al., in this publication). In November 2002, 82 cm deep section of peat was collected and dated using pollen and radiocarbon dating (Andrič et al., 2010). It was determined that sample from depth 65 cm correspond to year interval AD 1302–1338 with 300-year gap at depth 58.5 cm (Andrič et al., 2010), which could have been caused by Little Ice Age between the years AD 1550 and 1850 (Andrič et al., 2010). According to Maja Andrič (personal communication) one borehole to depth 711 cm shows there are lacustrine clay sediments under the peat layer. According to Jurkovšek (1987), glacial till sediments and Triassic carbonate rocks represent the bedrock of Šijec bog.

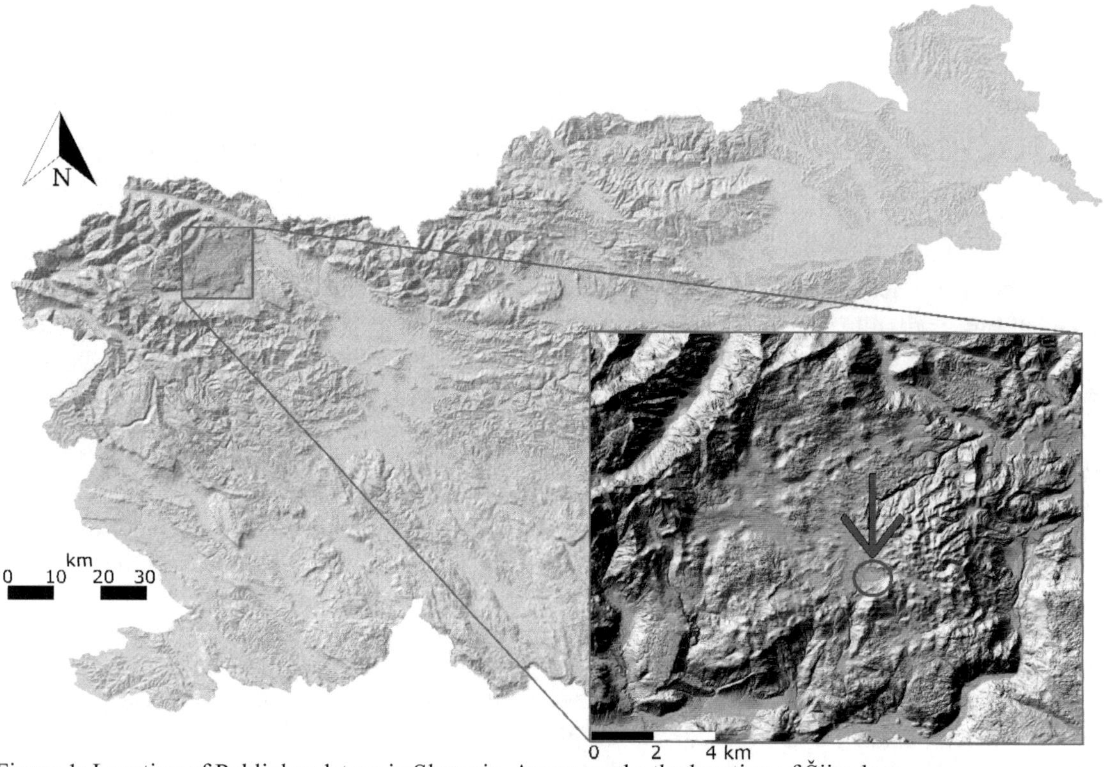

Figure 1: Location of Pokljuka plateau in Slovenia. Arrow marks the location of Šijec bog.

MATERIALS AND METHODS

In 1999 we started first geochemical study on Šijec peat bog. Five composite samples of different depth sections (0–10 cm, 10–20 cm, 20–30 cm, 30–50 cm and 50–70 cm) were taken from a 70 cm profile that was dug with a shovel. Samples were analysed in Bureau Veritas Mineral Laboratories at Vancouver, Canada. The air dried samples were ground to analytical grain size (<0.063 mm) and were analysed following the aqua regia (1 : 1 : 1 HCl : HNO_3 : H_2O) extraction.

Concentrations of following 36 elements were determined: Ag, Al, As, Au, B, Ba, Bi, Ca, Cd, Co, Cr, Cu, Fe, Ga, Hg, K, La, Mg, Mn, Mo, Na, Ni, Pb, S, Sb, Se, Sr, Te, Th, Ti, Tl, U, V, W, Zn. Sample from section 20–30 cm was used as a replica to determine the accuracy of analytical method. The error for elements Au, U, Cu, Zn were larger than 40 %. The changes with depth for these elements were still observed, though the results should be observed carefully. Error above 30 % was determined for elements Cd, Mg, K, Tl, Mo, Ag, Hg and Cr. Even though the error is large, we accepted the measurements, as they are all below 35 % error. The error can originate from not complete homogenisation of the composite sample.

RESULTS AND DISCUSSION

For major elements, the largest part represent Al, Ca and S. Aluminium has highest concentrations (measured 0.37 %) in depths from 20–30 cm and calcium has highest value (0.22 %) in lowest section from 50–70 cm, but also elevated values in upper sections (Figure 2). Sulphur has highest concentrations (measured 0.31 %) in upper sections, in 10–20 cm. Iron is also among more abundant elements in peat, with values around 0.1 %.

For minor elements, larger concentrations have Pb, Ba and Cu. All of them have their highest concentrations measured in section 10–20 cm (125.1 mg/kg Pb, 19.3 mg/kg Ba and 15.8 mg/kg Cu). Other elements, that have their higher values in mentioned section are Ag, Cd, Hg, Mo, Tl and W. From these, the most interesting are Cd with 1.46 mg/kg and Hg with 0.171 mg/kg (Figure 3) as they are well known indicators of anthropogenic influence. Higher values of cadmium and mercury in topsoil were found in the Slovenian Alps due to specific soil formation to the carbonate rocks (Gosar et al., 2019). Furthermore, processing of mercury ore from Idrija mine, located in western Slovenia, have an important regional influence on mercury contents in soil in western and northwestern Slovenia (Gosar et al., 2016).

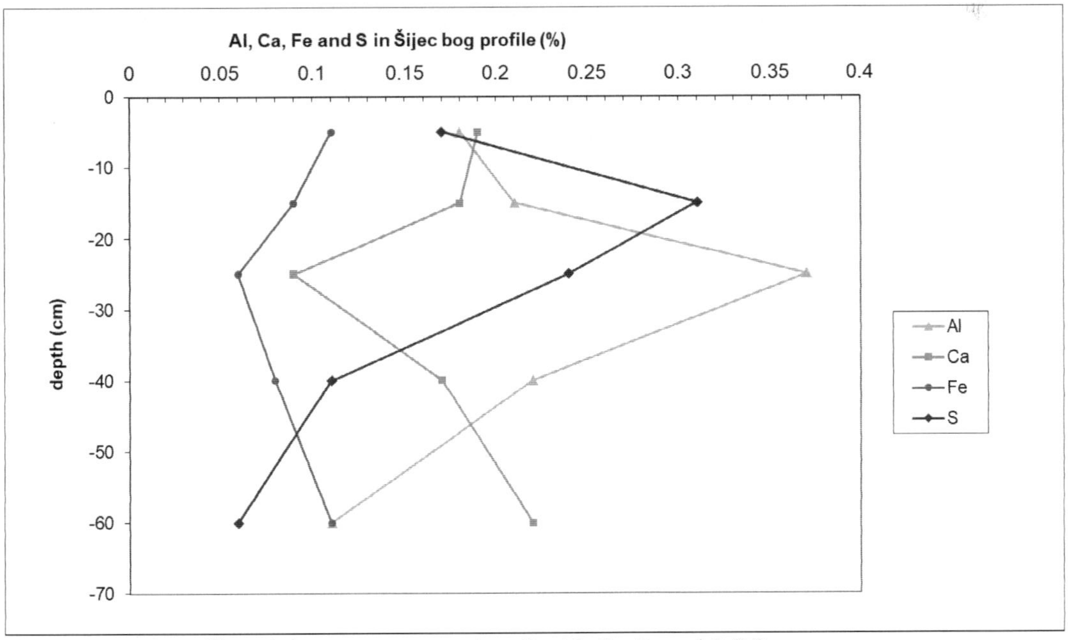

Figure 2: Depth profiles of element concentrations for Al, Ca, Fe and S (%).

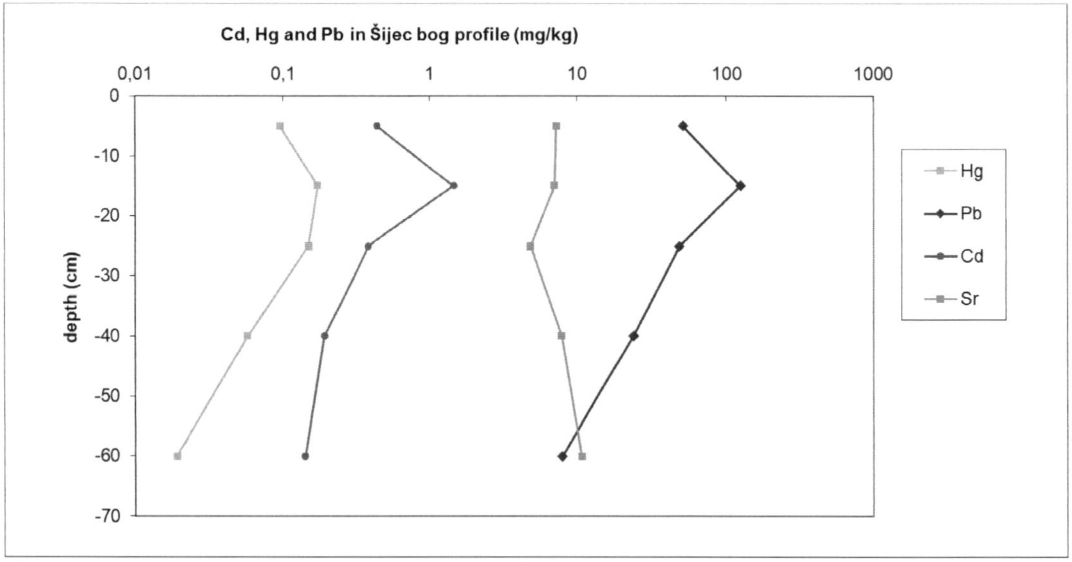

Figure 3: Depth profiles of element concentrations for Cd, Hg, Pb and Sr (mg/kg).

Elements Ca, Sr and Fe have their highest values in lower section (50–70 cm), which reflect the composition of geogenic inorganic material in peat and the surrounding soil and rocks. Except for Ca, they also show little changes throughout the profile. All of them show small decrease in concentration in section 20–30 cm. Magnesium concentrations, which are highest in first section (0–10 cm) also does not change drastically with depth and have geogenic origin.
Oppositely, the before mentioned PTE (potentially toxic elements), show important differences with depth, with most of them being enriched in layer 10–30 cm of peat. This includes elements Cu, Pb, Zn, Ni, Mn, Cd, Sb, Cr and Hg. Due to radiocarbon dating performed by Andrič et al (2010), where the age of peat at 30 cm is 1972–1974 AD, the anthropogenic activities in the last decades probably caused the higher values in these layers.
Most element concentrations are lower in the topmost layer that represents part of the living layer of peat.

CONCLUSION

Atmospheric dust accumulates in peatlands. Dust which represent the inorganic material in peat can reflect the geogenic and anthropogenic sources in the vicinity of the peatlands, as well as long-range transport from distant sources. Anthropogenic dust particles have become much more important in the last few hundred years as their concentration in the atmosphere increased. Consequentially, their concentration also increased in other mediums. Compared to accumulation of soils and rock formation, peatlands accumulate peat relatively quickly, which makes them appropriate medium for research of pollution. Though it must be considered that peatlands are specific, usually anaerobic, anoxic and waterlogged environments, where elements are subjected to different processes.

ACKNOWLEDGEMENTS

The presented study was funded by the Slovenian Research Agency (ARRS) in the frame of the young researcher programme and in the frame of the research programme Groundwater and Geochemistry (P1-0020).

REFERENCES

1. Andrič, M., Martinčič, A., Štular, B., Petek, F., Goslar, T. (2010) Land-use changes in the Alps (Slovenia) in the fifteenth, nineteenth and twentieth centuries AD: A comparative study of the pollen record and historical data. *The Holocene,* 20/7: 1023–1037. https://doi.org/10.1177/0959683610369506.
2. Biester, H., Knorr, K.H., Schellekens, J., Basler, A., Hermanns, Y.M. (2014) Comparison of different methods to determine the degree of peat decomposition in peat bogs. *Biogeosciences,* 11: 2691–2707. https://doi.org/10.5194/bg-11-2691-2014.
3. Charman, D. (2002) *Peatlands and Environmental Change*. John Wiley & Sons Inc., USA: 312 p.
4. Clymo, R.S. (1987) The ecology of peatlands. *Science Progress,* 71: 593–614.
5. Cocozza, C., D'Orazio, V., Miano, T.M., Shotyk, W. (2003) Characterization of solid and aqueous phases of a peat bog profile using molecular fluorescence spectroscopy, ESR and FT-IR, and comparison with physical properties. *Organic Geochemistry,* 34: 49–60.
6. Gosar, M., Šajn, R., Bavec, Š., Gaberšek, M., Pezdir, V. Miler, M. (2019) Geochemical backgroung and threshold for 47 chemical elements in Slovenian topsoil layer. *Geologija,* 62/1: 5–57. https://doi.org/10.5474/geologija.2019.001.
7. Gosar, M., Šajn, R., Teršič, T. (2016) Distribution pattern of mercury in the Slovenian soil: Geochemical mapping based on multiple geochemical datasets. *Journal of Geochemical Exploration*, 167: 38–48.
8. Jurkovšek, B. (1987) *Tolmač listov Beljak in Ponteba: L 33-51, L33-52, Osnovna geološka karta SFRJ. 1:100 000. [Explanatory book of Villach and Pontebba sheets: L 33-51, L33-52, Basic geological map of Yugoslavia. 1:100 000].* Zvezni geološki zavod, Beograd, 58 pp. (in Slovenian)
9. Lapen, D.R., Moorman, B.J., Price, J.S. (1996) Using ground-penetrating radar to delineate subsurface features along a wetland Catena. *Soil Science Society of America Journal,* 60: 923–931.
10. Nieminen, T.M., Ukonmaanaho, L., Shotyk, W. (2002) Enrichment of Cu, Ni, Zn, Pb and As in an ombrotrophic peat bog near a Cu-Ni smelter in Southwest Finland. *The Science of the Total Environment,* 292: 81–89.
11. Smieja-Król, B., Fiałkiewicz-Kozieł, B., Sikorski, J. Palowski, B. (2010) Heavy metal behaviour in peat – A mineralogical perspective. *Science of the Total Environment,* 408: 5924–5931.

ID 62645

SOCIAL FORESTRY CHALLENGES IN MANAGING PEATLAND: A CASE FROM NORTH KALIMANTAN

*Karlina F Kartika[1], Edy M Angi[2]

[1]*GIZ PROPEAT, Tanjung Selor, Indonesia*
[2] *Edy M Angi, Samarinda, Indonesia*

kaefka@gmail.com

SUMMARY

Tropical peat in Indonesia spread mainly in its three main islands namely Sumatera, Kalimantan and Papua. However, there is limited research regarding peatland situation and management in the North Kalimantan. Based on the indicative map of peat hydrological unit issued by the Indonesia Ministry of Environment and Forestry (MoEF), the youngest province has 13 peat hydrological unit which covers approximately 347.082 ha. This means the peat ecosystem play important role in supporting community life. The peatland in the North Kalimantan mostly located in two districts called Nunukan and Tana Tidung with more than 50% are within the concession area. The community has a room for managing the peatland through the social forestry schemes. Social forestry scheme aims to provide legal access for the local community towards forest resources. Unfortunately, there are some limitations in implementing the social forestry scheme in North Kalimantan. This study aims to identify the challenges in implementing the social forestry scheme especially in peatland area.

The study was conducted in November 2019 in Atap village of Sembakung sub district, Nunukan District which proposed the community forest scheme to get access for their farmer group. It located in the Sembakung watershed and known as the oldest village. The data was collected through Focus Group Discussion (FGD) and interview the key informants. The status of the community forest which covers the development of workplan, the institutional management and its challenge were analysed descriptively while SWOT analysis was used to identify the potential support and how to overcome the identified limitation. There were seven technical aspect identified in the implementation of the community forest. Those are institutional, technical assistance, planning, fund, human resources, business development, the involvement of other parties. The improvement of those technical aspect can be done with the support of relevant stakeholder especially in the context of capacity building for the farmer group.

***Keywords**: management, peat, social forestry*

INTRODUCTION

South East Asia has the largest area of peatland in the tropic zone, especially located in the lowlands of Indonesia and Malaysia (1). It has enormous function for community livelihood, source of biodiversity and climate regulation (2). Started in 2015 numbers of policy and regulation had been enacted to improve the management of peatland in Indonesia. It showed the attention of Indonesian government to tackle the peat fire disaster as well as improve the peatland governance. Having 865 peat hydrological unit, the government put an extensive effort to manage its natural resources. The engagement with the community is the primary tenet of community-based peatland management. The social forestry program launched by the Ministry of Environment and Forestry

(MoEF) in 2007 aiming to reduce poverty and imbalance forest management by the community. It is also part of the strategy in resolve the natural resource conflict in designation forest. The aim of this study is to promote the community-based peat management through social forestry scheme and highlight the challenges occur in the field.

MATERIALS AND METHODS

The study was conducted in Atap village of Sembakung Sub District which is part of the PHU area. Indonesia use the term of peat hydrological unit based on the importance of peat function in regulating hydrology system. PHU refer to the peat ecosystem between two rivers which creates extensive dome. Peat inventory is primary step in designation of peat ecosystem function and determine its management approach. Based on the analysis of peat depth indicative map, the peat depth in Atap village range from 100 cm to 800 cm. The community utilize their peatland area for agriculture with paddy rice as commodity.

The data collected through interview, series of FGD and field observation in November 2019. SWOT analysis was applied to identify the challenges of peatland management through social forestry scheme in this case known as *Hutan Kemasyarakatan* (HKm) or community forest.

RESULTS

The social forestry issue emerged in 2012 along with national target to grant 12,7 million ha of designation forest management to the community surrounds. On the contrary, the government halted new permit of pristine forest and peatland. This implied to the permit granted for the social forestry. However, in mid of 2020 the government enacted the regulation regarding social forestry in peatland. The community group of Atap formed in 2017 and it was allied of three forest farmer group. The identified problem from SWOT analysis showed that seven issues should be managed to achieve the essence of social forestry. Those are institutional, technical assistance, planning, fund, human resources, business development, the involvement of other parties. The improvement of those technical aspect can be done with the support of relevant stakeholder especially in the context of capacity building for the farmer group. The fact that most of the social forestry hindrance after receiving the permit showed that role of community facilitator to provide technical assistant is important.

Table 1. Evaluation on Technical Aspect of HKm in Atap village

Technical Aspect	HKm
1. Institutional	
Organization rule	Not Available
Organizational structure	Available
Secretariat/office	Not Available
Communication and coordination	Sufficient
2. Facilitator	
Availability	Available
Capacity	Sufficient
Allocated fund	Limited
Visitation	Short
Office	Not Available
3. Program	
Annual workplan	Available
Implementation	Limited
Knowledge	Limited
4. Funding	
Budget for activity	Not Available
Other fund source	Not Available
5. Human Resource (HR)	
HR for implementing SF	Limited
Capability	Limited
6. Natural Resources Development	
Local natural resources	Available
Local natural resources utilization	Not Available
Technology	Not Available
7. SF Business Group (KUPS)	
KUPS establishment	Available
Business plan	Not Available
Synchronize	Not Available
8. Stakeholder	
External support	Limited

The problems arose after the issuance of the HKm permit by the MoEF were mainly related to institutions, human resources, workplan, funding and so on. In the process of implementing the HKm activities, there were many obstacles hinder the implementation of planned activity. The formation of management structure was not based on the need of the forest farmer group and this imply to the commitment of the personnel itself. Lack of facilitation during the development of management structure affected the learning process of the HKm management board and member. This can be seen from number of members who did not fully understand the workplan of the institution. In addition, the lack of knowledge resulted confusion on how the management plan should be elaborated and implemented. These challenges should be addressed because HKm is part of community access to legal forest utilization and source of income to improve the economy of poor families.

CONCLUSION

The HKm management and members facing the institutional and technical aspect challenges to implement the social forestry scheme. It is important to other stakeholders look through and identify where they can contribute and complement with other activities.

ACKNOWLEDGEMENTS

This study was funded by GIZ Peatland Management and Rehabilitation Project. The content of paper does not represent the view of organization.

REFERENCES

1. Rieley, Jack & Page, Susan. (2016). Tropical Peatland of the World.
2. Osaki M, Suji, M. (2011) Tropical Peatland Ecosystems. *Springer*.

ID 61497

CONTROLLED DRAINAGE ON A CULTIVATED FEN

*Merja Myllys, Jaakko Heikkinen, Kristiina Regina

Natural Resources Institute Finland (Luke), Finland

merja.myllys@luke.fi

Controlled drainage diminishes the harmful environmental effects of peatland farming; water table is kept high when drainage is not needed but lowered for farming operations. This decreases greenhouse gas emissions and nutrient leaching. The aim of this study was to find out how controlled drainage works in practical field conditions.

The study was carried out on a cultivated fen with a thick peat layer. There were four study areas. Two of them were equipped with control wells where the level of the outlet could be adjusted. The water table on the four study areas was levelled before and after each adjustment of the outlet level. The reactions of the water table on the controlled areas were then compared to the natural water table fluctuation on the traditionally drained areas.

When the level of the outlet was raised, water table raised in rainy seasons. In dry seasons, it did not drop down as fast as on traditionally drained areas. Controlled drainage kept the water table at the most 20–25 cm higher than it was on the traditionally drained areas.

When the level of the outlet was lowered, water table on the controlled areas dropped 5 cm–20 cm more than on the traditionally drained areas indicating that water table on the controlled areas had been at a higher level before the lowering.

High water table reduced grain yields on normal and wet growing seasons but increased on dry seasons. Raising the water table by 10 cm diminished greenhouse gas emissions by 20 percentage. As a conclusion, controlled drainage works on a fen that topographically lies on a depression and gets water from the surroundings. Conditions on raised bogs are crucially different from fens, and therefore the result is not valid on raised bogs.

ID 62588

FARM MANAGEMENT OPERATIONS INFLUENCE THE VULNERABILITY OF CULTIVATED UK LOWLAND PEAT SOILS TO WIND EROSION

*Benjamin Freeman1, Giles Wiggs2, David Chadwick1, Christopher Evans3, David Jones1, 4

1 Bangor University, UK
2 University of Oxford, UK
3 Centre for Ecology & Hydrology, UK
4 The University of Western Australia, AU

b.freeman@bangor.ac.uk

Global peatlands store >600 Gt of Carbon but are highly vulnerable to degradation following drainage for agriculture. The extensively drained East Anglian Fens include half of England's most productive agricultural land, produce ~33% of England's vegetables and support a food production industry worth approximately £3 billion GBP. Substantial transport of wind-blown sediment can occur in the region, resulting in soil loss from fields and damaging/contaminating vegetable crops. Recent field measurements show sediment fluxes of 2.3 – 12.8 t ha^{-1} yr^{-1} from an East Anglian fen peat under arable management. There is interest in developing responsible management approaches to reduce sediment losses whilst maintaining economic productivity. In order to target mitigation efforts it is important to understand how spatial variation in erodibility is affected by farm operations. We undertook field measurements on sites at different stages of the crop management cycle (ploughed, prepared for planting, cropped, vehicle routes) and with a range of soil organic matter contents (11 – 76%). We used a portable in situ wind erosion laboratory (PI-SWERL) to measure dust emissions and threshold of entrainment. A range of physical properties were also determined to examine the effects of management on soil particle size distribution and the relationships between physical properties and erodibility. We found higher dust emissions from soils that had experienced more mechanical disturbance. This paralleled our finding that more intensively disturbed soils had a greater proportion of wind erodible material (particle diameter < 0.85mm). We conclude that crop management activities and farm traffic result in mechanical breakdown of soil particles and can increase the erodibility of agricultural lowland peat soils. It is hoped this study will help to inform the design of erosion mitigation strategies and encourage responsible management of UK lowland peat soil resources.

ID 62718

PUTTING PALUDICULTURE INTO PRACTICE – EXPERIENCES FROM FIELD-SCALE CATTAIL PALUDICULTURE IN NE GERMANY

*Sabine Wichmann[1], Kerstin Haldan[1], Nora Köhn[1], Kristina Kuprina[1], Josephine Neubert[1], Telse Vogel[2], Hans Joosten[1]

1 Institute of Botany and Landscape Ecology, University of Greifswald, Germany
2 Institute of Plant Production and Business Management, State Research Institute for Agriculture and Fisheries Mecklenburg-Vorpommern, Germany

wichmann@uni-greifswald.de

Paludiculture is the productive use of wet peatlands. In contrast to drained peatlands, rewetted peatlands have water levels close to surface, which ensure regulating services similar to those in natural peatland ecosystems. The cultivation of wetland plants provides promising options for sustainable farming on peatland. However, practical experiences with paludiculture is scarce and large-scale implementation remains challenging.

The Paludi-PRIMA project (2019-2022) puts paludiculture into practice. A core task is the establishment and investigation of a Cattail field of ~10 ha on a rewetted, formerly drained fen grassland. We gained valuable experiences on site selection, planning and approval processes (water and nature conservation law) and construction work (site preparation, water management). We planted commercially grown seedlings of two species (*T. latifolia*, *T. angustifolia*) with two planting densities (0.5 and 1 plant m^{-2}) using planting machines from forestry. Cattail is adapted to water-saturated soils, enables peat conservation and has a high value creation potential based on the material use of the biomass. Cost data of all implementation steps from site selection to harvest are collected to assess the economic viability in dependence of biomass quality and utilisation options. The field trial is also used for investigations on water demand, nutrient retention and biodiversity, and as a demonstration site for visitors. Mesocosm experiments with Cattail and Reed clones as well as genetic analysis investigate to which extend productivity and biomass quality are determined by species/genotypes, site conditions and management.

Barriers to the implementation of paludiculture are mainly related to the current EU Common Agriculture Policy, the protection of permanent grassland, the consideration of Cattail or Reed stands as protected habitat and the high investment costs. Lessons learned and research results are used to elaborate recommendations for farmers, authorities and policy makers in order to facilitate a large-scale implementation of paludiculture.

Further information: www.moorwissen.de/en/prima

ID 60782

PROFITABILITY OF INTENSIVE MANAGEMENT OF SCOTS PINE STANDS ON CUTAWAY PEATLANDS

*Lasse Aro, Anssi Ahtikoski, Jyrki Hytönen

Natural Resources Institute Finland (Luke), Finland

lasse.aro@luke.fi

The current peat production area in Finland is about 68,000 hectares. At present, annually approximately 2,500 hectares of peat harvesting areas are released for after-use in Finland. Harmful environmental effects, e.g. erosion and subsequent leaching of organic matter and nutrients into watercourses, may continue for many years after the cessation of peat production. In order to prevent this, rapid re-use of cutaway peatlands is recommended. Major after-use option of former peat harvesting areas has been afforestation, but in order to be successful it requires fertilization or soil preparation. Profitability of afforestation with Scots pine (Pinus sylvestris L.) was studied in 31-year old experimental stands in southern Finland. The stands were established by seeding and planting, and various fertilization treatments were tested. Financial performance for each plot was assessed in three stages. First, the costs occurred during the measurement time (i.e. between 0 and 31 years) were summed up according to their present value. Then, for the rest of the rotation (i.e. from the age of 31 onwards) stand management was optimized in order to maximize the net present value (MaxNPV). Finally, bare land values (BLV) were calculated by summing up the present value of costs and MaxNPV and converting the sum of series into infinity. Afforestation method did not affect mean annual increment (MAI; 9.2 - 9.5 m^3/ha/a). When interest rate was 5%, almost two thirds of the stands had negative BLV. However, at interest rate of 3% BLV was positive for all stands.

ID 61983

DRAINED RAE BOG – A UNIQUE NETWORK OF FOREST EXPERIMENTAL AREAS IN NORTH ESTONIA

*Katri Ots[1], Jaan Pikka[2]

[1] Institute of Forestry and Rural Engineering, Estonian University of Life Sciences, Tartu Estonia

[2] NPA Centre for Environmental and Forestry Development, Estonia

katri.ots@emu.ee

SUMMARY

The establishment of Rae experimental plantations (4.7 ha) was started in 1953, the main purpose of which was to find possibilities for afforestation of treeless bogs around Tallinn (North Estonia). The experimental area was drained in 1950. Prior to drainage, the thickness of the oligotrophic peat layer in the western part of Rae bog reached 6.8 m (the average is 5–6 m). Some of the experimental plots were fertilized in 1962–1973 repeatedly with NP-fertilizers; K-fertilizer was added on some plots and oil shale ash was used before afforestation (5–30 t ha^{-1}).
Cultivated tree species were Scots pine, Silver birch and Norway spruce. The purpose of establishing the experimental plots was to study factors that influence bog afforestation, such as the optimum distance between and depth of drainage ditches, proper methods of soil scarification, suitable main tree species and planting methods, initial plantation density and the effect of fertilization on tree growth, vegetation and on the process of soil formation.
The first results of the experiments were hopeful. Thus, in 1968, Tallinn forest enterprise established experimental plots also in Rae and Pääsküla bogs where a healthy forest is currently growing, providing the people of Tallinn with ideal conditions for exercise and leisure. Last measurements in 1994 showed that despite nutrient-poor peat, pine and spruce stands (320–330 m^3 ha^{-1}), but also birch (190 m^3 ha^{-1}) stands have produced adequate volume stock.
The Environmental Investment Centre will be financing (Project No 16363) repeated measurements of the total network of experimental areas after 25 years. The objective of the project will be to evaluate the condition of planted tree species, stand productivity, and changes in the soil and vegetation based on data gathered during fieldwork. Initial results indicate a continuously good growth of the stand.

Keywords: bog, afforestation, Betula pendula, Pinus sylvestris, Picea abies.

INTRODUCTION

The forest land of the Republic of Estonia forms about 50% of mainland. Approximately two-thirds of forests suffer from temporary or permanent excessive moisture. The intensive paludification process of forest lands and decrease in stand productivity in large areas are caused by humid climate. During the last 80 years the area of forest stands has doubled and growing stocks have increased more than 2.4 times caused by afforestation of agricultural lands but also by forest drainage. The volume of drainage operations peaked in 1969–1975, when about 150,000 ha of forest lands were drained; in the 1980s around 338,400 ha. According to various data, a total of 700,000 ha of forest lands have been drained in Estonia, 450,000 ha of which are in state forests.

Drainage of forest lands improves significantly the quality and production of stands. (www.rmk.ee)

The experimental area on Rae drained and fertilized peatland (5 km from the capital city Tallinn) was established in the 1950s to find out the factors that affect the forestation of peatlands and to investigate the possibilities of afforesting oligotrophic peat soils (Seemen et al., 2000). The first results of the experiments were hopeful. Thus, in 1968, Tallinn forest enterprise established experimental plots also in Rae and Pääsküla bogs where a healthy forest is currently growing, providing the people of Tallinn with ideal conditions for exercise and leisure. The uniqueness of the experimental area lies in the fact that the virtually sterile peat soil has managed to grow stands (Silver birch, Scots pine, Norway spruce) of 50–70 years (productive class II–IV). Last measurements in 1994 showed that despite nutrient-poor peat, pine and spruce stands (320–330 m^3 ha^{-1}), but also birch (190 m^3 ha^{-1}) stands have produced adequate volume stock.

In the course of establishing the experimental plantations in Rae bog, it was attempted to determine the factors that have hindered forestation of the bog throughout more than 5,000 years. The formation and development of the bog was explored as well as the trophicity of the moor soil, hydrological regime, microclimate, soil surface freezing and melting. The purpose of establishing the experimental plots was to study factors that influence bog afforestation, such as the optimum distance between and depth of drainage ditches, proper methods of soil scarification, suitable main tree species and planting methods, initial plantation density and the effect of fertilization on tree growth, vegetation and on the process of soil formation.

The Environmental Investment Centre will be financing (Project No 16363) repeated measurements of the total network of experimental areas after 25 years. The objective of the project will be to evaluate the condition of planted tree species, stand productivity, and changes in the soil and vegetation based on data gathered during fieldwork. Initial results indicate a continuously good growth of the stand.

MATERIAL AND METHODS

The experimental area (80 ha) is located in the northwestern part of Rae bog (1,080 ha) which was drained in 1950. The research area (4.7 ha) was divided into three plots which consisted of different sub-plots. The intensity of drainage and fertilization of the experimental area had a significant impact on the growth of young stands. The distance between ditches was 80 m and their depth was 1.5 m, supplementary ditches were dug in 1960. Prior to drainage, the thickness of the oligotrophic peat layer in the western part of Rae bog reached 6.8 m (the average is 5–6 m). The ash content of the poorly decomposed (10%), thick and nutrient-poor moor soil was 3%, $pH_{KCl} = 3.0$, N content – 0.7%, P_2O_5 – 0.07 %, K_2O – 0.07%, CaO – 0.4% (Seemen et al., 2000). Repeated chemical analyses in 2019 showed that $pH_{KCl} = 2.8–3.2$ and peat contained N 1.3–1.7%, P 98–145 mg kg^{-1}, K 163–309 mg kg^{-1}, Ca 1085–2242 mg kg^{-1} and Mg 185–400 mg kg^{-1}. (Seemen et al., 2000).

Rae bog was treeless with heather and *Sphagnum* species dominating the plant cover (Valk, 2005). Some of the experimental plots were fertilized in 1962–1973 repeatedly with NP-fertilizers; K-fertilizer was added on some plots and oil shale ash (OSA) was used before afforestation (5–30 t ha^{-1}) (Seemen et al., 2000) (Table 1).

RESULTS

Birch plantation was established with naturally regenerated plants, height of the seedlings was 20–40 cm. Before cultivation the sample plot was fertilized with oil shale ash (10 t ha^{-1} on stand No II-7 or 20 t ha^{-1} on stand No I-17); the fertilization combined NPK-fertilizer (on stand No I-17) which has a very good effect on the height growth of birches (Figure 1).

Table 1. Main characteristics of experimental plots (Seemen et al., 2000)

No of experimental plot	Tree species	Method of cultivation	Fertilization OSA (t ha^{-1})	Fertilization NPK	Quality class in 1997
I-17	Silver birch	Planting	20	9N3P1K	3
II-7	Silver birch	Planting	10	–	4
II-15	Scots pine	Planting	30	4N1P	2
II-15a	Scots pine	Planting	30	–	2
II-17	Scots pine	Planting	–	–	2
II-12	Norway spruce	Seeding	20	–	3
II-12a	Norway spruce	Planting	20	8N2P1K	2
II-14	Norway spruce	Seeding	–	–	4
II-14a	Norway spruce	Planting	–	–	3

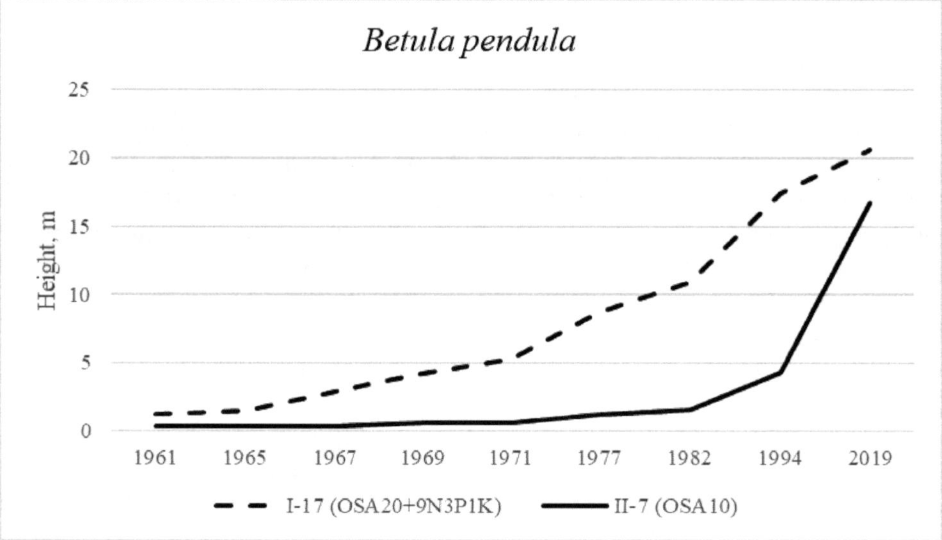

Figure 1. The 62-year-old Silver birch stand growth in Rae experimental areas fertilized with oil shale ash (10–20 t ha^{-1}) in 1957 and with the combined NPK-fertilizer in 1958–1983.

The height growth of fertilized pines was not bigger than that of pines growing on unfertilized sample plots; a small difference between the height growth of fertilized and unfertilized trees occurred only during the fast growth period of young stands (until the stands were 10–27 years old) in 1961–1978 (Figure 2).

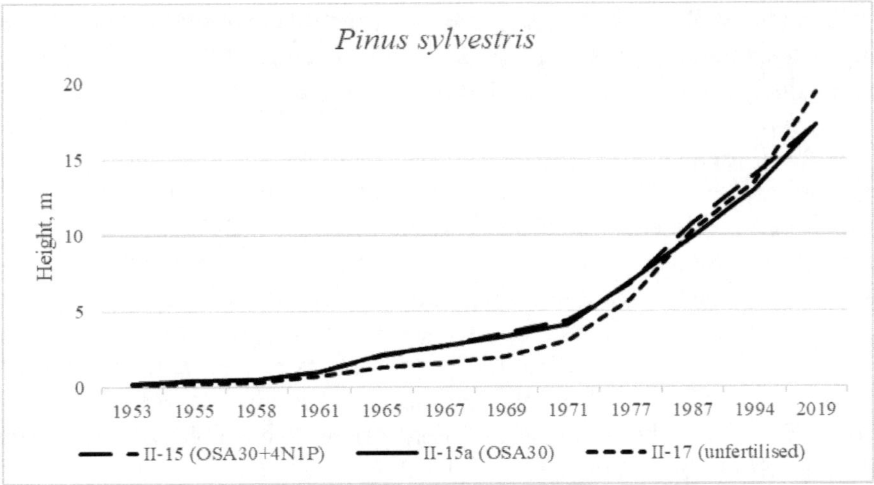

Figure 2. The 68-year-old Scots pine stand growth in Rae experimental area fertilized with oil shale ash (30 t ha^{-1}) in 1953 and with mineral fertilizers (4N1P) in 1968–1973.

The height of Norway spruce stands was measured at 47 years, which was significantly affected by the stand establishment method – the height of planted stands was 12.5–14.0 m, whereas the height of seeded spruces only reached 8.4–10.6 m (Figure 3).

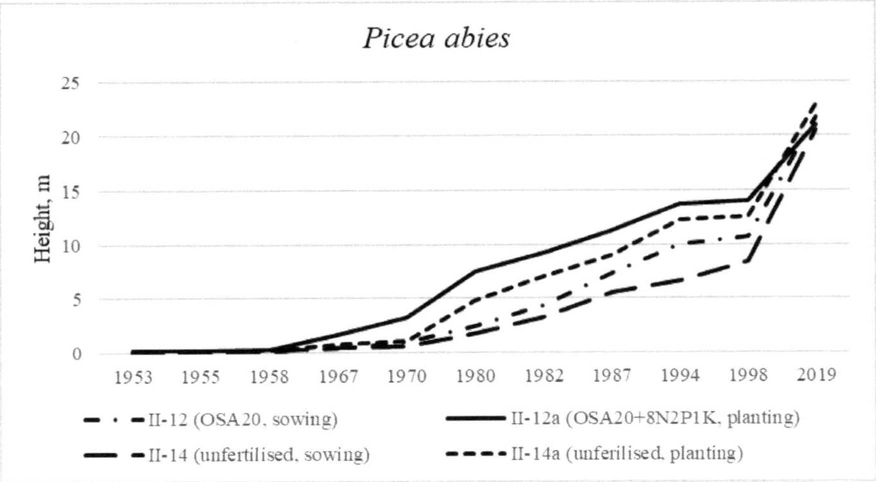

Figure 3. The 68-year-old Norway spruce stand growth in Rae experimental area fertilized with oil shale ash (20 t ha^{-1}) in 1953 and with mineral fertilizers (8N2P1K) in 1964.

DISCUSSION

Seemen and co-authors (2000) found good preliminary results of growing Christmas trees in Rae bog and were convinced that afforestation of oligotrophic peat bogs in the green zone of towns is possible. The oligotrophic peat-bog is the best area for studying tree growth processes and for experimental work because the soil conditions are very homogeneous. Phosphorus is especially important in the afforestation of raised bogs (Valk, 2005). The areas of Rae bog which demonstrated better growth, had a larger content of P in the surface layer of peat.

Fertilization in Rae drained bog has the strongest effect on the growth of birches, a fairly strong effect on the growth of spruces and a weaker effect on the growth of pine trees (Seemen et al., 2000). The combination of oil shale ash 20 t ha^{-1} and NPK-fertilizer on stand No I-17 has a very

good effect on the height growth of birches. The volume of unfertilized birch stands is very low – only 15 m^3 ha^{-1} in a 30-year-old stand (Seemen et al., 2000). The height growth of planted pines and spruces was better than the height growth of seeded trees; especially big differences occurred in growing stock. The application of oil shale ash 30 tons per hectare has a positive effect on the height growth of pines only for a short period.
The combination of oil shale ash and NP-fertilizer stimulates the volume growth of pines: the yield of wood was higher in a combined fertilized stand (330 m^3 ha^{-1} on stand No II-15) compared to a pine stand fertilized only with oil shale ash (259 m^3 ha^{-1} on stand No II-15a). In planted Norway spruce experimental plots where nitrogen was applied abundantly the variation parameters of trees increased: the number of trees with a small diameter was large. Refertilization was not needed, because the growth increment of the stand was sufficient. The natural cycling of nutrient elements from organic material arose. After thinning of Norway spruce serious elk damage can occur. Several experimental plots where a combination of oil shale ash and NP-fertilizer was used currently have thick spruce undergrowth. (Seemen et al., 2000)

CONCLUSION

The experimental area on Rae drained and fertilized peatland was established in the 1950s to determine the factors that affect the forestation of peatlands and to investigate the possibilities of afforesting oligotrophic peat soils. The uniqueness of the experimental area lies in the fact that the virtually sterile peat soil has managed to grow stands (Silver birch, Scots pine, Norway spruce) of 50–70 years (productive class II–IV) and there are no known analogues to that in the rest of Europe. Last measurements in 1994 showed that despite nutrient-poor peat, pine and spruce stands (320–330 tm ha-1), but also birch (190 tm ha-1) stands have produced adequate volume stock. Initial results indicate a continuously good growth of the stand, with planted stands having a growth advantage over seeded stands. Repeated measurements will be carried out in 2019–2021 as part of Project No 16363 financed by the Environmental Investment Centre.

ACKNOWLEDGEMENTS

This work was supported by the Environmental Investment Centre (Project No 16363). The authors are grateful to Jaak Pikk for consultations, earlier research materials and access to the measurement database.

REFERENCES

Seemen H, Pikk J, Valk U. (2000) The rae bog – a unique patch of experimental forestry. *Proceedings of the Estonian Academical Forestry Society XII. Studies of the history of Estonian forestry III*: 95–112

Valk U. (2005) *Estonian bogs*. Halo Kirjastus, Tartu: 314 p.

www.rmk.ee

ID 77320

CLIMATICALLY DRIVEN MULTI-ANNUAL GROWTH TRENDS OF SCOTS PINE TREES IN PEATLAND SITES OF ESTONIA, LITHUANIA, BELARUS AND SWEDEN

*Aleksei Potapov[1], Sandra Toomik[2], Maxim Yermokhin[3], Johannes Edvardsson[4], Marija Žukovskienė[5], Ando Lilleleht[1], Andres Kiviste[1], Tanel Kaart[6], Sandra Metslaid[1], Arvo Järvet[2], Maris Hordo[1]

[1] Institute of Forestry and Rural Engineering, Estonian University of Life Sciences, Estonia
[2] Institute of Ecology and Earth Sciences, University of Tartu, Estonia
[3] Institute of Experimental Botany of the National Academy of Science of Belarus, Belarus
[4] Department of Geology, Lund University, Sweden
[5] Geology and Geography Institute, Nature Research Centre, Lithuania
[6] Institute of Veterinary Medicine and Animal Sciences, Estonian University of Life Sciences, Estonia

aleksei.potapov@emu.ee

Long- and short-term growth dynamics of trees are affected by numerous factors. In peatlands, high groundwater level (GWL) can provide unfavourable soil aeration and result in suppressed tree growth. However, shifts in hydrological regime (long-term GWL fluctuations related to artificial drainage or climatic reasons) can induce changes in site conditions and consequently in growth trends of trees. Lowering of GWL as a result of ditching usually initiates an abrupt increase in growth rate of trees (growth release event). We can hypothesize that similar effect on tree growth can be observed in the case of climatically induced hydrological changes in peatlands.

Tree-ring data (processed according to the radial growth averaging method) of Scots pine sampled at peatland sites different in productivity and management history in 16 study areas in Estonia, Lithuania, Belarus, and Sweden were used to examine similarities between the sites in tree growth dynamics and timing of growth release events during the 20th century. Possible links to climatic drivers were explored using Self-calibrating Palmer Drought Severity Index (scPDSI).

Detected growth releases in the 1910s, 1930s, and around 1970 and 1990 were synchronous in both drained and undrained sites. Tree-ring chronologies developed for different peatland sites show common multi-annual growth trends, especially when comparing sites within and between Estonia, Lithuania and Belarus (in some cases also Sweden). Local factors (e.g. ditching) could trigger changes in growth dynamics and be detected in single tree-ring chronologies, however, common variations at multiple sites indicate the response to similar forcing mechanisms in different regions. Synchronous growth trends can be therefore linked to regional climate dynamics. Detected growth releases were possibly a result of climatically driven hydrological changes in the peatlands since there is an agreement between the trends in scPDSI time series and tree growth dynamics. Still, on drained sites tree growth was additionally determined by non-climatically induced changes in hydrology during post-drainage period.

ID 62707

PEAT EXTRACTION AND USE IN EUROPE – AN UDATE OF PREVIOUS IPS SURVEYS

Hannu Salo

The Bioenergy Association of Finland, Growing Media Finland

hannu.salo@bioenergia.fi

The IPS Expert Group on Growing Media is in the process of sending inquiries to the main countries extracting and using peat for various purposes during spring 2020. The aim is to collect updated figures on the amounts of volumes of peat used and also the areas in peat extraction. The data is mainly derived from national associations representing peat extraction, growing media organizations and other stakeholders using peat. Also expert estimations and official statistics are utilized. According to the preliminary results one can see a clear trend of peat extraction is in transition from energy peat to horticulture and other purposes in Europe continues. The share of peat used for growing media is increasing, and at the same time energy peat is declining.

ID 72797

PLANT BIOSTIMULANTS - A TOOL TO REDUCE FERTILIZATION IMPROVING QUALITY AND STRESS RESISTANCE OF SEEDLINGS IN PEAT-BASED SUBSTRATES

Costantino Cattivello

ERSA-FVG, Substrates laboratory, Pozzuolo del Friuli, (UD), Italy

costantino.cattivello@ersa.fvg.it

SUMMARY

A plant biostimulant is any substance or microorganism that is applied to plants with the aim of enhancing nutrition efficiency, abiotic stress tolerance and/or crop quality traits, regardless of its nutrient content.
Trials on plant biostimulants were carried out in order to evaluate the possibility of cutting in half the quantity of fertilizers used in peat based substrates for young horticultural plants. Moreover, the quality of seedlings produced in case of delayed transplanting (on cauliflower and fennel) was evaluated.
Five plant biostimulants, obtained from different raw materials, were tested on seedlings of four horticultural species. The following main indicators were measured in order to determine seedlings' qualitative characteristics: chlorophyll content (SPAD), fresh weight, foliage dry matter and compactness index. The use of plant biostimulants, together with halving the fertilizer added to the substrate, made it possible to obtain seedlings with quality characteristics that were comparable or better than those produced with the full dose of fertilizer. The results also confirmed the usefulness of plant biostimulants in the event of accidental prolongation of the seedlings' permanence in the plugs.

Keywords: *plug, vegetables, resilience, growing media, transplant*

INTRODUCTION

In 2015 there were almost 2.2 million hectares used for producing vegetables for fresh consumption and processing in the EU and nearly half of them were located in Italy (De Cicco - Eurostat, 2016). Unlike in the past, nowadays most vegetables crops are grown from transplanted seedlings. According to recent estimates, 15 billion seedlings are transplanted each year in Italy (Sansavini and Ranalli, 2012). Until recently nurseries were asked to produce high-quality seedlings suitable to be handled during transplanting phases, with a high chlorophyll content, right root/shoot ratio and an appropriate height. Moreover, nowadays nursery customers ask for plants that are more resilient and produced with organic methods or with a strong reduction of chemicals (fertilizers, pesticides, growth regulators, etc.).
Biostimulants are substances or microorganisms applied to plants with the aim of enhancing nutrition efficiency, abiotic stress tolerance and/or crop quality traits, regardless of their nutrient content. Therefore, they could be useful tools for reducing substrate fertilization, improving plant quality, ensuring good nutritional status, even in plug-aged seedlings, and decreasing the environmental impact of nursery crops.

Previous experiences have showed the potential of these products in substrates for horticulture (Brescon, 2010, Zamparo, 2018, Cattivello, 2019) in order to reduce substrate fertilization and to assure good nutritional status with a fast vegetative recovery of seedlings once transplanted in fields.
The aim of this work is to evaluate biostimulants obtained from different raw materials as tools to reduce substrate fertilization without detrimental effects on seedling quality also in case of delayed transplantation.

MATERIALS AND METHODS

Trials were carried out in a nursery located in northern Italy between 2019 and 2020. The same substrate for all treatments was prepared with fine peat (H3-H4), calcium carbonate for correcting the pH, wetting agents, and adding a full (1 kg m^{-3}) and halved dose (0.5 kg m^{-3}) of a ready-to-use chemical fertilizer (14% N -16% P_2O_5 -18% K_2O + t.e.). Five biostimulants were added to the substrates during the formulation, following the producer's instructions. In detail, we tested two products extracted from the seaweed *Ascophyllum nodosum* (*Actiwave G* and *MC Set* - Valagro Spa), one based on the seaweed *Ecklonia maxima* (*Kelpack* - AlzChem Group AG), one extracted from microalgae (*AlgaEnergy* - AgriAlgae SA) and one from leonardite (*Cytohumat* - Agrofarmica Srl). Four vegetables of different botanical families (tomato, lettuce, fennel, cauliflower) were grown both on control and on substrates enhanced with biostimulants. Seedlings were grown on plastic trays with plugs of different volumes, depending on species and ranging from 3.5 to 5 ml. Some important quality descriptors were evaluated: chlorophyll content (measured using the chlorophyll meter Minolta SPAD 502 Plus), foliage fresh and dry weight, dry matter, hypocotyl diameter, plant height, rooting and compactness index, calculated by the ratio ((hypocotyl diameter/plant height)x100). Data were collected at the end of a standard production cycle and, on cauliflower and fennel, also after an extended cycle of 10 days in order to simulate possible transplanting delays due to bad wheatear.

RESULTS

a) <u>*Young seedlings*</u> (Figure 1)

Biostimulants influenced the studied parameters in different ways without clear effects on rooting (data not presented). By adding the biostimulant *Actiwave G* to the growing media, we noted an improvement of SPAD (+6%), plant height (+10.6%), hypocotyl diameter (+5%), foliage fresh weight (+18.2%), in spite of a moderate decrease of compactness index (-5%) and dry matter (-6%). *MC Set* showed comparable performance except for a reduction of foliage dry matter (-3.2%). The biostimulant based on microalgae (*Agrialgae*) showed only a slight decrease in the fresh weight (-5%). Finally, *Kelpak* and *Cytohumat* also induced a plant behavior similar to the control, with differences only in terms of foliage fresh weight and chlorophyll for *Cytohumat* (+ 5%) and *Kelpak* (-3.7%) respectively.
A halved dosage of fertilizer decreased slightly the chlorophyll content (-5.6%), the plant height (-3.9%) and the foliage fresh weight (-7%) but improved the compactness index (+4.2%) and the foliage dry matter (+3.2%) (Table 1).

Table 1. Behavior of seedlings with different biostimulants and two fertilizer dosages on young seedlings (at the end of a standard production cycle).

FACTOR	SPAD	Plant height cm	Hypocotyl diameter cm	Compactness Index %	F. fresh weight g	Foliage dry matter %

Biostimulants (B)						
CONTROL	48.6 b	12.2 bc	0.39 b	3.20 a	49.0 c	9.5 a
Actiwave G	51.4 a	13.5 a	0.41 a	3.04 b	57.9 a	8.9 c
MC Set	48.2 b	12.3 b	0.39 b	3.17 ab	51.2 b	9.2 b
Kelpak	46.8 c	12.3 b	0.39 b	3.17 ab	48.9 c	9.6 a
Agrialgae	48.3 b	11.9 c	0.39 b	3.28 a	46.6 d	9.7 a
Cytohumat	47.7 b	12.4 b	0.40 ab	3.23 a	51.4 b	9.8 a
	***	***	**	**	***	***
Fertilizer (D)						
Full dosage	49.9 a	12.7 a	0.39 a	3.07 b	52.7 a	9.3 b
Half dosage	47.1 b	12.2 b	0.39 a	3.20 a	49.0 b	9.6 a
	***	***	n.s.	***	***	***
Interactions						
B x D	**	***	***	***	***	***
B x Species	n.s.	***	n.s.	***	***	***
D x Species	***	*	*	***	*	*
D x B x Species	n.s.	**	**	***	*	***

(***) P≤0.001; (**) P≤0.01; (*) P≤0.05; n.s. not significant

In many cases, aged plants grown in substrates with biostimulants in combination with reduced substrate fertilization gave results comparable with the control, overall in terms of compactness index and foliage dry matter, two important quality descriptors. *MC Set* and *Kelpak* showed the best results. The interaction analysis confirmed the same behavior of biostimulants with reduced fertilization in both species (Table 2).

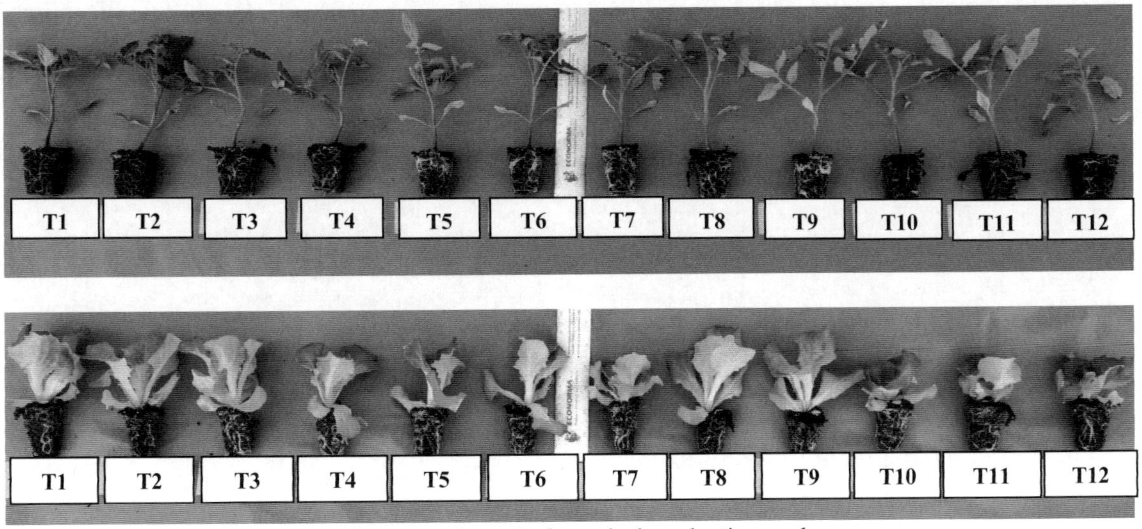

Figure 1. Seedlings of tomato and lettuce at the end of a typical production cycle.
From T1 to T6 full dosage of substrate fertilizer: Control (T1), Actiwave G (T2), MC Set (T3), Agrialgae (T4), Cytohumat (T5), Kelpak (T6).
From T7 to T12 halve dosage of substrate fertilizer. Control (T7), Actiwave G (T8), MC Set (T9), Agrialgae (T10), Cytohumat (T11), Kelpak (T12).

b) <u>*Aged seedlings*</u>

Table 2. Behavior of aged seedlings of cauliflower and fennel to different biostimulants and doses of fertilizer.

FACTOR	SPAD	Plant height cm	Hypocotyl diameter cm	Compactness Index %	F. Fresh weight g	Foliage dry matter %
Biostimulants (B)						
CONTROL (FD)	52.0 ab	15.7 b	0.288 ab	1.85 a	68.9 b	11.9 a

Actiwave G (HD)	52.6 a	16.7 a	0.29 a	1.79 a	76.9 a	11.1 b
MC Set (HD)	53.1 a	15.4 bc	0.28 bc	1.83 a	64.1 b	11.9 a
Kelpak (HD)	51.0 b	15.1 c	0.27 c	1.89 a	68.2 b	11.7 a
Agrialgae (HD)	50.5 bc	15.9 b	0.28 bc	1.79 a	65.0 b	11.6 ab
Cytohumat (HD)	49.3 c	15.9 b	0.28 bc	1.81 a	64.8 b	11.6 ab
	***	*	*	n.s.	**	*
Interactions						
B x Species	*	**	n.s.	n.s.	***	***

FD =Full dose fertilizer; HD = half dose fertilizer
(***) P≤0.001; (**) P≤0.01; (*) P≤0.05; n.s. not significant

DISCUSSION

Compared to control on young and aged plants, *Actiwave G* improved clearly the plant nutritional status in seedlings (high values of chlorophyll, plant height and hypocotyl diameter) in spite of a moderate reduction of foliage dry matter (-6.7%). *MC Set*, the other biostimulant obtained from *Ascophyllum nodosum*, gave the best results only on aged plants. *Actiwave G*, although obtained from the same seaweed as *MC Set*, seemed more interesting. These results could be due mainly to the presence of Caidrine, (a K vitamin derivate). It increases the absorption of nutrients through roots, by influencing the activity of the proton doors at cellular level and by promoting the introduction of nutrients in complex molecules (proteins, polysaccharides), whose synthesis is required for the growth of all plants.
The other biostimulants extracted by the seaweed *Ecklonia maxima* (*Kelpak*), by microalgae (*Algaenergy*) and leonardite (*Cytohumat*) gave results comparable with control in young and aged plants, overall in terms of compactness index and foliage dry matter. Finally, the half dose of fertilizer added to the growing media, combined with biostimulants based on different raw materials, assured a better quality in terms of rusticity and compactness in young and aged seedlings.

CONCLUSION

Trials were carried out on four vegetable species, in nurseries, and repeated in different seasons. Results confirm that biostimulants could be a valuable tool for reducing significantly the fertilization applied to a peat based substrate. They support the nutritional requirements also in aged seedlings with a final quality comparable or better than control represented by plants grown on substrates fertilized with a full dosage.

ACKNOWLEDGEMENTS

The author would like to thank all the people who were involved in these trials, the owner of the "Florodorico" nursery for his endless availability and colleagues Chiara Longo, Enrico Strazzolini and Valentino Cucit for their careful and stimulating conduction of the experimental activity.

REFERENCES

1. Anonymous (2018). Farms Catalogue - Valagro, Italy. https://www.valagro.com/usa/en-us/restricted/get-document/restricted_area/documents/ New_Leaflet_ACTIWAVE_en.pdf?id=1169.

2. Brescon G. (2010). Valutazione di substrati di nuova concezione su brassicacee per migliorare le caratteristiche

qualitative di giovani piante, in Italian (*Evaluation of new substrates in order to improve the quality of brassicaceous seedlings*). Bachelor dissertation, Università di Bologna, Italy.

3. Cattivello C. (2019). Evaluation of biostimulants in growing media for vegetable seedlings. Acta Horticulturae n° 1266. ISHS 2019. DOI 10.17660/ActaHortic.2019.1266.22

4. De Cicco A. (2016). The fruit and vegetable sector in the EU - a statistical overview. Eurostat. Online at: https://ec.europa.eu/eurostat/statistics-explained/index.php/The_fruit_and_vegetable_sector_in_the_EU_-a_statistical_review.

5. Sansavini S, Ranalli P. (2012). Manuale di ortofrutticoltura, in Italian, (*fruit and vegetable manual*), EdAgricole, Bologna, Italy, 323-324.

6. Zamparo L. (2018). Improving vegetable seedlings quality in peat based substrates: fertilizer mixes and biostimulants. Bachelor dissertation. University of Bologna, Italy.

ID 62482

TESTATE AMOEBAE RECORD OF HYDROLOGICAL CHANGES AT A UNIQUE PEATBOG IN THE CENTRAL PART OF THE POLESIE LUBELSKIE (SE POLAND); THE DURNE BAGNO CASE STUDY

*Joanna Jarosz[1], Irena Agnieszka Pidek[2], Mariusz Lamentowicz[3], Magdalena Suchora[2], Danuta Michczyńska[4]

[1] Department of Biology, University of Bialystok, Poland
[2] Department of Geomorphology and Paleogeography, Faculty of Earth Sciences and Spatial Management, Maria Curie-Skłodowska University, Poland
[3] Department of Biogeography and Palaeoecology, Faculty of Geographical and Geological Sciences, Adam Mickiewicz University, Poland
[4] Faculty of Environmental Engineering and Land Surveying, University of Agriculture in Krakow, Poland

jarosz.joa@gmail.com

The aim of the work was detailed identification of the paleohydrological changes registered in the lake-peat sediments of Durne Bagno site (E Poland), located in subregion Łeczna-Włodawa Lake District. The entire area is distinguished by its considerable lake density and the occurrence of numerous valuable peat ecosystems, including raised bogs.

The main research method was the analysis of subfossil testate amoebae. The results of this analysis are supported by the results of palynological NPPs (non-pollen palynomorphs) analyzes , lithology of the peat cores and peat decomposition degree. The chronology of events of lower and higher water table was established on the basis of radiocarbon datings. The determination ofsettlement phases ascertained by archaeologists (AZP) were also used to establish the chronology.

The results of the fossil testate amoeba studies on the Durne Bagno site allowed to indicate that the beginning of the peat bog formation is at the end of the Atlantic period. A total of 26 zones of amoebae assemblages were recorded in the profile, 10 NPPs zones, 27 zones of varying degrees of peat decomposition are marked by 13 episodes of increased anthropogenic pressure. On the basis of the obtained results, it can be stated that Durne Bagno peat bog has been subject to rapid changes in water level throughout the entire history. They reflect the vitality of the human population from the decline of the Mesolithic to the period after the 15th century. The driest conditions on the peatbog prevailed during Early Middle Ages, however, the Roman Period was also reflected as the period of drainage of the peat bog surface and generally since this period the water level on the bog has not increased to high levels. However, in the sections preceding the Roman Period there were alternately wet periods and dry periods.

ID 62365

CRITICAL RAINFALL TO EXTINGUISH PEAT FIRES

Shaorun Lin, Yau Kuen Cheung, Yang Xiao, *Xinyan Huang

The Hong Kong Polytechnic University, Hong Kong

xy.huang@polyu.edu.hk

Peat fire is one of the largest wildfires and most persistent fire phenomena on Earth. Here we assess the underlying mechanism of rain in suppressing the peat fire in the shallow soil layer through laboratory experiments. We show that the minimum rainfall intensity to extinguish the peat fire is roughly 4 mm/h, so that the persistent light rain cannot suppress such smoldering wildfire. The required rain duration (Δt in min) for extinguishing smoldering peat fire decreases with the rainfall intensities (I in mm/h), as $\log_{10}\Delta t=-1.2\ \log_{10}\square+3.3$, and is much longer than that for extinguishing flaming wildfire. We also identify that the required rainfall depth for extinguishing peat fire gradually decreases with the rainfall intensity and approaches a minimum value of 13 mm under violent rain. As rainfall intensity increases, the carbon emission flux from peat fire decreases. Therefore, we conclude that the short-term violent rain is most effective for suppressing the persistent peat fire. This research helps evaluate the impact of weather on the development of peat fire and improve the prediction of global carbon emissions from peat fire with the weather model.

ID 62422

POTENTIAL OF HYDROGEL TO MAINTAIN THE HYDROPHILIC PROPERTIES OF TROPICAL PEAT IN THE DRY SEASON

*Made Dirgantara, Adi Jaya

dirgantaramade@gmail.com

Indonesia is in the tropics, and has a variety of essential ecosystems that affect global environmental conditions, one of which is peatland. Tropical peatland plays an important role in carbon storage, water regulation in the rainy season, and preserving the biodiversity that lives on it. The problem that often arises in peat ecosystems is the decrease in surface water level and drought in the dry season, which causes a change in the characteristics of peat from hydrophilic to hydrophobic. This change causes peatlands to go on fire easily in the dry season, resulting in air pollution and high CO_2 emissions. After fire, peatlands are only able to absorb around 50% of the water it could in its original condition leading to flooding in the rainy season. Control and mitigation of peatland fires currently takes place through infrastructure development (boreholes and canal blocking) and response by local communities. The handling and mitigation are still not optimal, where major peatland fires occurred in Indonesia in 2019; therefore, alternative peatland fire mitigation is still needed. Using hydrogel, that can absorb 120 times its tweight in water there is the potential to help maintain hydrophilic peat, so it does not burn easily. In this study, a simulation was carried out to determine the effectiveness of hydrogel in this respect. The results show that hydrogel can help maintain peat moisture so that the hydrophilic nature is maintained.

ID 61444

RESTORATION DILEMMAS BETWEEN FUTURE ECOSYSTEM AND CURRENT SPECIES VALUES: THE CONCEPT AND A PRACTICAL APPROACH IN ESTONIAN MIRES

*Liina Remm, Urmas Sellis, Riinu Rannap
University of Tartu, Estonia

liina.remm@ut.ee

Ecosystem restoration is gaining political and economic support worldwide, but its impact on threatened species that inhabit the areas before restoration and live in the degraded ecosystems may remain unnoticed and unclear. A specific combination of uncertainties and options emerges when ecosystem restoration would negatively affect pre-restoration species conservation values. Such dilemma appears to be common, but largely ignored in restoration planning; for example, in historically drained wetlands that provide novel habitats for some threatened species. We present a framework for resolving the dilemma, and exemplify its application in extensive mire restoration in Estonia. Solution options include redistributing the risks by timing of the restoration works; relocating restoration sites; modifying restoration techniques; and managing for future habitats of the species involved. In our mire restoration project LIFE Mires of Estonia, we assessed these options based on spatially explicit mapping of expected future states of the ecosystem, the restoration works, and the distribution of species at risk. Such planning documentation, combined with follow-up monitoring and experimentation, can be used for adaptive management, by funding organizations, and for academic research. The presentation is based on a published article (Remm et al. 2019 Restoration dilemmas ... JEMA) but at the congress we will show also recent results about the short-term impact of careful restoration works on some species at risk, especially capercaillie.

ID 61531

CAUSE OF DECADE'S STAGNATION OF PLANT COMMUNITIES THROUGH 16 YEARS SUCCESSIONAL TRAJECTORY TOWARD FENS AT A CREATED WETLAND IN NORTHERN JAPAN

*Kazuo Yabe[1], Nobutake Nakatani[2], Tomotsugu Yazaki[3]

[1]*Sapporo City University, Sapporo, Japan*
[2]*Rakuno Gakuen University, Ebetsu, Japan*
[3]*Meiji University, Kawasaki, Japan*

k.yabe@scu.ac.jp

SUMMARY

Hiraoka is the created wetland constructed in 2000. We introduced fen and bog plants and monitored the hydrochemical conditions and species assemblage composition during the 16 years after construction (YAC).

The species richness indices resembled those of the target fens within 11 YAC, but the species assemblages did not match the target fens even after 16 YAC. The 0.1 m high artificial hummocks enhanced species richness 1.3 to 1.4 times more than the surrounding hollows and increased variety within species assemblages.

Water level were stable at around 0.00 to 0.05 m above the wetland surface, except during several-days floods. Mean pH values decreased from 6.9 in 1 YAC to 6.2 in 16 YAC and approached those of natural fens. The mean electrical conductivity (170–200 µS cm^{-1}) and concentrations of major minerals (Ca^{2+}, Mg^{2+}, and K^{+}) were consistently higher than those of natural fens, but dissolved phosphorus (0.00–0.04 mg l^{-1}) and nitrogen (0.12–0.48 mg l^{-1}) were lower. Since mineral content in Hiraoka was near the lower limit of calcareous rich fens, abundant minerals would be less effective in changing the species assemblage compositions. Accordingly, hydrochemical conditions were less effective for changing the species assemblage composition.

The trajectory of species assemblages quickly approached the target fen at least 5 YAC, but then changed between 5 and 11 YAC, before stagnating. Due to the dominance of eight initially introduced fen species, the trajectory turned in a different direction. Since the five fen dominants introduced at 8 to 9 YAC had not yet dominated, species assemblages are stagnated. Initial introductions, including species combinations of target fen, can shorten the time required to achieve natural fens.

Large emerged macrophytes did not dominate and did not competitively exclude fen species, probably because the water was oligotrophic and the wetland design did not include open water.

Keywords: *Annual plants, Artificial hummock, Exotic plants, Minerals, Non-metric multidimensional scaling (NMS), Two-way indicator species analysis (TWISPAN)*

INTRODUCTION

Ishikari Plain in northern Japan, where the city of Sapporo is located, once contained the largest bog areas in Japan, but landscapes such as continuous bogs and fens were lost by 1970, owing to large-scale agricultural development and subsequent urbanization. In 2000, Sapporo city constructed grounds for a created wetland using only easily obtainable base materials in Hiraoka park and began to attempt to create a lost landscape of mires in Ishikari Plain for citizens by establishing mire plant communities (Yabe and Nakamura, 2010). We set artificial hummocks made of coconuts fiber on the surface of the created wetland and tried to enhance habitat heterogeneity by reproducing the micro terrain on the surface of bogs. Sphagnum-dominated hummocks are ca. 0.1 m high on the bogs surface located in Ishikari Plain and other alluvial plains at the Sea of Japan Coast (Yabe and Uemura, 2001).

Since trajectory of species assemblage proceeded toward fens until 5 YAC and hydrochemical conditions were similar to those of fens, we decided fens as target of creation, and then, we transplanted fen dominants. However, until 11 YAC, the species assemblages changed the direction of trajectory different from target species assemblage and then, they are stagnating.

We, first, examine 16 years changes in species abundances of each life forms, origins (native or exotic), and trajectory of species assemblages and verify these indicators for assessing the success or failure of the fen creating project. We additionally evaluate the effectiveness of artificial hummocks made on the surface of created wetland using these indictors. Then we consider the cause of the changing direction and stagnation in trajectory in the progress of succession, in relation to the hydrochemical conditions and change in the occurrence pattern of dominant species. Finally, we propose the key points to achieve target communities within a short period.

MATERIALS AND METHODS

Hiraoka is the created wetland in Hiraoka Park (43.0° N and 141.5° E) located in urbanized district of Sapporo in Ishikari plain. Weather records of Sapporo weather station from 1981 to 2010 were used; monthly mean air temperature ranges from 22.3 °C (August) to -3.6 °C (January), annual precipitation is 1107 mm in a year, and monthly precipitations are small between March to July, ranging 47 to 81 mm, but largest in September (135 mm) and second largest in August (124 mm) owing to heavy rains caused by typhoon.

The base of created wetland (70 × 40 m, 2200 m^2) was constructed in February 2000 as a project of the Environmental Bureau Greenery Promotion Department, Sapporo City (Yabe and Nakamura, 2010). A stream with a pond adjoining the wetland on the way and two dams at the inlet and outlet of pond were also constructed. An impermeable sheet was laid over the base of wetland, pond, and stream. A 0.3 m-thick layer of volcanic gravels (Tarumae-a) was then spread over the sheet on the wetland and firmed twice with a stone-roller, and covered with 0.2 m thick erosion control blanket. In each site, hummock and hollow1 plots were set for the transplanting experiment. The hummock plot (0.9 × 0.9 m^2) consisted of nine square mats (0.3 × 0.3 m^2) of coconut husk and rose 0.1 m from surrounding surface.

We monitored hydrochemical conditions and composition of species assemblages on 4 times (1, 5, 11, and 16 YAC) until 2016. In order to compare composition of species assemblage with fens, coverage data (%) of fen species within quadrats were used for analyses. The 77 data of communities collected from the nearest six intact mires located in Yufutsu region of the Pacific coast, 45 km SSE from Hiraoka.

A TWISPAN was performed to classify species assemblages into community types. Occurrence patterns of species among the community types were examined by their frequency F% expressed as percentage of the plots in which the species occurred in a community type and coverage C% as the mean of coverage through the plots. Species showing 34.5% or more in the F and /or C values at one or more communities were listed. In order to examine the spatial arrangement of community types accounted for the difference of species composition, non-metric multidimensional scaling (NMS) was performed using Sørenson (Bray-Curtis) distance.

RESULTS

Change of hydrochemical environment through 16 years

Mean water levels form the ground surface (WL) among survey sites were low in 1 YAC, -0.11 to -0.10 m, but increased to+0.76 to +0.93 m in 5 YAC, and then became stable around wetland surface from 11 YAC (-0.55 to 0.00 m) to 16 YAC (-0.03 to 0.00 m). At the heaviest flooding on August in 16 YAC, the wetland submerged for only several hours (+0.46 m in WL), and the pond submerged (+0.62 m).

Both mean values and ranges of pH were decreasing through years from 6.9 (5.5-9.3) in 1 YAC to 6.2 (5.7-6.9) in 16 YAC, but those of EC, however, did not show any trends through respective years from 166 (59-490) to 196 (72-587) $\mu S\ cm^{-1}$. Composition of ions in the wetland and the pond were similar through years, except for high concentrations of NO_3^- in 0 YAC and 5 YAC and low concentration of NH_4^+ in 0 YAC in the pond. Concentrations of SO_4^{2-} and K^+ decreased in both the wetland and the pond, and Cl^- decreased in the wetland. The PO_4^{3-} concentration were low and NO_2^- were almost below the detection limit. Other ions did show a constant trend.

At the comparison with fens through Hokkaido island (Nakamura et al. 2002), water table fluctuation of Hiraoka was within the range in fens. Concentrations of dissolved phosphorus (0-0.04 mg l-1) and nitrogen (0.12-0.48 mg l^{-1}) was lower except for initial year of nitrogen (0.94 mg l^{-1} in 0 YAC). However, the mean values of EC and concentrations of major minerals (Na^+, Ca^{2+}, Mg^{2+}, and K^+) were consistently higher than fens. The pH values were higher at initial year but decreased afterward.

Changes of species richness in total, by life forms, and by origins

Mean species richness changed from 9.9 (5 YAC) to 8.2 (11 YAC) in hollows but changed from 14.2 (5 YAC) to 10.8 (11 AYC) on hummocks, which was higher than in same year's hollows. Since hummocks were collapsed until 16 YAC, species richness of only hollows could be examined to be 9.4 species in mean. As the whole, the change of species richness in the created wetland were relatively constant for 16 years, and nearly the same or slightly higher than fen communities (7.5 to 9.2).

Annual species showed the same tendency as exotic herbaceous species, because most of annuals were exotics. Both occurred many until 5 YAC, but then, decreased to less than half, which were nearly the same numbers as those of species occurred in fens. Perennials were increased from 30 to 49 until 5 YAC, and then showed constant numbers but slightly less than fens. Less number of trees (5 to 8 species) were migrated in Hiraoka.

Species assemblage

TWINSPAN extracted five types of community from the wetland and two from nearby fens. Each of seven communities has corresponding species groups characteristically occurred (Table 1).

The Cyperus difformis community covered all the plots in 1 YAC, then, the communities of Carex miyabei and Persicaria nepalensis covered almost all the plots in 5 YAC. After that, the communities of Juncus fauriei and Lysimachia thyrsiflora covered all the plots from 11 to 16 YAC. The C. miyabei community in 5 YAC and the L. thyrsiflora community in 11 YAC tended to occur on hummocks, but the communities of P. nepalensis and the J. fairiei in hollows of respective years.

Among major species, the 10 species were introduced much at the initial stage of the created wetland (0 and 1 YAC). Except for Nymphaea tetragona and Dorosera rotundifolia in species group B and C, the following eight species were showing the highest frequency values from 11 to 16 YAC: J. fauriei and Lythrum salicaria among four in species group D, and six out of seven species in group E, M. trifoliata, L. thyrsiflora, Schoenoplectus tabernaemontani, Rhynchospora alba, Eriophorum gracile, and Carex limosa. Five species in F and G, Equisetum palustre, Calamagrostis purpurea, Carex pseudocuraica, Thelypteris palustris and Carex lasiocarpa were the fen dominants transplanted into Hiraoka in 8 YAC. They began to occur from 11 YAC, but, they have not dominated in Hiraoka yet.
In the scattered diagram on maximum two axes of NMS, species composition of the created wetland was steadily heading to two fen communities year to year from 1 to 5 YAC, but suddenly changed to the different direction from fens until 11 YAC, and then stagnated.

DISCUSSION

Initial flora and their rapid changes

In the present study, richness of the native and exotic annual species in Hiraoka prevailed in the one year and five years after, while decreased to half until 11YAC and then became stable. The higher proportion of mesophytes in created wetlands would be owing to the disturbances occurred at the start of succession. In Hiraoka, indices of richness of life form and origin (exotic or native) saturated within 11 YAC, but species assemblages did not achieve those of fens. Accordingly, such richness indices for particular ecological groups are less effective than the assess of species assemblage on the ordination diagram, to assess the achievement toward the natural reference communities (Balcombe et al., 2005; Matthews and Spyreas, 2010).

Effect of artificial hummock

We tried to enhance the habitat heterogeneity of the wetland surface by setting artificial hummocks of coconut fiber. Mean species richness of hummock plots was 1.4 times higher than the hollow plots after five years but decreased to 1.3 after 11years. Species assemblages were different between hummocks and hollows. These results suggest that artificial hummocks can enhance the species richness and the variation of species assemblages especially at the initial stage of created wetland.

Effect of abiotic variables for the initial succession

Many cases of the marsh creation indicate that species assemblage often stagnated between the initial and target states where one or more of abiotic conditions was not met (Fagan et al., 2008). Much calcium and other minerals in the peat-pore waters cause the differentiation of species assemblage between poor and rich fens in limestone geology of Euro-America continent (Wheeler and Proctor, 2000). The pH values and relatively high concentrations of Ca^{2+} and other minerals in Hiraoka may be less effective for the stagnation in change of species assemblages toward fens. It is because pH values were within the range of Japanese fens and the mineral concentrations should be near the lower limit of the concentration range of rich fens.

Effect of initial introduction of fen species

The reason why trajectory changed direction until 11 YAC was the increase of initially introduced fen species. Owing to the dominance of these species, the dissimilar species assemblages from target fens are formed until 11 YAC. Five fen dominants transplanted at 8 YAC have not

dominated yet in 16 YAC. The floristic analysis of trajectory in Hiraoka strongly suggests that initial introduction of fen species considering combinations of species that reproduce the target species assemblages can shorten to reach the target fen.
In Hiraoka, P. arundinacea occurred but cannot grow thrivingly. P. australis also occurred, but, except for the margin next to the pond, its shoots showed stunt form (<1 m in height). Typha latiforia dominated in the submerged pond, but did not invade in the created wetland. We estimate that low concentration of inorganic forms of N and P in Hiraoka would restrict the monodominance of these competitive superiors.
In addition, controlling hydrological condition is also important, because monodominance of large emerged macrophytes, P. australis and T. latifolia, is often confined to the areas continuously submerged (Yabe and Onimaru 1997) because initially introduced hygrophytes suppress the competitive superiors by taking emerged habitats first (Matthews and Spyreas, 2010). We controlled the water level just above the wetland surface (0 to 0.05 m above), except for flooding periods, and prevented the formation of permanently flooded basin. This management would also ensure the occurrence of fen communities in Hiraoka.

CONCLUSION

Owing to the dominance of initially introduces eight fen species, the trajectory turns to different direction. Since five fen dominants transplanted at 8 YAC have not dominated yet, species assemblage stagnated between initial and target communities at least until 16 YAC. Accordingly, initial species introduction representing species combinations of target fens can shorten to achieve fens. At the 16 YAC, large emerged macrorophytes did not dominate and did not exclude fen species competitively, probably because of oligotrophic water chemistry and the wetland design without including open water.

ACKNOWLEDGEMENTS

We would like to thank Mr. T. Sawada, a chief in the management office of Hiraoka Park, and members of Hiraoka Acorn Forest for their help with the creation of the wetland.

REFERENCES

Balcombe, C.K., Anderson, J.T., Fortney, R.H., Rentch, J.S., William, N. G., Kordek, W.S. (2005) A comparison of plant communities in mitigation and reference wetlands in the mid-Appalachians. *Wetlands*, 25: 130–142.

Fagan, K.C., Pywell, R.F., Bullock, J.M., Marrs, R.H. (2008) Do restored calcareous grasslands on former arable fields resemble ancient targets? The effect of time, methods and environment on outcomes. *Journal of Applied Ecology*, 45: 1293–1303. https://doi.org/10.1111/j.1365-2664.2008.01492.x

Matthews, J.W., Spyreas, G. (2010) Convergence and divergence in plant community trajectories as a framework for monitoring wetland restoration progress. *Journal of Applied Ecology*, 47: 1128–1136. https://doi.org/10.1111/j.1365-2664.2010.01862.x

Nakamura, T., Uemura, S., Yabe, K. (2002) Hydrochemical regime of fen and bog in north Japanese mires as an influence on habitat and above-ground biomass of Carex species. *Journal of Ecology*, 90: 1017-1023. https://www.jstor.org/stable/3072308

Wheeler, B. D., Proctor, M. C. F. (2000) Ecological gradients, subdivisions and terminology of north-west European mires. *Journal of Ecology*, 88: 187–203. https://doi.org/10.1046/j.1365-2745.2000.00455.x

Yabe, K., Onimaru, K. (1997) Key variables controlling the vegetation of a cool-temperate mire in northern Japan. *Journal of Vegetation Science*, 8: 29–36. https://doi.org/10.2307/3237239

Yabe, K., Uemura, S. (2001) Variation in size and shape of Sphagnum hummocks in relation to climatic conditions in Hokkaido Island, northern Japan. *Canadian Journal of Botany*, 79:1318–1326.

Yabe, K., Nakatani, N., Yazaki, T. (2021) Cause of decade's stagnation of plant communities through16-years successional trajectory toward fens at a created wetland in northern Japan. *Global Ecology and Conservation*, 25: e01424. https://doi.org/10.1016/j.gecco.2020.e01424

Table 1 Seven community types classified by TWINSPAN using data of of the artificial wetland and fens. Species with >34.5% of Frequency (F%)and/or Coverage (C%) in one or more community are listed. In life form, annual (an), perenial (p), tree (t) and extotic (ex) are listed. Species having * on right upper was abundantly imported to initial stage of the artificial wetland .

Species group	Life form	Community type						
		Cy. difformis	*C. miyabei*	*P. nepalensis*	*J. fauriei*	*L. thyrsiflora*	*C. lasiocarpa -C. limosa*	*Ca. purpurea-C. pseudocuraica*
		F%	F%	F%	F%	F%	F%	F%
Species group A								
Echinochloa crus-galli (L.) P.Beauv. *var. crus-galli*	an ex	49	1	0	0	0	0	0
Cyperus difformis L.	an	59	1	0	0	0	0	0
Panicum bisulcatum Thunb.	an ex	36	6	0	0	0	0	0
Juncus decipiens (Buchenau) Nakai	p	41	3	5	0	4	0	0
Species group B								
Persicaria hastatosagittata (Makino) Nakai	an	5	58	3	2	0	3	0
Glyceria depauperata Ohwi var. *depauperata*	p	0	37	0	0	0	0	0
Bidens frondosa L.	an ex	13	91	50	8	11	0	0
Eriocaulon decemflorum Maxim.	an	3	61	20	10	11	0	0
Potamogeton berchtoldii Fieber	p	0	52	3	0	0	0	0
Nymphaea tetragona Georgi*	p	0	81	38	0	17	0	11
Carex miyabei Franch.	p	3	91	50	2	0	0	3
Persicaria sagittata (L.) H.Gross var. *sibirica* (Meisn.) Miyabe	an	3	78	13	48	24	31	0
Species group C								
Salix miyabeana Seemen	t	18	31	60	7	4	0	0
Persicaria nepalensis (Meisn.) H.Gross	an	3	76	95	5	7	0	0
Calamagrostis epigeios (L.) Roth	p	0	22	50	0	0	0	3
Drosera rotundifolia L.*	p	3	36	48	8	0	0	24
Persicaria hydropiper (L.) Delarbre	an	0	31	75	0	2	0	0
Persicaria thunbergii (Siebold et Zucc.) H.Gross	an	0	15	50	3	2	26	0
Species group D								
Juncus fauriei H.Lév. et Vaniot*	p	0	13	18	97	39	0	0
Lythrum salicaria L.*	p	23	6	3	79	39	13	5

Table 1 continued.

		Community type						
		Cy. difformis	*C. miyabei*	*P. nepalensis*	*J. fauriei*	*L. thyrsiflora*	*C. lasiocarpa -C. limosa*	*Ca. purpurea-C. pseudocuraica*
		F%	F%	F%	F%	F%	F%	F%
Galium trifidum L. subsp. *columbianum* (Rydb.) Hultén	p	0	0	0	72	52	28	0
Triadenum japonicum (Blume) Makino	p	0	0	0	41	24	18	41
Species group E								
Menyanthes trifoliata L.*	p	3	24	0	7	76	0	5
Lysimachia thyrsiflora L.*	p	3	9	8	77	89	10	8
Persicaria muricata (Meisn.) Nemoto	an	0	0	0	31	52	10	0
Schoenoplectus tabernaemontani (C.C.Gmel.) Palla*	p	0	1	8	8	48	0	0
Rhynchospora alba (L.) Vahl*	p	10	1	0	28	35	0	19
Eriophorum gracile K.Koch*	p	0	4	0	18	61	3	38
Carex limosa L.*	p	3	4	3	21	78	0	51
Species group F								
Equisetum palustre L.	p	0	0	0	26	41	46	8
Calamagrostis purpurea (Trin.) Trin. subsp. langsdorfii (Link) Tzvelev	p	0	0	0	2	2	82	22
Carex thunbergii Steud. var. appendi *-culata* (Trautv. et C.A.Mey.) Ohwi	p	0	4	0	0	0	59	14
Carex pseudocuraica F.Schmidt	p	0	0	0	2	4	69	8
Species group G								
Myrica gale L. var. *tomentosa* C.DC.	t	0	15	25	15	0	3	35
Alnus japonica (Thunb.) Steud.	t	8	6	0	10	4	5	35
Thelypteris palustris (Salisb.) Schott	p	0	0	0	11	0	31	43
Viola verecunda A.Gray	p	0	0	0	3	2	8	41
Carex lasiocarpa Ehrh. subsp. *occultans* (Franch.) Hultén	p	0	0	0	5	2	13	76
Phragmites australis (Cav.) Trin. ex Steud.	p	0	0	0	16	11	36	73

ID 61666

THE IMPACT OF WINDFARM INFRASTRUCTURE ON PEATLAND GEO-HYDROMORPHOLOGY AND CARBON STORAGE

*Guaduneth Chico, Ben Clutterbuck

Nottingham Trent University

guaduneth.chicoleon@ntu.ac.uk

Despite covering less than 3% of the Earth's surface, peatlands hold the largest store of terrestrial carbon and can act as carbon sinks when they are in pristine or restored status. The protection, restoration and conservation of peatland environments is, therefore, a key action in helping to mitigate climate change and could be synergistic with other approaches such as renewable energy production. However, locations for windfarm development often coincide with environments where globally rare blanket bog develop, but how windfarms are affecting blanket bogs is not fully reported.

This research mapped wind turbines and access tracks constructed over areas of blanket bog in Spain visible in the most recent 2017 aerial photography and used historical digital elevation data to determine the volume of peat removed to install and maintain one turbine at Malverde blanket bog in Cantabria (northern Spain). A peat core from Malverde was analysed to estimate the loss of long-term carbon storage for one wind turbine and 100 m of access track

In total 235 wind turbines and 60.1 km of tracks were mapped on protected blanket bogs, and a further 43 wind turbines and 11.9 km of tracks were mapped over unprotected blanket bog. At Malverde (a currently unprotected blanket bog), 225 t of carbon have been removed as consequence of a track 100 m long x 10 m wide and 322 t of carbon were extracted for a turbine foundation. Of additional concern, the access track has split a hydromorphological bog unit permanently altering the hydrological functioning of the peatland.

The blanket bogs in Spain represent the southernmost edge-of-range of this habitat in Europe and, in addition to the loss of long-term carbon storage, the installation of windfarms is removing endemic peatland species, a paleoenvironmental archive of 8,000 years and may reduce or prevent future carbon sequestration. The location of renewable energy installations needs careful consideration.

ID 62125

IMPLICATIONS OF PEATLAND RESTORATION IN VEGETATION COMMUNITIES AND PEAT LOSS

*Guaduneth Chico[1], Patxi Heras[2], José María Fernández-García[3], Marta Infante[2], Amador Prieto[4], Ben Clutterbuck[1], Maite Aguirre-Pascasio[5]

[1]School of Animal, Rural and Environmental Sciences, Nottingham Trent University, Southwell, United Kingdom
[2] Museum of Natural Sciences, Vitoria, Spain
[3] Hazi Foundation, Arkaute, Spain
[4] Independent researcher, Bilbao, Spain
[5] Bizkaia Provincial Council , Bilbao, Spain

guaduneth.chicoleon@ntu.ac.uk

Peatlands represent the largest carbon storage and a potential carbon sink when in pristine or restored status. Natural pressures such as aeolian or fluvial erosion contribute to the degradation process but anthropogenic pressures (e.g. burning, grazing, peat cutting or windfarm developments) are increasing this process. In Europe, large extensions of land are covered by blanket bog peatlands mainly located in United Kingdom, Ireland and Norway with some occurrence in Spain, Sweden and France.

Our research aims to (i) provide a description of the vegetation communities before and after restoration in Zalama blanket bog (Bizkaia/Burgos – Spain), (ii) quantify the surface changes in exposed peat surfaces and (iii) estimate the erosion rates and carbon loss. A traditional botanic survey was carried out after restoration to compare with previous surveys in order to describe the vegetation changes. Peatland surface changes were quantified using historical aerial (1977, 2002 and 2009) and UAV (2017) photographs. Finally, after restoration, surface changes were estimated using a Terrestrial Laser Scanner undertaking five surveys between May 2017 and June 2018, and the carbon loss was calculated through the analysis of the carbon content in a peat core.

An increase in the richness of plant species that demand wet soils has been recorded, demonstrating the impacts of the restoration actions to hold the water and increase the humidity. The peat surface exposed to degradation has been reduced from 0.66 ha in 1977 to 0.16 ha in 2017, and the current surface change in the still exposed areas is 2.3 cm/year, lower than another comparable but unrestored peatlands on the area.

Restoration actions in Zalama blanket bog are an example of good practices and positive impacts in peatland vegetation communities and peatland surfaces. However, as complete peatland functional restoration is achieved in the long-term, monitoring is key to fully understand the changes and the consequences of restoration actions.

ID 62605

MICROBIAL COMMUNITIES AND BIOGEOCHEMICAL FUNCTIONING IN NATURAL AND RECLAIMED PEATLANDS IN THE ATHABASCA OIL SANDS REGION OF CANADA: IMPLICATION FOR RECLAMATION AND MANAGEMENT

*Shaun Allingham[1], Felix Nwaishi[2], David Elliot[1], Roxanne Anderson[3], Louis Jamie Lamitt[4]

[1] Environmental Sustainability Research Centre, University of Derby, U.K.
[2] Department of Earth and Environmental Science, Mount Royal University, Canada
[3] Environmental Research Institute, University of the Highlands and Islands, Scotland. U.K.
[4] Syracuse University Department of Biology, United States

s.allingham@derby.ac.uk

Peatlands are essential for multiple ecosystem functions and play an important role in global biogeochemical cycles. Knowledge of the environmental drivers on soil microbial community structure and functioning can provide insights to enable effective and evidence-based management. However, it remains largely unknown how microbial diversity contributes to the functioning of belowground processes. Addressing this gap in knowledge will provide insights into predicting the provisioning of microbial-mediated processes in peatlands undergoing restoration or reclamation. We assessed the relationship between prokaryotic and fungal community structures via DNA sequencing as part of a Joint Genome initiative project led by Michigan State University. We evaluated soil function by measuring respiration on a range of substrates from three natural fen types (a treed rich fen, a poor fen and a Hyper saline fen) within the Athabasca Oil Sands region of Canada, and a constructed fen within nearby post-mining landscapes. There was no significant difference in microbial aerobic respiration between fens, but the microbial communities were different. Relative abundance of fungi and prokaryotes was highest in the treed rich fen and microbial community composition was significantly different between fens. Redundancy analysis revealed that pore water pH, plant richness and ammonium were the main factors affecting functional activity (as determined by substrate utilisation capacity). Pore water pH, plant richness and ammonium were the main factors structuring fungal communities while pore water pH, temperature and extractable ammonium were the main factors structuring prokaryotic communities. Although differences in total microbial aerobic respiration was negligible across fens, forms of inorganic N may be important in structuring soil communities and activity potentially leading to improved functionality. Further studies are necessary to assess microbial driven processes in the long term and future models of reclaimed peatlands should consider the dynamic interaction between communities and functionality which this study forms a useful baseline.

ID 62741

EFFECT OF HYDROTHERMAL COMBINATION AND ENZYME ACTIVITY ON SOIL ORGANIC CARBON AND ITS COMPONENTS IN A DEGRADED HERBACEOUS PEATLAND

Guangyuan Xu[1,2], *Hongyan Zhao[1,2], Shengzhong Wang[1,2], Hongkai Li[1,2], Tianyu Zhang[1,2]

[1] Key Laboratory of Geographical Processes and Ecological Security in Changbai Mountains, Ministry of Education, Northeast Normal University, Changchun, 130024, China
[2] Institute for Peat & Mire Research,State Environmental Protection Key Laboratory of Wetland Ecology and Vegetation Restoration, Northeast Normal University, Changchun, 130024, China

hyzhao@nenu.edu.cn

SUMMARY

Over recent decades, drainage for mining peat, agriculture or afforestation have resulted in widespread degradation of temperate peatlands in China. In order to reveal effect of hydrothermal combination and enzyme activity on soil organic carbon and its components in a degraded peatland, a 50 cm herbaceous peat profile from a drained peatland in the Changbai Mountians, Northeast China was put in the incubator to simulate its decomposition in situ. Soil organic carbon (SOC), organic matter components and enzyme activity in every 10 cm peat samples were analyzed from May to October in 2017 in the lab of School of Geographical Sciences, Northeast Normal University. The results show that SOC decreased in the non-flooded layer (NFL, 0–30 cm) where the activities of polyphenol oxidase, peroxidase and β-Glucosidase increased in summer, while SOC in the fluctuation layer of water table (WTFL, 30–40 cm) and the flooded layer (FL, 40–50 cm) did not change much. Not hydrolyzed organic matter decreased by 93% while hydrolyzate increased by 10% in the NFL under the dominant action of polyphenol oxidase. Refractory and not hydrolyzed organic matter decreased by ~50% and ~90% respectively while hydrolyzate changed little in the FL where peroxidase was extremely active. β-Glucosidase, which can decompose refractory, played a main role in the WTFL and FL. This research has certain guiding significance for the identification and restoration of degraded peatlands.

Keywords: *degraded peatland; soil organic carbon; Northeast China; enzyme activity; decomposition*

INTRODUCTION

The northern peatlands, which accounting for about 3% of the land area, storing nearly 1/3 of soil organic carbon and 10% of liquid water worldwide (Yu et al, 2003; 2010) play an important role in climate change and carbon cycle. The peatlands in the Changbai Mountain, northeast China, one of the concentrated distribution areas of peatlands in China. are located in the southern margin of the northern peatland distribution area. The coverage of the peatlands is 0.76%, dominated by herbaceous peatlands. The peat layer is generally 1 ~ 2 m thick and the maximum thickness is 12 m. The reserve of peat is about 1.22×10^8 tons. Since the 1960s, some peatlands have been drained for agriculture, forestry, and peat ores mined for soil fertilizers, plants growth agents and soil improvers (Xiu Chai, 1990). Surface vegetation has been severely damaged. The degradation of the peatlands not only damage the structure of the peatland ecosystems, but also has a great impact on the function of the ecosystems, which has greatly changed environmental and economic benefits of the peatlands (Joosten H & Clarke D, 2002). In order to restore the function of the degraded peatland, the Chinese government has implemented the project of returning farmlands, woodlands and peat ores to wetlands. However, it is not clear whether peatlands continue to degrade and change from carbon dioxide sinks to carbon dioxide sources in the context of global warming. This paper selects a herbaceous peatland developed extensively in the Changbai Mountains to explore the effects of hydrothermal combinations and enzyme activities on soil organic carbon and its component changes in degraded peatlands under natural conditions.

MATERIALS AND METHODS

Donggou peatland, which is located in Dunhua basin of the Changbai Mountains, is a typical degraded peatland. A monolith of peat soil was dug out of Donggou peatland by hook machine on 3rd May 2017. The soil samples were wrapped with plastic film in site, and then taken into a plastic backet with a height of 50 cm and a diameter of 14 cm. The mire surface water samples in this peatland were collected by a plastic backet from the drainage ditches and they were used for soaking the peat soils. The simulation experiment on decomposition of peat soil was conducted in a biochemical incubator in the laboratory of School of Geographical Science, Northeast Normal University. The temperature in the biochemical incubator was set according to the monthly average temperature in Dunhua weather station in recent 50 years, and they are 14°C, 19°C, 21°C, 21°C, 14°Cand 5°C, respectively. The depth to water table was set based on the values measured in the peatland in the growing season (from May to October). The simulation experiment started in May and ended in October of 2017.

The samples at intervals of 10 cm were monthly taken from the above peat column in the biochemical incubator to test organic carbon and enzyme activities. Organic components at intervals of 10 cm were test at the beginning of the simulation experiment and after 6 months of incubation. Soil organic carbon was measured using potassium dichromate volumetric method (NISCAS, 1977). Systematic analyses of organic matter components were based on the method proposed by Ministry of Geology and Mineral Resources of the People's Republic of China (1983). The enzymatic activities of polyphenol oxidase (PPO), peroxidase (PER) and glucosidase (βG) were measured by microplate fluorescence method using SynergyH4 multifunctional microplate reader (BIOtec, USA).

RESULTS

Effects of different hydrothermal factors on the decomposition of herbaceous peat

As shown in Table 1, the content of organic carbon in the peat samples at the non-flooded layer (NFL, 0–30 cm) decreased over time from May to October while the content of organic carbon at the water level fluctuating layer (WTFL, 30–40 cm) and the flooded layer (FL, 40–50 cm) did not change much. The closer to the surface, the greater decrease of the organic carbon occurred. In addition, the content of organic carbon in surface peat decreased faster with the increase of temperature in summer.

Compared to the content of benzene-extracted organic matter in May, the content of benzene-extracted organic matter increased at 0–10 cm and 30–40 cm, and decreased at 10–20 cm, 20–30 cm and 40–50 cm in September (Table 1). The content of hydrolyzed organic matter also increased in 0–10 cm, 10–20 cm and 20–30 cm layers in September (Table 1). The content of refractory hydrolyzed organic matter in September was generally lower than that in May (Table 1). The content of not hydrolyzed organic matter in September was generally lower than that in May (Table 1).

Table 1 Percentage change in organic composition and organic carbon after 6 months of decomposition

Depths	benzene-extracted organic matter	hydrolyzed organic matter	refractory hydrolyzed organic matter	not hydrolyzed organic matter	organic carbon
0-10cm	10.98%	6.15%	-30.72%	-96.43%	-17.89%
10-20cm	-34.48%	18.61%	-88.57%	-93.05%	-27.23%
20-30cm	-78.94%	17.28%	-80.96%	-93.59%	-5.86%
30-40cm	94.89%	-1.01%	-49.09%	-91.35%	9.35%
40-50cm	-55.50%	-0.88%	-54.85%	-93.13%	-1.78%

Changes of enzyme activity during peat decomposition

The activity of PPO at different depth of the profile varied with decomposition time (Fig. 1a). The activity of PPO in NFL (0–30 cm) increased at first and then decreased. The PER activity of FL (40–50 cm) was significantly higher than that of other layers in the early stage (from May to July), and showed a linear downward trend, while the PER activity of other layers was higher in summer (from July to September). The analysis of variance showed that the PER activity in the FL was significantly different from that in other layers ($p < 0.05$) (Fig. 2). The activity of βG in the lower peat (30–50cm) was significantly higher than that in the NFL in summer (from June to August) (Fig. 1c). The βG activity in the FL showed a downward trend, and the analysis of variance revealed that there was a significant difference in the enzyme activity between the FL and the NFL ($p < 0.05$) (Fig. 3). The enzyme activity increased with the increase of temperature, for example, the PPO activity in the surface layer (0–20cm) increased significantly in summer (August), which was significantly different from that in spring and autumn (from May to October) (Fig. 4a); βG has similar properties and was sensitive to temperature change in the deeper layer (> 20cm) (Fig. 4c).

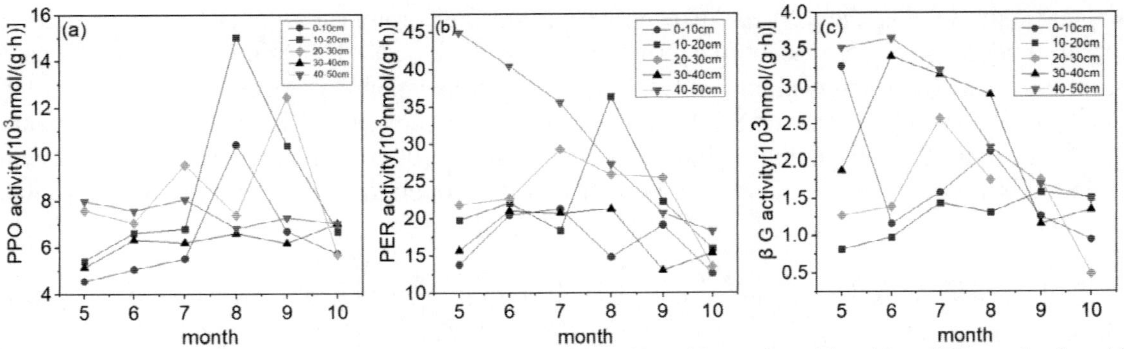

Fig.1 The activity changes of polyphenol oxidase(a), peroxidase(b) and beta-glucosidase(c) at different depths with time

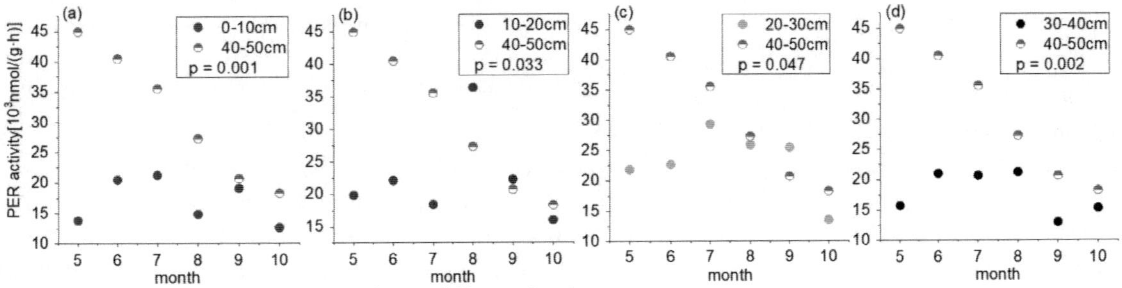

Fig.2 Comparison of peroxidase activities at different depth

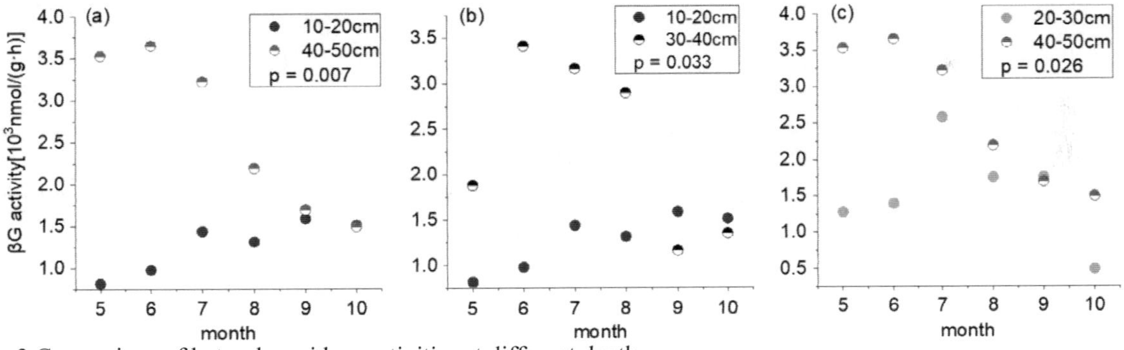

Fig.3 Comparison of beta-glucosidase activities at different depth

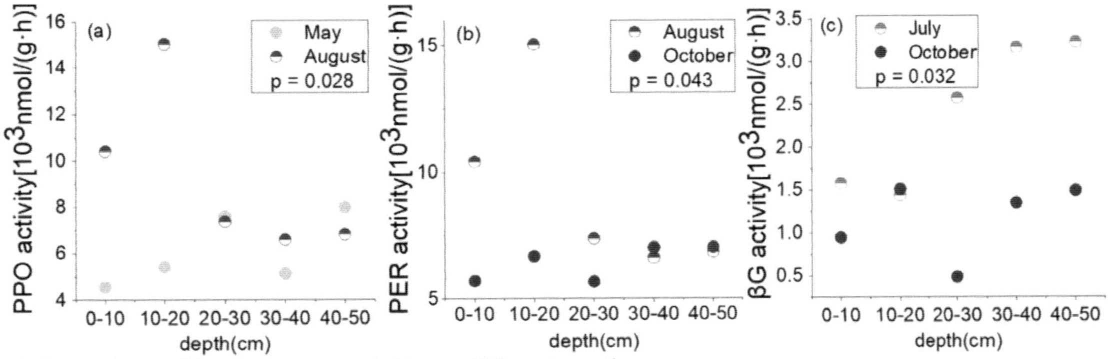

Fig.4 Comparison of three enzymes activities at different month

DISCUSSION

Our study shows that the content of organic carbon and organic components in peat samples decreased along with the decomposition of herbaceous peat. This suggests that the carbon accumulation in Donggou peatland is decreasing and this peatland has been degrading (Joosten et al, 2002). We speculate that variability in organic carbon content and its components in peat are related to hydrothermal combination (Nikonova et al, 2019). The effect of hydrothermal combination on degraded peatland may be carried out through the action of enzymes (Freeman et al, 2004).

It is well known that soil enzymes are closed with soil microbe and have own specificity. The role of soil enzymes is to catalyze decomposition of organic matter (Kim, 2015). In the NFL, the content of organic carbon decreases rapidly because of no stagnant water, which leads to PPO to have strong activity in this layer (Fig. 1a), especially in summer (Fig. 4a). The closer to the surface peat, the more oxygen content, the more serious the decomposition of organic carbon. Of course, the effect of PER and βG should not be ruled out. Under the action of three enzymes, complex compounds, for example phenols, are converted into simple small molecular compounds, thus promoting the decomposition of organic components.

The changes of organic components and enzyme activities were different in different soil layers and different composition time (Fig. 1). The increase of benzene-extracted organic matter in 0–10 cm may be due to the transformation of spore and pollen substances buried on the surface in the process of decomposition. Except for the increase of benzene-extracted organic matter, the other three kinds of organic components decreased at WTFL. We speculate that the increase of benzene-extracted organic matter in this layer may be due to the re-synthesis of decomposition products of 10–30cm plant residues. The activity of βG increased (Fig. 3), especially in the months with frequent summer precipitation (Fig. 4c), resulting in the decrease of non-hydrolysate and refractory hydrolyzed organic matter (Bonnett, 2006). All the tested organic components were reduced, and the enzyme activities was the strongest at FL layer. However, the content of organic carbon does not change much. We speculate that the peat at FL layer has been submerged for a long time, and anoxic environment inhibited the decomposition of peat. In summary, different depths to water table represent different redox conditions, and different months represent different temperature. Hence, temperature and moisture are two important environmental factors, which jointly affect the activities of microorganisms and enzymes, and then affect the decomposition of organic components in peat.

CONCLUSION

Decomposition of herbaceous peat is characterized by decreased content of organic carbon and transformation of organic components through the indoor simulation experiment of typical degraded herbaceous peatland in the Changbai mountains. Variability in content and composition of organic matter are mainly affected by enzyme activity, which is mainly restricted by hydrothermal environmental factors. The much more organic carbon is decomposed by polyphenol oxidase at the non-flooded layer under the condition of sufficient oxygen. Peroxidase and β-glucosidase had great influence on peat decomposition at flooded layer. Their activity was the highest at the beginning of growing season, and then decreased all the time, which indirectly reflected slower and slower decomposition of organic carbon and organic components at flooded layer. The relatively high temperature in summer increases three enzyme activity, which is beneficial to the decomposition of organic matter and degradation of a peatland. This study suggests that the high surface humidity or water level of peatland should be maintained in order to avoid the degradation of peatland, which further convert a peatland from sink of a carbon dioxide into a source of carbon dioxide. This research will lay a foundation for addressing the mechanisms of peatland degradation.

REFERENCES

3. Bonnett, S.A.F., Ostle, N, Freeman, C. (2006) Seasonal variations in decomposition processes in a valley-bottom riparian peatland. *Science of the Total Environment*; 370 (2–3): 561–573
4. Dommain R, Couwenberg J, Joosten H. (2011) Development and carbon sequestration of tropical peat domes in south-east Asia: links to postglacial sealevel changes and Holocene climate variability. *Quaternary Science Reviews*; 30: 999–101
5. Freeman C, Ostle N J, Fenner N, *et al*. (2004) A regulatory role for phenol oxidase during decomposition in peatlands. *Soil Biology & Biochemistry*; 36(10):1663–1667
6. Joosten H, Clarke D. (2002) Wise use of mires and peatlands. *International Mire Conservation Group and International Peat Society*; 48–91
7. Kim, H. (2015) A review of factors that regulate extracellular enzyme activity in wetland soils. *Korean Journal of Microbiology*; 51 (2): 97–107
8. Nikonova, LG, Kurganova, IN, Lopes De Gerenyu, *et al*. (2019) Impact of abiotic factors on the decomposition of litter of peat-forming plants in the incubation experiment. *Vestnik Tomskogo Gosudarstvennogo Universiteta, Biologiya*; (46):148–170
9. NISCAS (Nanjing Institute of Soil at Chinese Academy of Science). (1977) Physicochemical analyses of Soil. *Shanghai Science and Technology Press*; 593 (in Chinese)
10. Xiu Chai. (1990) Peat Geoscience. *Geological Publishing House*; 276–295 (in Chinese)
11. Yu Z, Loisel J, Brosseau D P, *et al*. (2010) Global peatland dynamics since the Last Glacial Maximum. *Geophysical Research Letters*; 37 (13): L13402
12. Yu Z, Vitt DH, Campbell ID, *et al*. (2003) Understanding Holocene peat accumulation pattern of c continental fens in western Canada. *Canadian Journal of Botany*; 81 (3): 267–282

ID 62747

CAN MOSS REMOVAL REVERSE UNDESIRED SUCCESSION UNDER DIFFERENT NUTRIENT LEVELS IN RICH FENS?

*Patrícia Singh, Petra Hájková, Tomáš Peterka, Zuzana Plesková, Eva Šmerdová, Michal Hájek

Masaryk University, Czech Republic

patadurcanova@gmail.com

Rich fens, considered as a biodiversity hotspot, are declining globally due to increased acidification, eutrophication and climate change. Brown-moss communities, forming initial stages of rich fens ecosystems, harbour number of rare specialised species and are disappearing in the last decades. One reason is the ongoing expansion of Sphagna in Europe, which may suppress competitively weak brown-mosses. The potential improvement may be to reverse undesired succession by removing strong competitive Sphagna and/or initiate succession by reintroducing of target brown mosses fragments to design patches. This procedure was applied in 2015 in Bohemian Massif fens (Czech Republic) to Tatra Mts (Slovakia and Poland) on an extensive set of experimental plots in fens with different macro-nutrient availability.

This experiment tests the rate and direction of succession after the Sphagna removal along the fertility gradient and assesses the limits of brown moss reintroduction. We hypothesised that: (1) after the removal of dominant Sphagna species, succession starts with more calcium-tolerant species; (2) in nutrient-richer fens, primary succession after Sphagna removal proceeds faster and some successional stages can even miss; (3) the current occurrence of calcicole brown mosses is limited by competition with expanding calcifobe Sphagna or by water chemistry. This study will evaluate the efficiency of Sphagna removal as a countermeasure of ongoing undesired succession.

ID 62948

INDICATION OF PEAT ACCUMULATION AFTER ECOSYSTEM RESTORATION INTERVENTIONS IN THE ARCTIC

*Tatiana Minayeva[1], Oxana Cherednichenko[2], Dmitry Moseev[3], Liudmila Sergienko[4], Olga Lavrinenko[5], Sergey Uvarov[6]

[1] Care for Ecosystems UG, Germany/Centre for Conservation and Restoration of Peatland Ecosystems RAS, Russia
[2] Lomonosov Moscow State University, Biological Faculty, Russia
[3] The North-Western Branch of the P.P.Shirshov Institute of Oceanology, Russia
[4] Petrozavodsk State University, Russia
[5] Komarov Botanical Institute RAS, Russia
[6] Ltd "Rubus" Naryan-Mar, Russia

tatiana.minayeva@care-for-ecosystems.net

Peatland ecosystems restoration projects are eligible for reporting under climate change mitigation and adaptation activities. The indicator for the success of peatland ecosystem restoration would be the peat formation process which is recognised by an excess of the ecosystem production over the respiratory processes and displacement of not decomposed organic material from the ecosystem biogeochemical cycle for example due to anaerobic conditions. The numeric data on the positive NEE is often used as criteria for peat formation. In the Arctic, the direct measurements of NEE by GHG fluxes demand high temporal and spatial variability of testing points. The conditions and ecosystem response are permanently changing depending on the current weather situation and permafrost status. We had undertaken the attempt to develop the set of not complicated, measurable integrative indicators for peat formation based on the vegetation and soil physical characteristics. The pilot areas for ecosystem restoration have been set up in the Russian Arctic: Bolshezemelskaya tundra in 2013-2017 and the Yamal Peninsula in 2019. The survey of the numerous testing plots resulted in the data on plant species composition and abundance (including vascular plants, lichens and mosses), surface temperature and soil moisture gradients, water table and permafrost level, soil texture and depth of the organic layer. The Spearman correlation between species abundance and physical factors demonstrated that very few plant species meet the set of criteria identified for the direct indication of the peat presence and more plant species show statistically proved correlation with the specific parameters of the environment compatible with peat formation conditions. The species-indicators are regionally specific and should be identified for every specific case for the MRV purposes in peatland restoration projects.

ID 62954

SUCCESSION OF FUNGAL COMMUNITIES IN RESTORED PEAT BOGS

*Martina Vašutová[1], Kamila Vítovcová[1], Markéta Šandová[2], Sujan Balami[1], Alžběta Manukjanová[1], Karel Prach[1]

[1]Department of Botany, Faculty of Science, University of South Bohemia, České Budějovice, Czech Republic
[2] Mycological Department, National Museum, Prague, Czech Republic

mvasutova@prf.jcu.cz

SUMMARY

Most studies of restored peat bogs are focused on plant communities. Fungi, although significantly affecting the whole system as decomposers, symbiotrophs or pathogens, have so far received little attention. Our aim was to find out whether the succession of fungal communities in restored peat bogs corresponds to the succession of vegetation, and what are ecological requirements of fungal species typical of undisturbed peat bogs which could be used as indicators of successful restoration.
In the Šumava Mts. (SW part of the Czech Republic) we established permanent plots (9 x 9 m) in three succession stages of 2 restored (24 plots) and 2 undisturbed peat bogs dominated by *Pinus rotundata* (8 plots), where we described vegetation, regularly monitored fungal fruit bodies (6 times per season) and sequenced peat and Sphagnum to identify non fruiting part of fungal community (1 per season). Fungal communities seemed to reflect well vegetation changes. As the best indicators of successful restoration appeared the following species: *Arrhenia oniscus, Arrhenia gerardiana, Cortinarius chrysolitus* and *Galerina hybrida*.

***Keywords**: fungi, Illumina sequencing, peatland, indicator*

INTRODUCTION

Central European peatlands are isolated unique ecosystems, most of them having persisted continuously at the same sites and approximately in the same extent since the early Holocene period (1). Biodiversity of undisturbed peatlands is especially determined by the long-term persistence and isolated character of the habitat with relict populations of different biota.
Human-made disturbances had and have detrimental effects on these fragile ecosystems. The most destroying is the large-scale industrial peat harvesting, accompanied by profound changes in water regime. Possibilities for restoration of such deeply disturbed bogs are limited and their success is mostly evaluated in terms of vegetation and presence of rare plant species.
Fungi, although significantly affecting the whole system as decomposers, symbiotrophs or pathogens, have so far received little attention. Moreover, disturbed and undisturbed bogs were mostly studied separately (e.g. 2, 3). Studies focusing on restoration of fungal communities were mainly based on environmental sequencing but not dealing with individual species (4), so their results are difficult to interpret and to apply in nature conservation.
Our aims were to find out whether the succession of fungal communities in disturbed peat bogs corresponds to the succession of vegetation and tends to undisturbed bogs. Furthermore we wanted to know the ecological requirements of fungal species typical of undisturbed peat bogs which could be used as indicators of successful restoration.

MATERIALS AND METHODS

In the Šumava Mts. (SW part of the Czech Republic) 32 permanent plots (9 x 9 m) within three successional stages (10-15 years, 15-25 years, 25-35 years) in 2 restored (24 plots, Soumarský Most – SM, 48°54'11"N, 13°50'5"E, Vlčí Jámy – VJ, 48°55'8"N, 13°46'58"E) and 2 undisturbed reference raised bogs dominated by *Pinus rotundata* (8 plots, Malá Niva + Velká Niva, REF, 48°54'48"N, 13°48'50"E, 48°55'6"N, 13°49'32"E) were established. We described vegetation by phytosociological relevés, regularly monitored fungal fruit bodies (6 times per season) and sequenced peat and Sphagnum samples to identify non fruiting parts of fungal communities (1 per season). DNA was extracted from mixed samples of peat (9 cores per plot), fungal ITS2 was amplified and sequenced on Illumina MiSeq as described in (5). Two from 8 undisturbed peat bog plots were removed due to unsuccessful sequencing.

To assess ecological requirements of fungal species typical of undisturbed peat bogs, 3 moderately frequent species indicating undisturbed raised bogs (6) were selected. To include mycorrhizal symbionts we added 1 indicator species for other bog forests. All these species were associated with Sphagnum and they were never found on bare peat. Altogether 44 localities (altitudinal range 420-1250 m s.l.) in Šumava Mts and in the surroundings were visited in 2019-2020 (mostly repeatedly) and vegetation in close vicinity (2 x 2 m) of fruit bodies was described.

Detrended correspondence analysis (DCA) in Canoco 5 (Microcomputer Power, Ithaca, NY, US) was used to present the successional trend in fungal communities of disturbed raised bogs (Fig. 1) and vegetation of microsites with records of fruit bodies of fungal species typical of undisturbed peat bogs (Fig.2). Site characteristics (cover of vegetation layers, litter, dead wood, bare peat) and environmental variables (pH, altitude) were used as supplementary variables (7).

RESULTS AND DISCUSSION

In total 241 species forming fruit bodies were found on permanent plots in 2019. On average 11 species per plot were in young stages, 18 in middle stages, 27 in old stages and 20 in REF. Environmental sequencing of peat revealed 217 OTUs (operational taxonomic units) with higher abundance than 0,01% sequences per sample. Approximately third of them was not possible to identify into species level, mainly because of missing reference sequences in public databases. There were no differences in average number of OTUs per plot category (19 OTUs in young stages, 17 in middle stages, 18 in old stages, 19 in REF). The most common species per plot category are summarized in Table 1.

Table 1. The most common species/OTUs per plot category

	Fruit bodies	OTUs
Stage 1	*Laccaria proxima*	*Pezoloma ericae*
	Paxillus involutus	*Suillus bovinus*
	Jaapia argillacea	*Solicoccozyma terricola*
Stage 2	*Gymnopus androsaceus*	*Lactarius rufus*

	Laccaria proxima	*Amanita fulva*
	Lactarius rufus	*Pezoloma ericae*
Stage 3	*Mycena metata*	*Elaphomyces muricatus*
	Mycena cinerella	*Penicillium spinulosum*
	Russula ochroleuca	*Cenococcum geophilum*
Reference	*Collybia cirrata*	*Lactarius rufus*
	Mycena galopus	*Suillus variegatus*
	Hebeloma incarnatulum	*Tylospora fibrillosa*

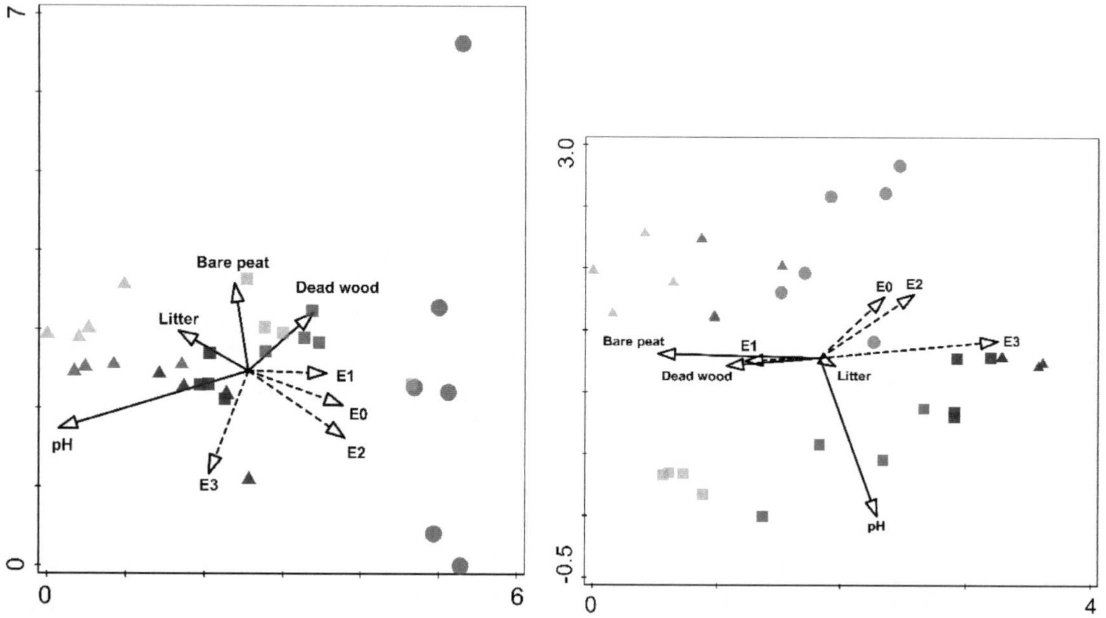

Fig.1 DCA of plots (yellow – stage 1, orange – stage 2, red – stage 3; square – SM; triangle – VJ; grey circle – REF) based on presence of fruit bodies (a) and sequence abundance of fungal OTUs (b). Site characteristics (vegetation layers, bare peat, dead wood, litter) and environmental variable (pH) were supplementary projected.

DCA diagrams based on presence of fruit bodies (Fig. 1a) and sequence abundances (Fig. 1b) show differences between sites (SM, VJ, REF). Bare peat prevails in young stages, a high cover of E3 is characteristic of old stages. However, in agreement with successional trend in vegetation (8) the old stages do not resemble REF. Data on fungal fruit bodies (Fig. 1a) reflect vegetation pattern better than sequence data, because they include many specialized saprotrophs living on dead plant litter or wood. On the other hand, sequence data from peat (Fig. 1b) show mainly underground relationships. Dominant OTUs were i) molds and yeasts probably associated with peat, ii) ectomycorrhizal (ECM) species - often the same species were associated with *Pinus* spp in old stages and REF and iii) ericoid mycorrhizal fungi (i.e. *Pezoloma*, *Oidiodendron*) associated with ericoid shrubs. ECM fungi were captured by both methods, because they often produce many fruit bodies and are also common on roots underground. Although each of the chosen methods showed only a part of the present fungal diversity, both indicated differentiation between the successional stages of fungal communities.

To get more reliable data about potential indicators of successful restoration we recorded 43 microsites with fruit bodies of *Galerina hybrida*, 25 microsites with *Arrhenia gerardiana*

(=*Omphalina gerardiana, Omphalina sphagnicola*), 21 with *Cortinarius chrysolitus*, and 13 with *Arrhenia oniscus* (syn. *Omphalina oniscus*) in the Šumava Mts. and surroundings. Vegetation analysis (Fig. 2) confirmed our field observation that these species differ in ecological requirements. *Galerina hybrida* has a broader ecological niche, it grows in *Sphagnum* spp. in transitional mires (upper left part of the diagram) as well as in raised bogs but avoids forests. *Cortinarius chrysolitus* has similar requirements. As a mycorrhizal species, it is associated with *Picea abies*, *Pinus sylvestris* or *Pinus mugo* complex but prefer open habitats, i.e. solitary trees, forest margin or open forests. *Arrhenia gerardiana* and *A. oniscus* prefer treeless raised bogs and higher altitudes.

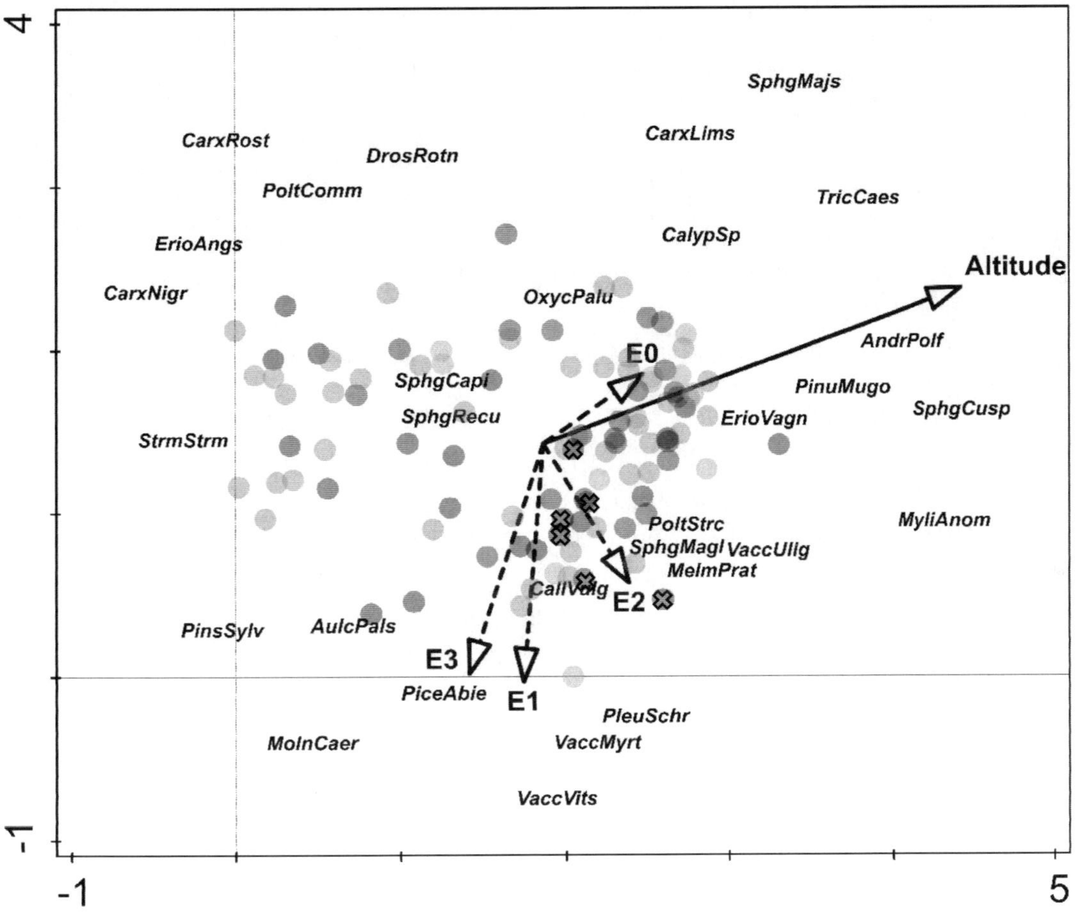

Fig.2 DCA vegetation. Supplementary projected environmental variable Altitude and site characteristics (vegetation layers - E0, E1, E2, E3). 30 plant/moss species with highest weight are projected. *Legend:* blue – *Cortinarius chrysolitus*; green – *Galerina hybrida*; red – *Arrhenia gerardiana*; yellow – *Arrhenia oniscus*, microsites in REF bogs (see Fig. 1).

Fruit bodies of all these species were found in REF bogs (750 m.a.s.l.), although *A.oniscus* and *G. hybrida* not in the studied period. DCA diagram (Fig. 2) shows that REF microsites are within ecological niches of all species. Their possible occurrence in disturbed peat bogs would be a good indicator of successful restoration. With regards to the broader niche and the altitudinal range, *G. hybrida* and *C. chrysolitus* are expected to appear earlier than *Arrhenia* species.

CONCLUSION

Succession of fungal communities corresponds to the vegetation succession. However based on one-year data, succession of fungal communities of disturbed raised bogs is not moving towards undisturbed ones. Fruit body data and sequence data mirror different parts of fungal communities. *Galerina hybrida* and *Cortinarius chrysolithus* have a broader ecological niche than *Arrhenia* species and therefore are supposed to occur in successfully restored peat bogs earlier than *Arrhenia* species.

ACKNOWLEDGEMENTS

Pavlína Matysková, Hedvika Synková and Aleš Jirsa are thanked for their help in the field, Jiří Košnar for his support in molecular laboratory. The authors thank the Administration of the Šumava National Park for a permit to access the study sites. Research was supported by the Grant Agency of the Czech Republic (Grant No. 31-19-15031S).

REFERENCES

1. Horsák, M., Hájek, M., Spitale, D., Hájková, P., Dítě, D., Nekola, J. C. (2012) The age of island-like habitats impacts habitat specialist species richness. *Ecology*; 93(5): 1106–1114
2. Laber, D. (2009) Die Funga der Moore des Hochschwarzwaldes. *Beihefte zur Zeitschrift für Mykologie*. Band 11; 1–208
3. Zíbarová, L. (2014) Závěrečná zpráva z mykologického průzkumu v okolí Hory sv. Šebestiána v l. 2013-2014. Ms.
4. Xue, D., Liu, T., Chen, H., Liu, J., Hu, J., Liu, L. (2021) Fungi are more sensitive than bacteria to drainage in the peatlands of the Zoige Plateau. *Ecological Indicators*; 124: 107367
5. Vašutová, M., Jiroušek, M., Hájek, M. (2021) High fungal substrate specificity limits the utility of environmental DNA to detect fungal diversity in bogs. *Ecological Indicators;* 121: 107009
6. Hofmeister, J., Hošek, J. (2016) Seznamy indikačních druhů živočichů a hub pro jednotlivé typy přírodních stanovišť podle Katalogu biotopů ČR. https://www.mzp.cz/C1257458002F0DC7/cz/seznamy_indikacnich_druhu_katalog/$FILE/OZUOPK-Priloha_metodiky_-_Seznamy%20indikacnich%20druhu-20170203.pdf
7. Šmilauer, P. and Lepš, J. (2014) Multivariate Analysis of Ecological Data Using Canoco 5. Cambridge: Cambridge University Press.
8. Vítovcová K., Lipárová J., Manukjanová A., Vašutová M., Štechová T., Vrba P., and Prach K. (2021). Biodiversity restoration of formerly mined raised bogs – vegetation succession and recovery of other trophic groups. In preparation.

ID 72800

SOCIO-ECOLOGICAL RESTORATION OF SOUTH EAST ASIA PEATLANDS

Stuart W. Smith[1], Yuti Ariani Fatimah[1], Nur Estya Rahman [1], Teo Pei Yun[1], David A. Wardle[1], Kwek Yan Chon[2], *Janice Ser Huay Lee[1,3]

[1] Asian School of the Environment, Nanyang Technological University, Singapore
[2] Department of Biological Sciences, National University of Singapore, Singapore
[3] Earth Observatory of Singapore, Nanyang Technological University Singapore

janicelee@ntu.edu.sg

To develop a restoration method that will generate lasting effects, both ecological and social aspects should be considered. Simply selecting the species with highest survival rate is not enough; the restoration effort should also be adapted based on the site's history, local community and context. Such pertinent information could then be conveyed from one researcher to the next to improve the likelihood of successful ecosystem restoration. Here, we present a summary of our research project that examines the role of community participation in Indonesia's peatland restoration. We used mixed methodology of combining qualitative data gathered through secondary data, semi-structured interviews, and observation to understand the relationship between unintended feedbacks from restoration activities and the institutional setting of the local community, with quantitative data on survivability, flammability, and decomposition of peatland species to understand species selection. The findings of our project have implications for both the academic community and policy makers in the science and practice of peatland restoration. We present preliminary results from both disciplinary and interdisciplinary research projects from the ecological and social sciences on restoration of tropical peatlands in South East Asia.

ID 72802

PEATSWAMP FOREST REVEGETATION: LESSONS LEARNT FROM A SYSTEMATIC REVIEW

(*) First two authors contributed equally to the development of the study

*Stuart W. Smith[1], *Nur Estya B. Rahman[1], Mark E. Harrison[2], Shiodera Satomi[3], Lahiru S. Wijedasa[4], Randi Agusti[5,6], Wim Giesen[7], David A. Wardle[1], Kwek Yan Chong[1], Maija Lampela[1], Pei Yun Teo[1], Thian Nam Teng[8], Yuti A. Fatimah[1], Laura L. B. Graham[9], M. Jahangir Alam[10], Katsumi Kojima[11], Kitso Kusin[12], Faizah B. H. Metali[13], Marlide B. Nahor[7], Richard R. P. Napitupulu[14], Darmae Nasir[12], Tapan K. Nath[10], Mariko Norisada[11], Dony Rachmanadi[15], Henti H. Rachmat[16], Purwanto B. Santosa[17], Rahayu S. B. H. Sukri[13], Benjamin Tay[18], Wardah B. H. Tuah[13], Takashi Yamanoshita[11], Janice S. H. Lee[1]

[1] Nanyang Technological University, Singapore
[2] College of Life and Environmental Sciences, University of Exeter, UK, & School of Geography, Geology and the Environment, University of Leicester, UK
[3] Centre for Southeast Asian Studies, Kyoto University, Japan & Research Institute for Humanity and Nature, Japan
[4] National University of Singapore, Singapore
[5] National University of Singapore, Singapore
[6] Natural Kapital Indonesia, Pontianak, Indonesia
[7] Euroconsult Mott MacDonald, Netherlands
[8] Department of Earth Sciences, University of Oxford, UK
[9] Borneo Orangutan Survival Foundation, Indonesia
[10] School of Environmental and Geographical Sciences, University of Nottingham Malaysia, Malaysia
[11] Asian Natural Environmental Science Center, The University of Tokyo, Japan
[12] Centre for the International Cooperation in Sustainable Management of Tropical Peatlands, University of Palangka Raya, Indonesia
[13] Universiti Brunei Darussalam, Brunei Darussalam
[14] University of Jambi, Indonesia
[15] Plantation Forest Research and Development Institute of Eastern Indonesia, Banjarbaru, Indonesia
[16] Forest Research and Development Center, Indonesia
[17] Forestry Research Institute of Banjarbaru, Indonesia
[18] Peoples Movement to Stop Haze, Singapore

another.swsmith@googlemail.com

Plant species selection is a critical initial step in the revegetation of degraded peatlands. Knowledge of survival and growth from previous revegetation projects should help guide future species selection. Yet, after several decades of tree plantings on degraded tropical peatswamp forests across South East Asia, there has been no quantitative synthesis of survival and growth of planted species. To address this knowledge gap, we conducted a meta-analysis on survival and growth of tree species planted on degraded peatlands. To acquire the necessary monitoring data, we undertook a systematic review of both peer-reviewed studies (journal articles, book chapters, conference proceedings) and unpublished studies or 'grey literature' (reports, theses, datasets). We screened in detail almost 200 articles, yet found desirable information for our meta-analysis was often missing. Missing details or issues with reporting encompassed broadly and in no priority order: (1) site descriptions (i.e. location, date, durations); (2) propagation materials (i.e. seedling source and size, provenance, nursery details); (3) experimental design (i.e. replication or numbers planted, original tree size, planting densities); (4) maintenance (i.e. hydrological management, weeding, treatments); (5) presentation of data (i.e. time series, species identity, averaging data); (6) environmental conditions (i.e. drainage, canopy exposure, site history); (7) social and economic factors (i.e. community engagement, land ownership, planting and maintenance costs), and (8) wider monitoring (i.e. biodiversity recovery, carbon storage, neighbouring areas). The absence of such information limits the scope of syntheses on peatswamp forest revegetation. For our own meta-analysis, this limited the identification of underlying reasons for large variability in species survival and growth. To improve future syntheses, we present a checklist of information that should be included when reporting peatswamp revegetation projects. Incorporating these recommendations in reporting will improve knowledge sharing, synthesis and ultimately the collective effort of peatswamp forest revegetation.

ID 72826

PEAT WATER TABLE DEPTH AND SOIL MOISTURE RELATIONSHIP IN SOUTH SUMATRA AND CENTRAL KALIMANTAN OMBROGENOUS PEATLAND

*Dede Sulaeman[1], Ihsan Hafiyyan[1], Hidayah Hamzah[1], Desti Ayunda[1], Dimas Alfred Prasetia[2], Salira Vidyan[2]

[1]World Resources Institute Indonesia, Jakarta, Indonesia
[2]Wetlands International Indonesia, Bogor, Indonesia

dede.sulaeman@wri.org

SUMMARY

Peat fires have become an enormous problem in recent decades and caused peatland degradation in Indonesia. Peat fires event in 2015 burned more than 600,000 hectares of peatland scattered mainly Sumatra and Kalimantan. Excessive drainage leads to the depletion of water table depth and soil moisture in the surface and makes peat soil highly flammable. The Indonesian Government, through the Peatland and Mangrove Restoration Agency/BRGM, carries out rewetting activities in the form of canal blocking and canal back-fillings implementation. The main objective of rewetting activities is to prevent excessive water drainage from the peatlands and keep peatlands water table at a specific elevation to control soil moisture and avoid peat fires. The peat water table is known to correlate with surface peat soil moisture through capillary movements. This study aims to understand peat soil moisture's characteristics and its relationship with water table depth, especially in ombrogenous peatlands, and to develop an empirical equation to estimate peat soil moisture based on water table depth data. Soil moisture and peat water table depth data were obtained by field observation in four Peat Hydrological Units (PHUs) in South Sumatra and Central Kalimantan. The relationship between soil moisture and water table depth was analyzed using correlation analysis. Results showed that soil moisture correlates sufficiently against daily water table depths with the coefficient determination (R^2) value of 0.8. This relationship took a quadratic pattern, with water table fluctuation and soil moisture variation ranged from -1.6 m – 0 m and 5% - 84%, respectively. With these findings, it is expected that activities to monitor peat wetness can be carried out more efficiently by using peat water table data as a reference in predicting peat soil moisture and thus preventing fires.

Keywords: *peat fires, rewetting, soil moisture, water table, Indonesia*

INTRODUCTION

Peatland is a rich biodiversity-ecosystem made of organic matter accumulation due to incomplete decomposition under permanent water saturation for over thousands of years. The ecosystem plays an important role in carbon sequestration, contains much more organic carbon than other terrestrial ecosystems. Tropical peatlands are widely known to be globally significant deposits of terrestrial organic carbon, with estimates ranging from 50 to 105 GtC, equivalent to about 15% of the carbon stored in peat globally (Warren *et al.*, 2017). Natural peatlands also have a vital role in the retention, purification, and release of water and the mitigation of droughts and floods (FAO, 2014).

Tropical peat swamp forests are threatened by large-scale deforestation and peat swamp forests conversion mainly into oil palm or Acacia plantations. It requires draining to make the naturally waterlogged condition ecosystem more suitable for agricultural plants to grow. The peat water table depth will decrease as peatland gets drained. Then, it will decrease the peat soil moisture, increase microorganism decomposition activities that cause oxidation of the peat and, which consequently releases large carbon emissions into the atmosphere.

Indonesia is home to more than 14 million hectares of peatland (Osaki et al., 2016), approximately 23 percent of the world's total tropical peatlands. The forest fires in 2015 were one of the worst disasters to hit Indonesia in recent decades, burning at least 2.6 million hectares of forest and land (Purnomo *et al.*, 2017), including more than 600 thousand hectares of peatland. In response to the disaster, the Indonesian Government constructed thousands of peat rewetting infrastructure to decrease peat degradation by fires. The restoration activities aimed to raise peat water table depth and keep the soil remains moist to prevent the peatland fires from occurring.

Water is one of the most critical components in the peatland ecosystem and water table depth (WTD) is of hydrological condition indicators that can increase forest fire susceptibility when it decreased drastically. WTD influences peat soil moisture in the unsaturated zone through capillary forces. The capillary connection of the surface soil moisture to the water table depends on the peat's physical properties (hydraulic conductivity and water retention characteristics), which are highly variable and depend, e.g., on peat type and degree of decomposition. Currently, few studies (Chandra, 1989; Widarso *et al.*, 2020) have predicted water table depth dynamics and soil moisture content in tropical ombrogenous peatland in Indonesia. Hence, this research aims to formulate an empirical equation to estimate surface peat soil wetness (*soil moisture*) based on the peat water table depth.

MATERIALS AND METHODS

Study Area

This study was carried out in 4 Peat Hydrological Units (PHUs) in South Sumatra and Central Kalimantan Province. Two sites in South Sumatra are located in Burnai-Sibumbung (BS) and Musi-Penukal (MP) PHUs in Ogan Komering Ilir and Pali Regency, respectively. Other two sites in Central Kalimantan are located in Kahayan-Sebangau (KS) PHU (Pulang Pisau Regency) and Kapuas-Barito (KB) PHU (Kapuas Regency), see Figure 1. Research areas in those four sites are categorized as ombrogenous peatland, the type of peatland that is hydrologically isolated and entirely dependent on precipitation for water and nutrient supply. None of these sites were affected by brackish water, direct backflow feed, or lateral flow input from adjacent sloping land. Therefore, we assume only rainfall that acts as the sole input in the water balance.

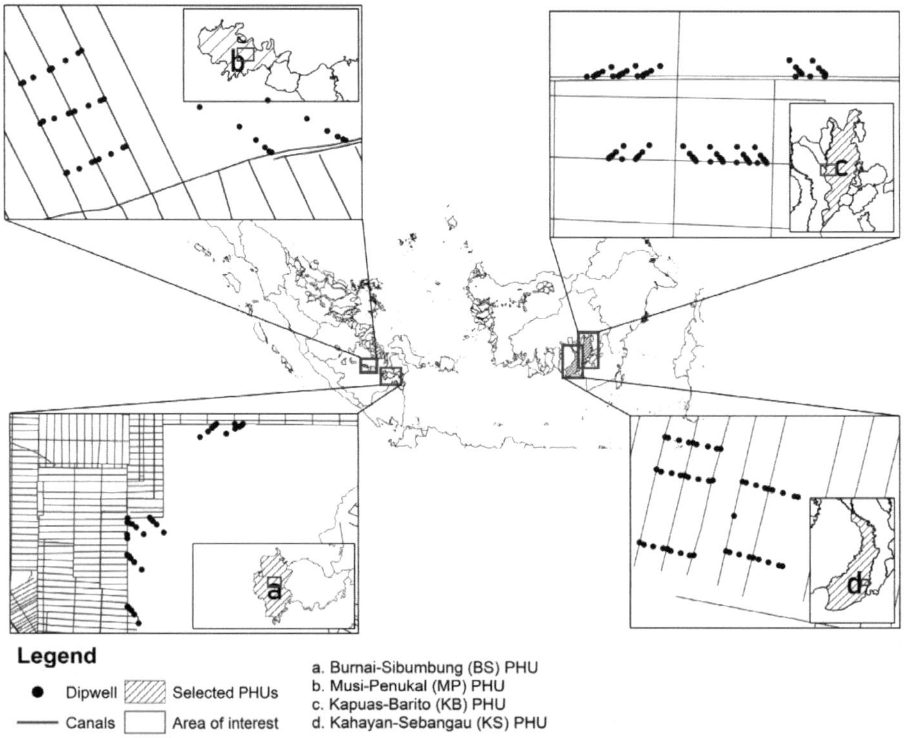

Figure 1. Research Locations

In this study, peatland region situated on lowland area where maximum elevations do not usually exceed 20 meters (above mean sea level) and surface slopes rarely exceed 0.1 percent. The plane/basal contacts of peat soils in the area mainly consist of tertiary marine clay, or sandy clay, or quaternary tidal mudflat deposits with very low hydraulic conductivity.

Water Table Depth Data Measurement

Water table data were obtained using a combination of manual and automatic measurements at dipwells installed along transects. Dipwells were set closely-spaced near canals and gradually set at larger intervals as the distances get farther from the canals. The first dipwells of the transects were installed at about 25 – 40 meters from canals. The next dipwell-intervals were 50, 100, 200, and 400 meters, respectively. Manual measurements were performed at 2-weekly intervals using a scaled rod with 1 mm resolution. Automatic measurements were performed by using pressure-based water level loggers (HOBO with 1 mm accuracy and 20 meters hydrostatic pressure tolerance) that were set at 30 minutes time interval. Furthermore, the 30-minute logger data series were averaged over 24 hours to derive mean daily values. There were six transects with 31 dipwells installed in BS site, five transects with 29 units dipwells in MP site, five transects with 31 dipwells in KS site, and 11 transects with 57 units in KB site (Figure 1).

Rainfall Data Measurement

Daily precipitation data were measured using Neta rain gauges (250 mm catchment diameter) at the MP, KS, and KB sites and Stratus rain gauges at the BS site. Measurements were taken daily from 07:00 to 08:00 am.

Surface Soil Moisture Data Measurement

Surface soil moistures were collected in the field using soil moisture testers SM-150 Theta Kit from Delta-T and PMS 714 from Lutron at the top of peat soils (20 cm below surface) every two weeks at several random points within 30 meters from dipwells. We calculated SM-150 equivalent values of PMS 714 readings based on a regression analysis of a dedicated number of paired measurements (i.e., readings from the two instruments at the same spot and time). We represented all soil moisture data in SM-150 equivalent values using the equation below:

$\theta_{SM} = 3.0723 \times \theta_{PMS} - 3.7816$; where

Θ_{SM} : Soil moisture content based on SM 150 Theta Kit reading (%, v/v); percentage of volume per volume

Θ_{PMS} : Soil moisture content based on PMS 714 reading (%, v/v); percentage of volume per volume

Water Table Depth and Soil Moisture Correlation Analysis

The relationship between soil moisture against water table depth data was analyzed by employing standard correlation analysis, providing soil moisture as the dependent variable. No presumed relationship patterns were held prior to the analysis. The best-fitting curves were chosen first based on visual inspections, followed then by regression analysis. The individual water table depth data need to be grouped into 'bin' that is generally called data binning, to minimize the 'noise' before correlation analysis is performed. Binning criteria depend on their individual value and how they are going to be presented. In this study, water table depth is grouped by values of 2 cm.

RESULTS AND DISCUSSION

The Dynamics of Peat Water Table Depth

This study showed that water tables responded quickly to rainfall inputs. Water table depletions were more gradual following aquifer storage withdrawals by evapotranspiration and groundwater flow toward channels and rivers. Water table depths averaged over dipwell positions are shown in Figure 2 – Figure 5. These graphs reflect water table dynamics in BS, MP, KS, and KB sites, respectively.

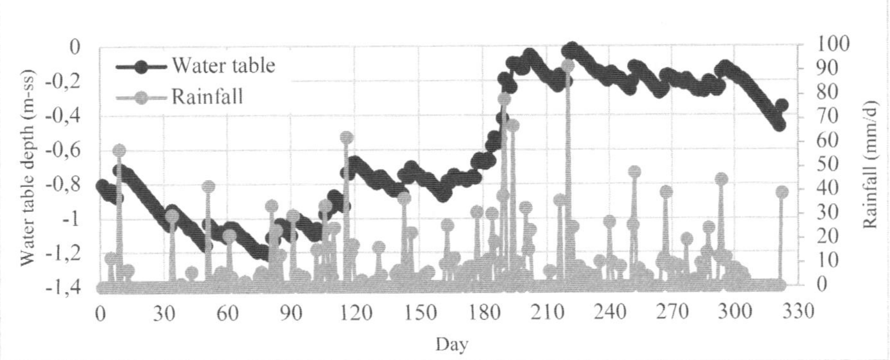

Figure 2. Water table depths daily data averaged for site BS (26 September 2019 – 12 August 2020)

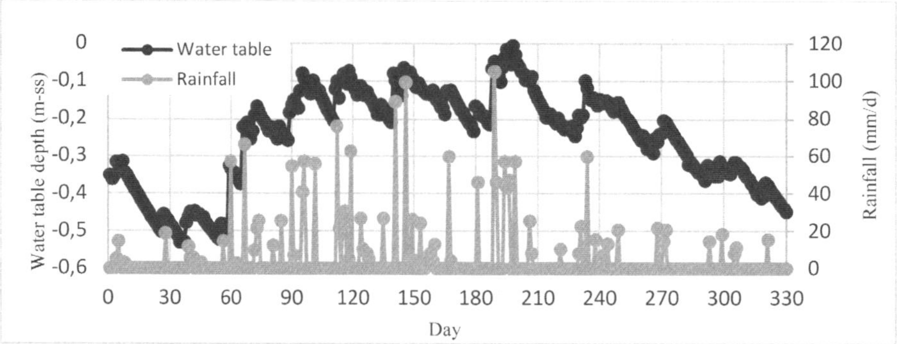

Figure 3. Water table depths daily data averaged for MP site (21 September 2019 – 11 September 2020)

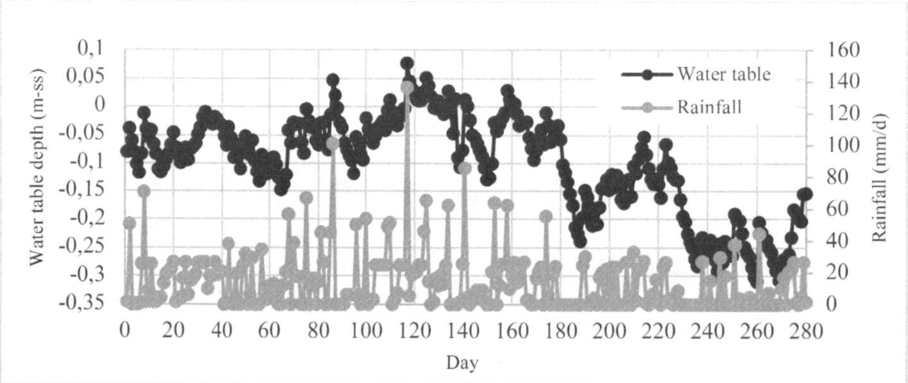

Figure 4. Water table depth daily data averaged for KS site (10 December 2019 – 14 September 2020)

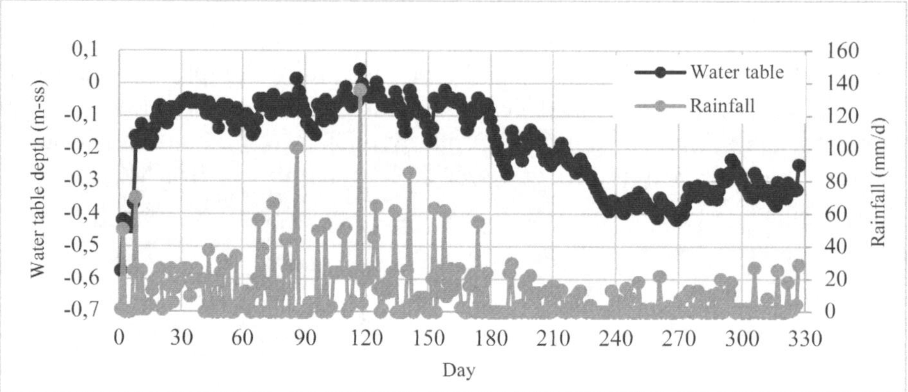

Figure 5. Water table depth daily data averaged for KB site (10 December 2019 – 31 October 2020)

This study also found that WTDs were extremely low at the BS site during the dry season, especially at positions closer to canals. Dipwell positions in BS site are distributed closer to canals than to the middle of the site. This configuration reasonably returns lower minimum water table depths (about -1.2 meters below soil surface) compared to the other sites. Furthermore, canal depths at the BS site are also very deep, up to 3 meters below the soil surface; meanwhile, crest levels of the existing canal blocks, as evident in the field, were not constructed high enough to lift canal water levels sufficiently. The average minimum water table depths reached moderately, ranging from about -0.3 to -0.8 m below the surface in the other three sites.

Soil moisture

Soil moisture is an indicator of the amount of water present in the soil. Peat soil is known for its characteristic to hold water to a greater degree than mineral soils due to the high content of organic matter. Figure 6 described the average of soil moisture data at 20 cm below the peat surface in all sites that ranged between 15-17%. The maximum soil moisture content could reach 84% and drop to 5% following the peat water table fluctuation. A highly decreased water table depth could disturb the capillary water flow to the surface of the peat. In the dry season, the capillary water flow possibly could not reach the surface layer of peat, and the peat became irreversibly dry, causing the peat vulnerable to fire.

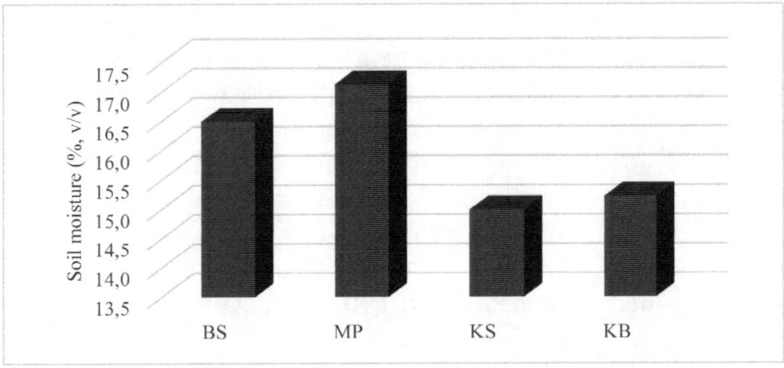

Figure 6. Soil moisture data average at 20 cm below the peat surface

Water Table Depth and Soil Moisture Correlation

The study found that soil moistures of peat soils at the upper 20 cm correlate sufficiently against daily water table depths. This relationship took a quadratic pattern/second-order polynomial for water table range up to 0 cm of water table upper limit. The individual data plot can be seen in Figure 7 below. The grouped plot showed a positive correlation between soil moisture and water table on these tropical peatlands with an R^2 value of 0.81. Another study stated that the polynomial regression model developed by Chandra (1989) is a valid approach to predicting water table depth and soil moisture in peatlands (Widiarso et al., 2020).

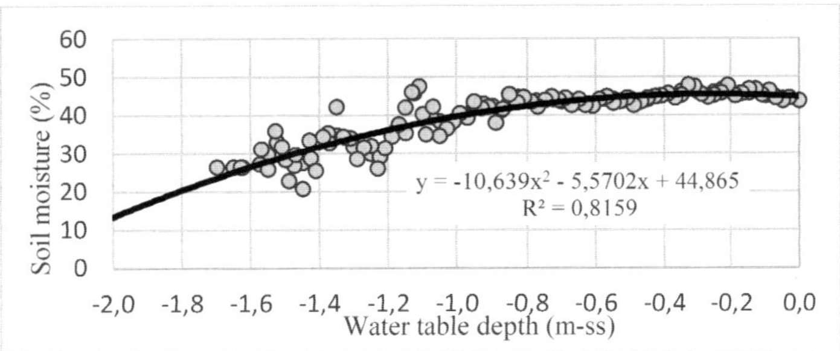

Figure 7. Relationship between water table depth and soil moisture content of upper 20 cm of peat soils (n = 4904)

CONCLUSION

Water table depth fluctuates following rainfall data in ombrogenous peatland since it is the only source of water for this type of peatland. The average minimum of water table depths in MP, KS, KB sites ranged between -0.3 to -0.8 m below the surface. Meanwhile, water table depth in BS site could reach -1.2 m below the surface. Water table depth dynamics affect peat soil moisture through peat capillary movement. The average soil moisture data at 20 cm below the peat surface in all sites ranged between 15-17%. This study also shows that soil moisture and water table relationships are in a quadratic form with an R^2 value of 0.81. It can be concluded that the greater water table depth value comes greater soil moisture with a parabolic/quadratic trend. The equation resulted from this study can be used to predict peat soil moisture for peat restoration or peat fire prevention purposes. However, it should be noted that this equation resulted from this study is limited for ombrogenous peatlands in general. Further research on other types of peatland is strongly recommended.

ACKNOWLEDGEMENTS

We thank the Government of Norway and the United Nations Office for Project Services (UNOPS) for supporting the research through PRIMS (Peatland Restoration Information and Monitoring System) project activities. The research is part of peat rewetting impact research under PRIMS project. Therefore, we would also like to thank Peat and Mangrove Restoration Agency (BRGM) for the consultancy during the research and for allowing us to conduct the research in their peat restoration area.

REFERENCES

Asmuß, T., Bechtold, M., and Tiemeyer, B. 2019. *On the potential of sentinel-1 for high resolution monitoring of water table dynamics in grasslands on organic soils*. Remote Sensing. 11: 1659. doi:10.3390/rs11141659

Chandra, T. O. (1989). Simulasi pola fluktuasi muka air tanah daerah pasang surut. Bogor: IPB University

FAO. 2014. *Towards climate-responsible peatlands management*. Rome: Mitigation of Climate Change in Agriculture (MICCA)

Osaki, M., Nursyamsi, D., Noor, M., Wahyunto, and Segah H. 2016. *Tropical peatland ecosystems*. Springer Japan. JICA-JST Project Report

Purnomo, H., Shantiko, B., Sitorus, S., Gunawan, H., Achdiawan, R., Kartodihardjo, H., and Dewayani, A.A. 2017. *Fire economy and actor network of forest and land fires in Indonesia*. Forest Policy and Economics. 78: 21-31

Warren, M., Hergoualc'h, K., Kaufman, J.B., Murdiyarso, D., and Kolka R. 2017. *An appraisal of Indonesia's immense peat carbon stock using national peatland maps: uncertainties and potential losses from conversion*. Carbon Balance Manage. 12:12. doi: 10.1186/s13021-017-0080-2

Widiarso, B., Minardi, S., Komariah, Chandra, T.O., Elmahdi, M.A., and Senge M. 2020. *Predicting peatland groundwater table and soil moisture dynamics affected by drainage level*. Journal of Soil Science and Agroclimatology. 17(1): 42-49

ID 72835

EARLY STAGES OF REVEGETATION AFTER TWO YEARS OF REWETTING AN EXTRACTED PEATLAND IN SWEDEN

Eva Weber[1,2], Örjan Berglund[1], Sabine Jordan[1]

[1] Swedish University of Agricultural Sciences, Uppsala, Sweden
[2] Technical University of Munich, Freising, Germany

eva.weber@slu.se

SUMMARY

Introduction: The recolonization by peat-forming plant species after rewetting is crucial for the restoration of terminated extracted peatlands. The aim of this study was to investigate the early stages of revegetation in Ekeby Mossen, a former extracted peatland (originally a bog) in south-central Sweden, to receive an insight in the dynamics of this process.
Material and Methods: Before rewetting the site in autumn 2018, Sphagnum fragments were spread as propagules on reference surfaces. From that time on, a general vegetation mapping was carried out continuously and data was additionally collected from drone flights. Vegetation surveys were carried out along a transect throughout the vegetation period in 2020 (May to October).
Results: Along the shoreline of the newly established shallow lake, plants re-colonized the area very fast, with leaving only smaller patches of bare peat. At the central lake area, where former ditches were situated, Typha latifolia and Phragmites australis already established in vast populations in May 2019. Along the transect, the coverage of higher plants generally increased throughout 2020, although it was less dense during the very dry and warm month of August. The plant species richness was rather low, even for bog or fen vegetation. The two species that covered most of the area and had the highest biomass increase were Juncus effusus and Carex canescens. Rumex acetosella had a high abundance as well, but decreased drastically towards the end of the vegetation period. In the contrary, Sphagnum species increased in abundance in general, with being present in seven out of nine plots along the transect.
Conclusion: The fast re-colonization by peat-forming species (Phragmites, Carex and Sphagnum) indicates, that rewetting is a good measure for restoring extracted peatlands as long as large water table fluctuations will be avoided. Long-term observations will show which peat-forming species will dominate the prospective landscape.

***Keywords**: peat-forming species, restoration, Sphagnum, landscape development, shallow lake*

ID 62500

SPHAGNUM MOSSES FROM REWETTED EXTRACTED PEATLANDS FOR GROWING MEDIA

*Sabine Jordan[1], Örjan Berglund[1], Nargish Parvin[1], Johannes Koestel[1]

[1] Swedish University of Agricultural Sciences, Uppsala, Sweden

sabine.jordan@slu.se

INTRODUCTION

In general, we aimed to investigate if peat-forming Sphagnum (peat mosses) can be a competitive growing media to peat. We were particularly interested in which mixing proportions Sphagnum provide the best conditions for a high quality plant establishment and how the substrate will change over time in the pot.

***Keywords**: changes in macroporosity, surface and fractal dimension over time; S. papillosum; S. squarossum; S. riparium; S. fallax; X-ray tomography*

MATERIALS AND METHODS

The growing experiment was done in a climate-controlled environment (16 h sunlight, 20°C) during March and June 2019 in the SLU greenhouse at campus Ultuna.

Four peat moss species (S. papillosum, S. squarossum, S. riparium, S. fallax) from rewetted extracted peatlands in Sweden have been tested for growing media against fertilised white peat (conventional horticultural substrate). To obtain a homogenous substrate, the peat mosses were cut into 0,5 cm small fragments. To avoid hydrophobicity of the peat and the peat mosses, the samples have not been dried. Neither were the samples hygienised (steamed) for weed control. The peat mosses were investigated in different peat:Sphagnum-mixtures of 0, 25, 50 and 100 %, from pure white peat to pure Sphagnum, for the purpose, if peat mosses gradually could substitute the conventional peat or if a pure (100 %) Sphagnum growing media would give successful results compared to the conventional peat. For the mixtures, conventional, but unfertilised, white peat was used. Both, the peat mosses and the white peat have been fertilised with 1,5 kg NPK (11, 5, 18) plus micro nutrients per m3 and 8 kg limestone powder per m3.

All substrates have been grown in replicates with basil (3 plants per pot) or with Tagetes (1 plant per pot). For the first 14 days after the start of the experiment, the pots were watered daily with 20 ml of ordinary tap water. After that and until the end of the experiment, 30 ml of Wallco liquid plant nutrients (51, 10, 43) have been added. The establishment of the plant above ground was observed visually and phenologically (such as germination, leave development, inflorescence emerge, flowering and colour) and by quantitative methods (weight of substrate and plant, length, width). With X-ray tomography, changes in macroporosity, surface and fractal dimension of the substrate have been detected two times: one at the initial stage and one at the 3-leaf stadium.

RESULTS AND DISCUSSIONS

Peat mosses can become a competitive substrate for plant cultivation. Basil and Tagetes have grown in all pots of peat mosses and their mixtures. All plants grown in the conventional substrates (fertilized and unfertilized low-humified peat) were nearly similar in length, number of leaves and inflorescences. Tagetes grown in pure peat mosses and moss-peat-mixtures had a greater variance in appearance (from compact to long, feathery plants with a strong vegetative growth and only a few inflorescences). How qualitative the seeds were have only been tested by a parallel germination experiment. Thus, the characterisation of each plant can be more influenced by genetic properties of the seed as from the peat moss substrate. However, most of the plants grown in the pots with peat mosses were similar to the plants grown in the conventional substrates.
The appearance of the basil plants was uniform across the entire population. The leaves were well developed in all substrates. In some pots with 100 % S. squarossum (Tagetes and Basilica) and S. riparium (Tagetes), weeds have been grown. In some cases, the weeds suppressed the Basilica growth. For large-scale horticultural use of peat mosses as growing media, a hygienic pre-treatment (steaming) of the moss material should be taken into account.

With three-dimensional image analysis (X-ray tomography), it was possible to relate soil properties to three-dimensional soil structures, such as macroporosity in the various peat-moss-mixtures and how it has changed over time. In the first image analysis at the start of the experiment, it was clearly seen that the macroporosity in the pure (100 %) peat mosses was 20 to 30 % higher than in the conventional peat (S. fallax and S. riparium had 5 to 10 % higher macroporosity as S. squarossum and S. papillosum). This quality parameter guarantees good conditions for root development of the cultures.
In the second image analysis 3 weeks later, the macroporosity of the peat had decreased while it increased in the peat mosses (more in S. squarossum and S. papillosum as in S. fallax and S. riparium). This process occurred at the same time with an increased surface area and a higher fractal dimension in the peat moss substrate. Even though the peat mosses were cut into fragments, some samples continued to grow during the experiment. Being a living substrate for growing media is the biggest difference in substrate properties between peat mosses and the conventional used white peat. As long as the water supply is sufficient, we see this as an advantage over the peat because the peat mosses will not be as sensitive to oxidation as the peat. As a renewable growing media, peat mosses can absorb CO_2 from the atmosphere and thus build up new substrate again. The question for the horticultural industry is whether the peat moss substrate meets the requirements for a homogeneous growing medium when it can grow above the rim of the plant pot.

ACKNOWLEDGEMENTS

We thank KSLA, SLF and SLU for financial support and Matthias Krebs and Mira Kohl from Greifswald University for help and nice company during peat moss sampling.

ID 73670

SUITABILITY OF THE POPLAR CLONE WESTEN FOR ESTABLISHING OF PLANTATION FORESTS ON FORMER PEAT MINING AREAS

Sindija Zigure, *Dagnija Lazdina, Santa Neimane, Toms Arturs Stals, Juris Zalmanis

dagnija.lazdina@silava.lv

After peat extraction, it is not always possible to restore mire ecosystem, mire restoration is not possible in areas neighbouring with active peat extraction fields because the drainage system is still operating. Afforestation ensures both economic benefits and carbon sequestration in tree biomass. In 2017 a demo site was established in the central part of peat extraction area. In a sector where peat extraction was completed leaving at least 50 cm deep residual peat layer (raised bog peat, pH 5–5.5), poplar clone Vesten were planted. Soil was improved using wood ash. To evaluate vegetation recovery and growth of the planted trees in relation to peat layer neutralization and influence of added macro-elements (phosphorus, potassium) and micro-elements in the ash, several experimental plots were established where 0, 5, 10 un 15 t ha-1 of wood ash were spread across the topsoil. In the first vegetation season, more diverse vegetation was found in sampling sites where the highest amount of wood ash was applied. In the second year, the highest number of plant taxa was found in plots where 10 t ha-1 of wood ash were applied. In areas where soil was improved using wood ash, the highest growth increment was observed for poplars. In the former production fields where wood ash was not applied, lack of nutrients was observed in poplar plantations where survival rate was by 10% lower and no fertilized trees died at the third year after planting reached average height of 1.9 meters. While survival rate of fertilized trees (5,10,15 t wood ash per ha) after third year were accordingly 70, 81, 79 % and height of trees reached in average 2.5, 3.13 and 3.13 meters. Clone Vesten are suitable for plantations on former peat mining area if fertilizers are used.

ID 62341

DETERMINING PEAT DEPTH USING GROUND PENETRATING RADAR AND ELECTRICAL RESISTIVITY TOMOGRAPHY (ŠIJEC BOG, NORTHWEST SLOVENIA)

*Valentina Pezdir[1], Teja Čeru[1], Barbara Horn[2], Mateja Gosar[1]

[1] Geological Survey of Slovenia, Ljubljana, Slovenia
[2] GEARH d.o.o., Maribor, Slovenia

valentina.pezdir@geo-zs.si

SUMMARY

Šijec bog on Pokljuka plateau in northwest Slovenia is among southernmost ombrotrophic peatlands in Europe and covers an area of approximately 0.15 km^2. Located at elevation of 1194 meters, its climate is colder than the regional climate of the area. Bedrock on Pokljuka plateau consists of Triassic and Jurassic limestone and dolomite. On Šijec bog, the bedrock is covered with lake sediments that are, based on previous research, at least 13,000 years old. Based on previous research, boundary between peat and lake sediments is found at depth of 6 meters, where the sediments are approximately 11,000 years old. Our research aims to improve accuracy of depth at which lake sediments appear as well as to determine at which depth bedrock occurs. With these data we can create a geomorphological model of the peat bog that will be used as a base for further geochemical analyses.

For determining the depth of sediments and bedrock we conducted measurements with the ProEx (MALA Geoscience, Sweden) ground penetrating radar with an RTA (Rough Terrain Antennas) unshielded 50 MHz bistatic antenna. Depth of ground penetrating radar measurements will be referenced with manual probing. We also applied 2-dimensional electrical resistivity tomography (ERT) survey, using ARES equipment with 48-electode system. ERT determines the true distribution of the subsurface resistivity, from which it is possible to determine the depth of lake sediments and bedrock.

***Keywords**: Ground penetrating radar (GPR), Electrical resistivity tomography (ERT), peat depth, peat*

INTRODUCTION

Šijec bog on Pokljuka plateau in northwest Slovenia is one of the southernmost ombrotrophic peatlands in Europe (Kutnar, 2000). It is located 1194 meters above sea level and covers approximately 15 hectares. There have not been many studies on peat depth of the Šijec bog. Previously, it was assumed that the peat depth reflects the surface topography. Therefore, it was supposed that peat is thickest in the central part where a slight depression was observed. Based on one borehole, boundary between peat and lake sediments is found at depth of 6 meters, where the sediments are approximately 11,000 years old (personal communication M. Andrič). The depression actually has its lowest point in northwest part of the bog and is surrounded with small ridges, covered with pine bushes (Figure 1). Southern part is elevated and is covered with higher pine bushes. According to Šifrer (1952), there are glacial till sediments from last ice age located on the southern and eastern edges of the peat bog, while older glacial till sediments can be found on western parts of the Šijec bog. In the base of the glacial till sediments are Triassic carbonate rocks (Jurkovšek, 1987).

Geophysical methods used in this study were the first attempt to determine the peat depth and depth of the bedrock in ombrotrophic peatland environments in Slovenia.

Geophysical methods were applied to estimate the thickness and characterize the subsurface topography of peat deposits and to reveal the topography of bedrock. Due to the contrasts in dielectric properties between peat and underlying clayey sediments, we expected to detect the boundary between peat and underlying lake sediments with ground penetrating radar (GPR) and the bedrock with electrical resistivity tomography (ERT).

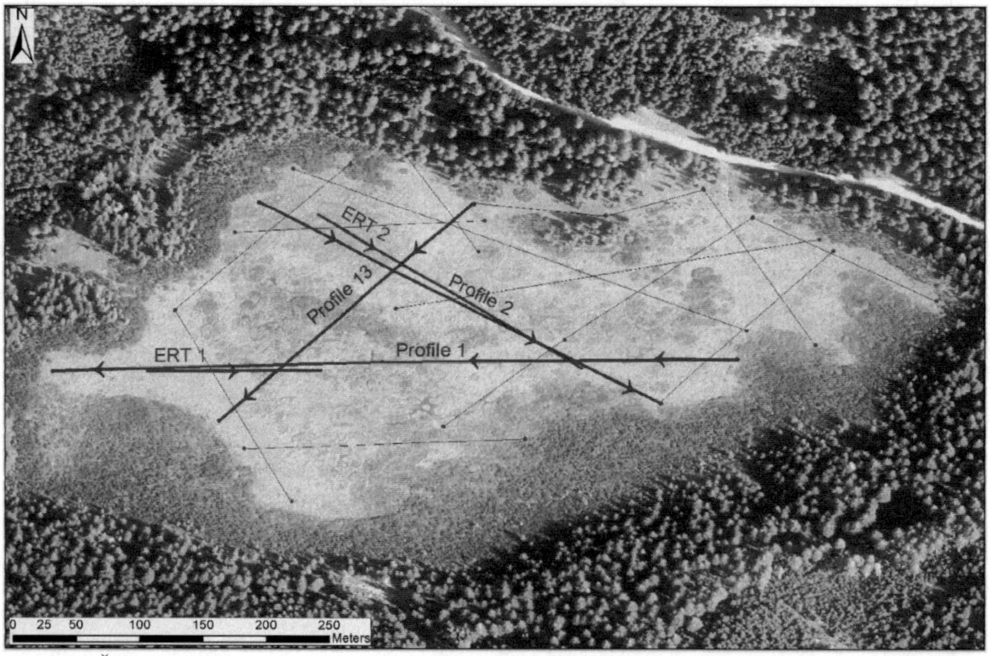

Figure 1: Šijec bog with measured profiles. GPR profiles mentioned here are marked red and ERT profiles are marked blue. Arrows mark the direction of the profile.

GEOPHYSICAL METHODS AND FIELD MEASURING

Ground penetrating radar

Ground penetrating radar (GPR) is a non-destructive established method that emits short pulses of electromagnetic waves into the subsurface and detects reflected signals from the interfaces between materials with different electromagnetic properties (Blindow et al., 2007). In addition to various applications GPR is also used for estimating the thickness and volume of peat deposits (Sass et al., 2010; Lowry et al., 2009; Slater & Reeve, 2002; Ryazantsev & Mironov, 2018). Peatland are generally not ideal environments for GPR due to the higher water contents which can strongly attenuate the radar signal. However, there are many studies, especially in ombrotrophic peats, where GPR provides good results (Jol, 2009). Generally, lower-frequency (<200 MHz) antennas are typically used to profile peatlands. In our study, we used two different antennae, an unshielded 50 MHz RTA (Rough Terrain Antenna) and a shielded 250 MHz antenna. At study site only 50 MHz antenna provide good results due to better depth penetration needed for detecting peat boundary with underlying sediments. Penetration depth of 250 MHz antenna was around 2–3 m, which was insufficient to detect the peat thickness.

GPR measurements were performed during winter when the upper surface layers were frozen and manoeuvring is available. In the rest of the seasons surface water pools disable the GPR measurements. Profiles were acquired in longitudinal and cross lines to cover the entire surface of the bog. GPR profiles were adjusted to the field condition due to the dense shrubs inside the bog (Figure 1).

All GPR profiles were processed and analysed using the Reflex-Win software by Sandmeier Geophysical Research. The following processing steps were employed: editing, subtract-mean (dewow), time zero correction, background removal, gain (Automatic Gain Control), bandpass filtering and topographic corrections.

Electrical resistivity tomography

The electrical conductivity of rocks and sediments is generally dependent on the amount of water in the medium, the conductivity of water and the way water is spread (porosity, the degree of saturation, cementation factor, fracturing) (Kowalczyk et al., 2014). Laboratory measurements of soil and sediment show high dependence of resistivity on the sample's moisture content (degree of saturation) and porosity (e.g., Kowalczyk et al., 2014; Merritt et al., 2016).

In order to estimate the thickness of the clayey sediments below the peat layer and to obtain the information on the deeper geological composition of the Pokljuka raised bog Šijec we have measured two 2-D ERT profiles (Figure 1). Dipole-dipole array, which is more sensitive for detecting vertical structures such as depressions and can yield better resolution images compared to other conventional arrays (Dahlin and Zhou, 2004), was applied at both profiles, with 2 m electrode spacing in profile ERT-1 (94 m length), and 3 m electrode spacing in profile ERT-2 (189 m length, roll-along technique). After integrating the topography data and removing the bad data points both pseudosections were inverted using the l1 norm smoothness-constrained Gauss-Newton least-squares optimization method, where the absolute difference (or the first power) between the measured and calculated apparent resistivity values is minimized (Claerbout and Muir, 1973), known also as a blocky inversion method (Loke et al., 2003).

RESULTS AND DISCUSSION

All GPR profiles (3 profiles presented here of all 16) clearly show strong reflector at the peat and clayey lake sediments interface (Figure 2). Even though that in most published studies frequencies between 100 and 200 MHz have been the most suitable, in our study only 50 MHz antenna gave information about base of peat layer. Depth penetration of 50 MHz antenna depends on the thickness of peat. Radar signal suddenly attenuate at the peat/lake sediments interface due to the presence of clay content.

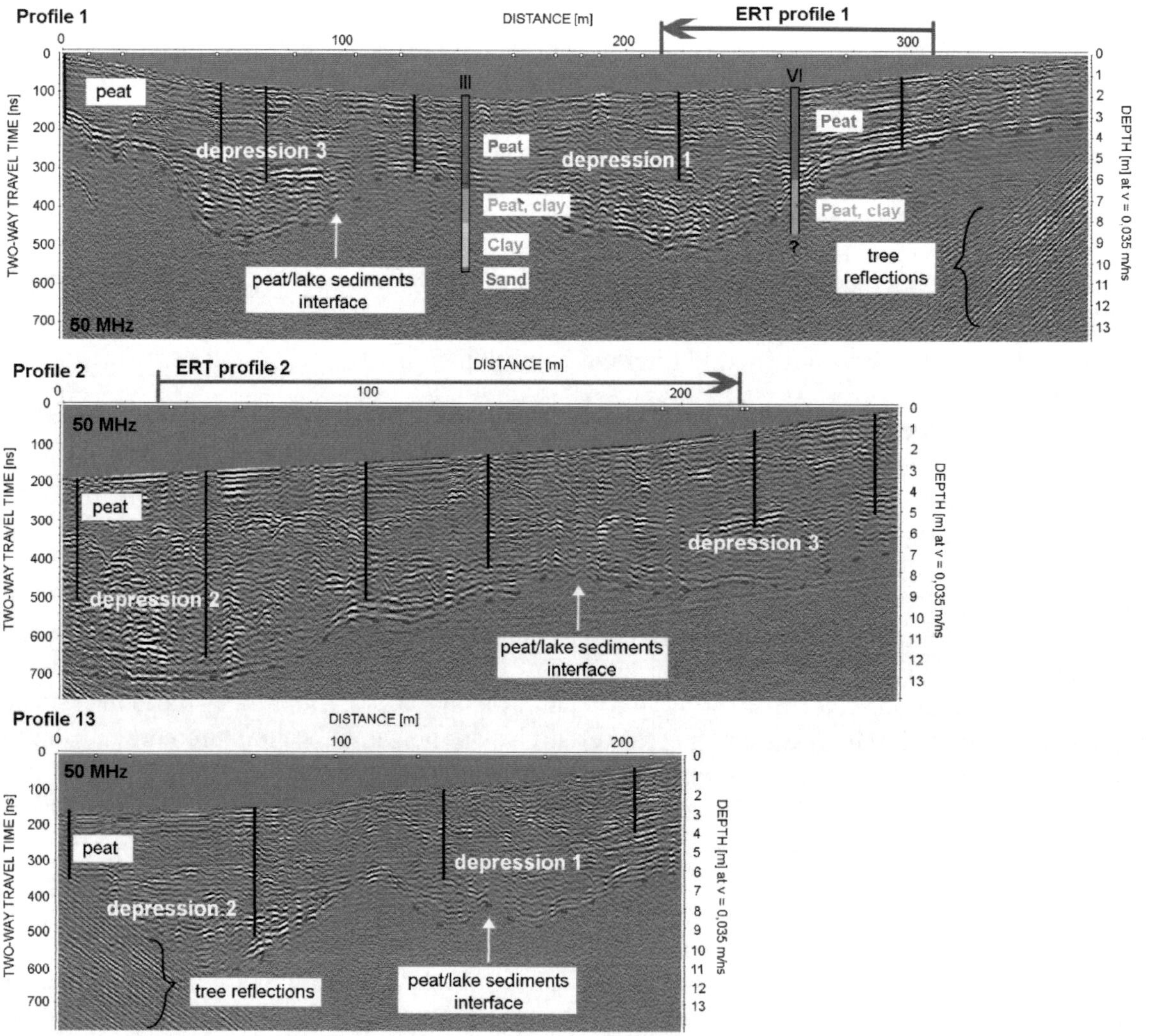

Figure 2: GPR profiles with high-amplitude reflectors revealing the morphology of peat deposits. Sections of ERT profiles are marked in Profiles 1 and 2.

GPR results of 13 profiles reveal the heterogenous morphology of peat deposit. Dense network of GPR profiles (Figure 1) reveal 4 deeper bowl-shaped depressions. This finding is in contrary to the previous prediction of maximum peat depth located in the middle of the Šijec bog. Peat layer is ranging from 2 to 9 m in depth. Deeper depressions are of different size, two larger (160–190 m in diameter) in northern part and two smaller (60–100 m in diameter) in southern part. Between them are areas with 4–6 meters of peat, which are also areas with denser vegetation and higher bushes. Beside the strong reflection at interface, some stronger heterogenous reflections are visible within depressions and are probably related to glacial till material. Further manual investigations (coring, peat probing) will be compared to geophysical data. The shallower wavy reflector at the depth around 1.5–2.5 m is also visible. It can present the boundary between minerotrophic and ombrotrophic peat (when moss grew a dome, so surface water runoff lost its connection). The thinnest parts of peat layers are in areas outside of the depressions and represent the edge part of the bog. Surface and subsurface morphology indicate that the bog most probably developed from the individual smaller ponds.

The resistivity distribution on both inverse ERT models shows three well contrasted resistivity bodies (Figure 3), which are described in terms of geological layers. A sharp resistivity contrast is present between the peat layer (P: 200–600 Ωm) and underlying clayey deposits (C, D1, D2: 20–70 Ωm) at both inverted ERT models. The resistivity contrast is less sharp and occasionally gradual (particularly in lateral direction) between the clayey deposits and medium resistivity body (MRB: 100–200 Ωm) of a yet unconfirmed lithology.
The peat layer gradually thickens along with a slight lowering of the surface, from 2 to 6 m towards east on the profile ERT-1 and from 3 m up to 10 m towards northwest on profile the ERT-2. The thickness of the clayey layer (C) above the medium resistivity body (MRB) is 4–7 m at ERT-1 location and 5–11 m at ERT-2 location. Below the thickest peat deposits at both locations, low resistivity depressions (D1, D2) are present down to final depths of investigation. According to the low resistivity values (50–70 Ωm) we can assume that both depressions are filled with mostly clayey sediments, which can contain also some silty and/or sandy fraction.

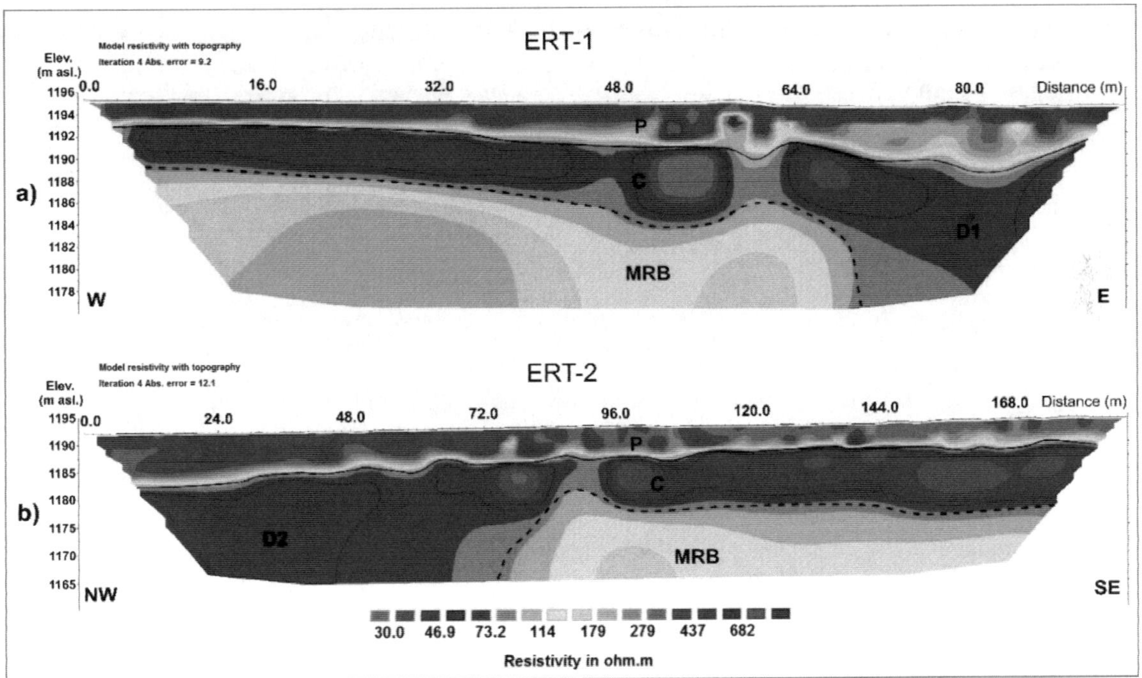

Figure 3: Inverted resistivity models of profiles: a) ERT-1 and b) ERT-2. Marks: P – peat layer, C – clayey deposits, D1 and D2 – clayey deposits in deeper depressions, MRB – medium resistivity body.

The peat layer (P) has significantly higher resistivity values than underlying clayey sediment and can be very well followed throughout the profiles with a sharp resistivity contrast. As observable on ERT results, low resistivity clayey deposits (C) are present throughout both profiles above the medium resistivity body (MRB) and are also present in two deep depressions (D1, D2), which could indicate the existence of the older lake in the past. However, it is not possible to discern between the Pleistocene and Holocene clays on a basis of ERT results.
The resistivity values of the medium resistivity body (MRB) ranges from 100 to 200 Ωm, which can be, according to some authors, attributed to fractured and saturated limestones (e.g. Telford et al., 1990). Although, far more typical resistivity values for various limestones in Slovenia and

elsewhere are significantly higher, from at least 500 Ωm and up to several thousand Ωm, with average higher than 1000 Ωm (e.g. Horn et al., 2018; Žebre et al. 2019). Resistivity values within the interval 100–200 are usually connected to unconsolidated and to some degree saturated Quaternary sediments, such as till, diamicton, sand and gravel (e.g. Žebre et al. 2019).

CONCLUSION

GPR results provided very detailed data about the depth of peat deposits and delineating peatland surface morphology. Strong reflector is visible at the contact between peat and lake sediments, from which it is possible to determine the shape of the peat body. Peat formed in four larger depressions where the thickness of peat is approximately 7–9 meters in its deepest point, while peat depth on the edges ranges from 2–4 meters. The depth values are estimated to most probable value for dielectric constant from literature and will be evaluated with manual probing. ERT results provided data about lake sediments and bedrock of the Šijec bog. Deep clayey depressions could be present under all four peat depressions, but that cannot be confirmed based on only two ERT profiles. For a more accurate determination of the lithology of the MRB and age of clayey lake sediments further research is needed.

ACKNOWLEDGEMENTS

The presented study was funded by the Slovenian Research Agency (ARRS) in the frame of the young researcher programme and in the frame of the research programme Groundwater and Geochemistry (P1-0020).

REFERENCES

13. Blindow, N., Eisenburger, D., Illich, B., Petzold, H., Richer, T. (2007) Ground penetrating radar. In: Knödel, K., Lange, G., Voigt, H.J. (Eds.) *Environmental Geology. Handbook of Field Methods and Case Studies.* Springer, Berlin: pp. 283–335.
14. Claerbout, J.F., Muir, F. (1973) Robust modeling with erratic data. *Geophysics*, 38: 826–844.
15. Dahlin, T., Zhou, B. (2004) A numerical comparison of 2D resistivity imaging with 10 electrode arrays. *Geophysical Prospecting*, 52/5: 379–398. https://doi.org/10.1111/j.1365-2478.2004.00423.x.
16. Horn, B., Mušič, B., Črešnar, M., Basar, P. (2018) Geofizikalne raziskave v kraškem okolju: rezultati električne upornostne tomografije in nizkofrekvenčne elektromagnetne metode na primeru utrjene naselbine Gradišnica pri Dolenjem Gradišču. [Geophysical research in the karst environment: electrical resistivity tomography and low-frequency electromagnetic method results, case study of the fortified settlement Gradišnica near Dolenje Gradišče]. *Arheo*, 35: 7–31. (in Slovenian)
17. Jol, H.M. (2009) *Ground Penetrating Radar: Theory and Applications*. Elsevier Science, Amsterdam, 544 p.
18. Jurkovšek, B. (1987) *Tolmač listov Beljak in Ponteba: L 33-51, L33-52, Osnovna geološka karta SFRJ. 1:100 000. [Explanatory book of Villach and Pontebba sheets: L 33-51, L33-52, Basic geological map of Yugoslavia. 1:100 000].* Zvezni geološki zavod, Beograd, 58 pp. (in Slovenian)
19. Kowalczyk, S., Maślakowski, M., Tucholka, P. (2014) Determination of the correlation between the electrical resistivity of non-cohesive soils and the degree of compaction. *Journal of Applied Geophysics*, 110: 43–50. https://doi.org/10.1016/j.jappgeo.2014.08.016.
20. Kutnar, L. (2000) Spruce mire types on the Pokljuka plateau, Slovenia. *Phyton (Austria),* 40/4: 123–128.
21. Loke, M.H., Acworth, I., Dahlin, T. (2003) A comparison of smooth and blocky inversion methods in 2D electrical imaging surveys. *Exploration Geophysics*, 34: 182–187.
22. Lowry, C.S., Fratta, D., Anderson, M.P. (2009) Ground penetrating radar and spring formation in a groundwater dominated peat wetland. *Journal of Hydrology*, 373: 68–79.
23. Merritt, A.J., Chambers, J.E., Wilkinson, P.B., West, L.J., Murphy, W., Gunn, D., Uhlemann, S. (2016) Measurement and modelling of moisture-electrical resistivity relationship of fine-grained unsaturated soils and electrical anisotropy. *Journal of Applied Geophysics*, 124: 155–165. https://doi.org/10.1016/j.jappgeo.2015.11.005.
24. Ryazantsev, P., Mironov, V. (2018) Study of peatland internal structure by the Ground Penetrating Radar. *17th International Conference on Ground Penetrating Radar (GPR)*: 1–4.
25. Sass, O., Friedmann, A., Haselwanter, G., Wetzel, K.F. (2010) Investigating thickness and internal structure of alpine mires using conventional and geophysical techniques. *Catena*, 80: 195–203.
26. Slater, L.D., Reeve, A. (2002) Investigating peatland stratigraphy and hydrogeology using integrated electrical geophysics. *Geophysics*, 67: 365–378.
27. Šifrer, M. (1952) Obseg zadnje poledenitve na Pokljuki. [The extent of the last ice age on Pokljuka]. *Geografski vestnik*, 24: 95–114. (in Slovenian)
28. Telford, W.M., Geldart, L.P., Sheriff, R.E. (1990) *Applied Geophysics* (Second Edi). Cambridge University Press.
29. Žebre, M., Jež, J., Mechernich, S., Mušič, B., Horn, B., Jamšek Rupnik, P. (2019) Paraglacial adjustment of alluvial fans to the last deglaciation in the Snežnik Mountain, Dinaric karst (Slovenia). *Geomorphology*, 332: 66–79. https://doi.org/10.1016/j.geomorph.2019.02.007.

ID 61081

THE DIGITAL DATABASE OF ESTONIAN PEAT INVESTIGATION RESULTS

*Mall Orru, Monika Aarniste

Institute of Geology, Tallinn University of Technology, Estonia

Mall.Orru@taltech.ee

Estonia is rich in peatlands, covering 22.3% of its territory. Peat is an important mineral resource, amounting to 2.37 billion tons, of which 1.0–1.2 million tons per year are extracted. It is necessary to analyse the sustainability of peat mining and to develop innovative peat uses (balneology, activated carbon, peat wax, humic substances, fertilizers, etc.).

Systematical studies on Estonian peatlands have been carried out from 1966, chiefly by the Geological Survey of Estonia. So far, 550 peat deposits are well studied. More than 50000 peat samples have been collected from manuscript reports. Their botanical composition, degree of humification, pH, natural moisture and ash content have been determined. Calorific value, trace element content, organic matter composition, and the peat formation have been described, as well. All the Estonian peat samples have been analyzed using a uniform methodology. Samples have been collected throughout the whole peat sequence.

The project "The digital database of Estonian peat investigation results", financed by the Estonian Environmental Investment Centre, was initiated in 2016 and will be accomplished in 2020. Compilation of a digital database is an essential step towards efficient use of a vast amount of valuable data.

The database structure:

1. Scanned maps of 550 peat deposits, accompanied by their characteristics.
2. Laboratory analysis results in a table format. A search engine for finding information on plant species is provided, being useful e.g. in interpreting climate changes.
3. Georeferenced peat deposit maps, matching with the map layers of the Estonian Land Board. XYZ coordinatesof 30000 sample points.
4. Areas of protected species.
5. Estonian peatland districts and their genetic types.
6. Appendices (reports of investigations on abandoned peat fields, the book Trace Elements in Estonian Peat).
7. Letter of explanation and a manual (in Estonian and in English).

Open Access to the database: http://turvas.geokogud.info/.

ID 62250

INTEGRATED IDENTIFICATION APPROACH OF GROUNDWATER DEPENDENT ECOSYSTEMS

*Elve Lode, Martin Küttim, Raimo Pajula, Reimo Rivis, Jaanus Terasmaa

Institute of Ecology, School of Natural Sciences and Health, Tallinn University, Estonia.

elve.lode@tlu.ee

There are three types of water input to the groundwater depending ecosystems (GDEs): a) precipitated water, b) surface water and c) groundwater. Discharge of mineral groundwater (GW) to such systems usually is considered a relatively stable feature in comparison with the big variety in precipitation and surface water supply. However, some variation of the GW input to the GDEs exists due to higher GW recharges in spring and autumn and due to water deficit during the dry periods. The winter water supply strongly depends on snow conditions during the season. Identification of GDEs, being valuable part of terrestrial ecosystems, is also important for assessment of quality and quantity status of the local GW conditions.

Presence of flood tolerant vegetation, their composition and zonality are common criteria for identification of conditional level of such systems on the ground. Several *Modules* in GIS provide a powerful tool for identification and analyses of the GDEs. However, remote sensing has it limits and specifics for identification of such ecosystems.

The purpose of this work is to present the results of *remote sensing-ground level integrated survey* of South-Estonian Matsi spring mire, whereas both the aerial images of Estonian Land Board and the drone images of the GroundEco project are used. Based on both, the remote sensing data and the ground level studied plant cover pattern, as a reflection of the mire annual water dynamics and the long-term soil formation, the identification scheme of the GDEs is compiled. This approach will be illustrated via maps and graphs of two parts of the Matsi spring mire, differing mainly by the hydro-topological disturbance conditions.

Approach for identification of GDEs was developed within the EstLat62 GroundEco project ("Joint management of groundwater dependent ecosystems in transboundary Gauja-Koiva river basin") of the Interreg Estonia-Latvia cooperation programme, and funded by the ERDF.

ID 62294

PRIMS-BOT: AN EARLY WARNING SYSTEM CHATBOT FOR FIRE INDICATION IN PEATLAND CASE STUDY INDONESIA

Mochammad Fadhli Zakiy

World Resources Institute Indonesia, Indonesia

fadhli.zakiy@wri.org

Indonesia, a home for the second largest tropical peatland, had faced tragic forest and land fires in 2015 which ravaged more than 2,6 million hectares and caused transboundary haze pollution towards neighbouring countries. Since then monitoring fire occurrences in peatland has been prioritized, one of it is by harnessing technology. Rapid growth of technology enabled information exchange via mobile phone fast and convenient, therefore WRI Indonesia created a peatland fire indication early warning system chatbot called PRIMSbot. PRIMSbot is a Telegram messenger based chatbot that can provide latest information as well as historical data of fire indication occurred within peatland area in interactive way or spreadsheet format for seven rich-peatland provinces across Indonesia. PRIMSbot is an add-on application for Peatland Restoration Information and Monitoring System (PRIMS) coined by the Peatland Restoration Agency of Indonesia (BRG - Badan Restorasi Gambut). The fire indication is updated automatically every three hours from Indonesia Space Agency (LAPAN) MODIS catalog portal which comprises VIIRS and MODIS satellite data overlaid with peatland area in Indonesia. PRIMSbot also supports subscription to enable daily push notification for peatland fire early warning system.

ID 62787

PEATLAND PROBABILITY MAP OF THE CARIBBEAN COAST

*Cristina Malpica-Piñeros[1], Laura Villegas-Mejia[2], Cosima Tegetmeyer[3], Alexandra Barthelmes[3], Jan Peters[4]

[1] University Greifswald, Institute for Botany and Landscape Ecology, Germany

[2] Peatlands team REDD+/NFM Cluster Forestry Department/FAO, Italy

[3] University Greifswald, Institute for Botany and Landscape Ecology, Germany

[4] Michael Succow Foundation for the Protection of Nature, Germany

cris.malpica@greifswaldmoor.de

Coastal tropical peatlands have an important role as nature-based solutions for coastal protection, climate change regulation, as wildlife refuges, and landscape hydrology, as well as having recreational and cultural values. However, the knowledge on their location and extent is scarce in the Caribbean coastal regions and peatland science is weakly developed. Several studies are stating information that could indicate the presence of peat formation, nevertheless, only a few studies compile and integrate archive data to identify peatlands explicitly. Based on existing information on soil, vegetation, flooding period and soil organic carbon from national and global sources, we used a semi-automatic approach to identify and locate landscapes and areas that potentially could host peatlands in regions with scarce explicit data. Our estimates suggest that 130,000 km^2 probable peatland area exists along the Caribbean coast, where Nicaragua harbours the largest area on the sub-continent with 39,000km^2, followed by Honduras with 16,000 km^2 and Cuba the largest area of the islands with 23,900 km^2. We compare our results with three peatland maps, located in different areas of the Caribbean, our approach allowed us to identify the three of them, nevertheless, the total size and cover did not resemble completely the source and a downscaling is needed, especially in small peatland areas. The results of this study could prioritise further field research to confirm peatland occurrence on the ground and support decision making for management, monitoring plans and project design. The applied probabilistic approach is a valuable tool to identify peatland areas in regions with limited information, allowed us to integrate national and global data. Additionally, it has shown to be a fast, efficient tool, which is easily adaptable to different landscapes and ecosystems.

ID 72810

NATIONAL SCALE PEATLAND LAND USE MAPPING USING GOOGLE EARTH ENGINE AND LANDSAT DATA – A CASE STUDY OF IRELAND

*Wahaj Habib, John Connolly

Department of Geography, Trinity College Dublin, Ireland

habibw@tcd.ie

Globally, peatlands have been under severe strain for centuries due to management related activities (land use). In Ireland, peatlands span over approximately 14600 km2, and 85 % of which has already been degraded to some extent. Recent legislative changes (2018) in the EU's 2030 climate and energy framework calls for the inclusion of greenhouse gas (GHG) emissions and removals accounting from land use, land-use change and forestry. Under this legislation, Ireland has set a precedent by voluntarily including peatlands into that system, which takes effect from this year. Despite this, there is a lack of information about land use and associated GHG emissions on peatlands. Having mentioned that, the identification of land use on peatlands is ever more important.

Google Earth Engine ((GEE), a cloud-based geospatial analysis platform) offers a good prospect for mapping peatland land use at a national scale. In this study, GEE was used with medium-resolution multispectral satellite imagery (Landsat-5). A cloud-free image mosaic was created for Ireland (images collected between 2004-2006). The most recent map of peatland extent in Ireland was used to constrain the imagery for further analysis and classification. Moreover, a land use classification taxonomy is in development to assess land use at multiple spatial scales (medium (30m) to fine (sub-metre)). In this work, the taxonomy was implemented at the medium scale. An analysis was conducted using the taxonomy to identify several peatland land use classes: cutaway, cutover, forestry, grassland, water bodies, remnant peatlands and residual peatlands, using the mosaicked imagery. Preliminary results are presented here. When finalised these results may be used as baseline data to aid Ireland's national GHG accounting commitments from wetlands. It could also be used for quantification of land-use change on peatlands. Lastly, this could also assist in peatland rehabilitation/restoration/rewetting activities and effective land use management of degraded peatlands.

ID 62452

CRITERIA AND INDICATORS FOR TROPICAL PEATLAND RESTORATION: A PRELIMINARY ACCOUNT

*Daniel Murdiyarso[1], Haruni Krisnawati[2], Daniel Murdiyarso[2]

[1] Center for International Forestry Research, Indonesia; Department of Geophysics and Meteorology, IPB University, Indonesia

[2] Forest and Environment Research and Development and Innovation Agency, Indonesia

d.murdiyarso@cgiar.org

Although the global area of tropical peat swamp forests is disproportionately small, they are very important ecosystems in the global carbon cycle as they store the largest carbon stocks per unit area on earth. Yet, these ecosystems experience high rates of deforestation and degradation causing enormous greenhouse gas (GHGs) emissions. Peatlands also provide numerous ecosystem services ranging from regulating (climate, flood, and pollution), provisioning (food, fiber, water, medicine, genetic resources), supporting (biodiversity, primary production, nutrient cycling) to cultural and social (cultural use, social use, recreation, education, research) services. Peatland degradation has been affecting all areas of these services worldwide, including tropical peatlands. At the same time substantial efforts have been made to reverse the direction of change. However, there is no such practical and yet scientifically sounds basis to evaluate the process. Criteria and indicators for these massive efforts are needed. A preliminary account is presented here based on general category of effort, such as returning water table, original vegetation covers, and the associated socio-economic implications. Quantifiable peatland ecosystem services are considered to develop tangible criteria and range of indicators are proposed for further scrutiny and test.